Automating vSphere

with VMware vCenter Orchestrator

VMware Press is the official publisher of VMware books and training materials, which provide guidance on the critical topics facing today's technology professionals and students. Enterprises, as well as small and medium-sized organizations, adopt virtualization as a more agile way of scaling IT to meet business needs. VMware Press provides proven, technically accurate information that will help them meet their goals for customizing, building, and maintaining their virtual environment.

With books, certification and study guides, video training, and learning tools produced by world-class architects and IT experts, VMware Press helps IT professionals master a diverse range of topics on virtualization and cloud computing and is the official source of reference materials for preparing for the VMware Certified Professional Examination.

VMware Press is also pleased to have localization partners that can publish its products into more than 42 languages, including, but not limited to, Chinese (Simplified), Chinese (Traditional), French, German, Greek, Hindi, Japanese, Korean, Polish, Russian, and Spanish.

For more information about VMware Press, please visit
http://www.vmware.com/go/vmwarepress

Automating vSphere

with VMware vCenter Orchestrator

TECHNOLOGY HANDS-ON

Cody Bunch

vmware PRESS

Upper Saddle River, NJ • Boston • Indianapolis • San Francisco
New York • Toronto • Montreal • London • Munich • Paris • Madrid
Capetown • Sydney • Tokyo • Singapore • Mexico City

Automating vSphere

With VMware vCenter Orchestrator

Published by Pearson Education, Inc.

Publishing as VMware Press

Warning and Disclaimer

Corporate and Government Sales

ISBN-13: 978-0-321-79991-3

ISBN-10: 0-321-79991-7

Text printed in the United States on recycled paper at RR Donnelley in Crawfordsville, Indiana.

First printing, March 2012

VMWARE PRESS PROGRAM MANAGER
Andrea Eubanks de Jounge

ASSOCIATE PUBLISHER
David Dusthimer

ACQUISITIONS EDITOR
Joan Murray

DEVELOPMENT EDITOR
Susan Zahn

MANAGING EDITOR
Sandra Schroeder

SENIOR PROJECT EDITOR
Tonya Simpson

COPY EDITOR
Keith Cline

PROOFREADER
Megan Wade

EDITORIAL ASSISTANT
Vanessa Evans

INDEXER
Lisa Stumpf

BOOK DESIGNER
Gary Adair

COMPOSITOR
Bumpy Design

This book is dedicated to Julie, my love, forever and always.
Also to our children and to my parents. Without their neverending drive
and support, this book would not have been possible.

Contents

Preface

This book is the first edition of *Automating vSphere: With VMware vCenter Orchestrator* and one of the first books to be published by VMware Press.

About This Book

Virtualization has changed the face of the IT industry as we know it. Along the way, VMware has pioneered various virtualization technologies that allow for the consolidation of workloads and reductions in cost for IT operations. This, along with the ease in which an administrator can now stand up a virtual machine, has led to administrators being responsible for an ever-increasing number of servers, services, and infrastructure. Couple these trends with the pressure for IT groups to manage as efficiently and cost-effectively as cloud service providers and you find yourself in a world where orchestrating your systems becomes not just a good idea, but a necessity.

This book is a guide down the path of automating your vSphere environment using VMware vCenter Orchestrator. The version of Orchestrator, a.k.a. vCO, used in this book is 4.2. You'll notice that this is not in lockstep with the current vSphere release numbers, and that is because during this release cycle, the vCO team has broken away from the vSphere platform for releases, allowing greater flexibility in pushing bug fixes and new features.

How to Use This Book

This book is divided into three parts: Introduction, Installation, and Configuration; Working with vCenter Orchestrator; and Real-World Use Cases.

The following is a brief overview of the parts and chapters contained within.

Part I: Introduction, Installation, and Configuration

Part I of this book provides the foundation on which we build our automation and introduces you to vCO.

Chapter 1, "Introducing VMware vCenter Orchestrator"

A brief introduction to vCO and discussion of who should use it, what vCO can do, and why you should be using it.

Chapter 2, "Installing vCenter Orchestrator"

Chapter 2 dives into various installation scenarios for vCO. These cover everything from installing alongside vCenter to building vCO for scalability.

Chapter 3, "Configuring vCenter Orchestrator"

Chapter 3 picks up just after the installation and provides you with the steps and guidance necessary to configure and begin using vCO.

Part II: Working with vCenter Orchestrator

Part II provides a conceptual foundation for working with vCO. Because a vCO installation involves a number of moving parts, having a firm grasp of the fundamentals is key.

Chapter 4, "Identifying the Moving Parts"

This chapter provides an overview of the various parts of vCO, including workflows, actions, packages, plug-ins, and more.

Chapter 5, "vCenter Orchestrator Plug-Ins"

Because vCO derives quite a bit of power and flexibility from the use of plug-ins, Chapter 5 delves deep into the ins and outs of vCO plug-ins.

Chapter 6, "Introduction to Workflow-Fu"

Perhaps the component of vCO that you will spend the most time working with is the workflow. Therefore, Chapter 6 provides some additional insight into workflows, including how to organize, use, and build them.

Part III: Amazing Smoothies, Inc. (a.k.a. Real-World Use Case)

Part III of this book is where the vCO rubber meets your virtual road and we start building on both the installation from Part I and the concepts of Part II to formulate workflows to solve your real-world problems.

Chapter 7, "Your First Day at Amazing Smoothies, Inc.: Network Orientation"

Chapter 7 provides the "real-world" company for which we will build workflows. It covers who they are, what they do, and what some of their needs are.

Chapter 8, "Amazing Smoothies Day 2: Dealing with Snapshots"

This chapter explains how Amazing Smoothies currently handles snapshots and how to better that process with vCO.

Chapter 9, "Amazing Smoothies Day 3: VM Provisioning"

Chapter 9 covers how to work with the VM provisioning process and build a "VM factory" for Amazing Smoothies, up to and including post-installation configuration.

Chapter 10, "Amazing Smoothies Day 4: VM Decommissioning"

For obvious reasons, you need to know how to bring a VM back offline after it has outlived its usefulness. Chapter 10 breaks out the low-orbit ion cannon and shows you how to use vCO to remove VMs, as well.

Chapter 11, "Amazing Smoothies Day 5: Other VM Management"

This chapter wraps up VM management by covering some additional workflows for the regular care and feeding of VMs. This includes managing VMware tools and removing orphaned VM files.

Chapter 12, "Amazing Smoothies Day 6: New Hardware"

This chapter tackles the challenge of bringing new hypervisors into the Amazing Smoothies environment and adding them to your existing vSphere clusters.

About the Author

Cody Bunch is a private cloud architect hailing from the hill country just outside San Antonio, Texas. Cody was recognized as a VMware vExpert in 2009, 2010, and 2011 and has been involved in the VMware community since late 2007. Cody has also spoken on virtualization and automation at VMworld 2011 and the Virtualization Congress 2009. Cody shares his nuts-and-bolts operations and automation guidance on his website ProfessionalVMware.com.

Acknowledgments

Before we delve into vCenter Orchestrator, I want to acknowledge the folks who worked tirelessly behind the scenes to make this book a reality. First and foremost, my wife, Julie, my sun and stars; without her tireless efforts to herd our small litter of kittens to give me the time needed to write this book, well, it'd just not exist.

Up here, somewhere between first and second, is this space… first and a half or so, and in it I want to thank my parents for their tireless support and for putting my seventh grade "He'll never do anything worthwhile in his life" English teacher into his place while encouraging me to keep doing what it is I do.

Second, I want to thank Thomas Corfman, Christophe Decanini, Burke Azbill, and all the other members of the VMware vCenter Orchestrator team. During the writing process, this group provided feedback on both the content that got included and, more importantly, that which didn't. Further, they responded to all manner of questions around the clock. Another invaluable resource was Joerg Lew of VCOPortal.de, who, like the vCO team, has provided guidance, feedback, and corrections along the way.

Third, I want to thank all the folks at Pearson/VMware Press who helped this first-time author through the process. I did not fully appreciate the village that goes into writing and producing a book of any size. In no particular order, the folks at Pearson who made this volume possible: Joan Murray, Susan Zahn, Sandra Schroeder, Stephane Nakib, Jamie Adams, Emily Nave, and many others I'm sure I didn't name.

Finally, I want to call out Jim, Patrick, John O, and John E, who encouraged me to start blogging, which set me down the path that led to this book.

We Want to Hear from You!

As the reader of this book, *you* are our most important critic and commentator. We value your opinion and want to know what we're doing right, what we could do better, what areas you'd like to see us publish in, and any other words of wisdom you're willing to pass our way.

As an associate publisher for Pearson, I welcome your comments. You can email or write me directly to let me know what you did or didn't like about this book—as well as what we can do to make our books better.

Please note that I cannot help you with technical problems related to the topic of this book. We do have a User Services group, however, where I will forward specific technical questions related to the book.

When you write, please be sure to include this book's title and author as well as your name, email address, and phone number. I will carefully review your comments and share them with the author and editors who worked on the book.

Email: VMwarePress@vmware.com

Mail: David Dusthimer
Associate Publisher
Pearson
800 East 96th Street
Indianapolis, IN 46240 USA

Reader Services

Visit our website and register this book at Pearsonitcertification.com/register for convenient access to any updates, downloads, or errata that might be available for this book.

Part I

Introduction, Installation, and Configuration

Chapter 1

Introducing VMware vCenter Orchestrator

Where to begin when introducing VMware vCenter Orchestrator? At the beginning, I suppose. Like any new relationship, it helps to get to know one another. So, that is what we do here with VMware vCenter Orchestrator. VMware vCenter Orchestrator (vCO) is one of VMware's most powerful but best kept secrets. In fact, you have likely picked up this book because you know it exists but have any number of questions about what vCO can do, if you can make vCO work for you, or whether vCO is even a good fit for your environment. This chapter answers the following questions:

- What is vCO?
- What can vCO do?
- Why should you use vCO?
- Who should use vCO?
- When should you use vCO?
- Where does vCO fit?
- How do I get started?

Yes, that is quite a number of questions, and I intend to answer them all if you'll bear with me. Ready to begin your vCO adventure?

What Is VMware vCenter Orchestrator?

What better way to start a book about VMware vCenter Orchestrator than to tell you what it is we're talking about? If you already have a pretty good grasp of what vCO is, feel free to skip ahead. Otherwise, welcome aboard, and let's go!

The VMware website describes vCO as follows:

> VMware vCenter Orchestrator provides out of the box workflows that can help administrators automate existing manual tasks. Administrators can utilize sample workflows from VMware vCenter Orchestrator's workflow library and provide a blueprint for creating additional workflows.

That statement is rather broad but gets right to the meat of the matter: vCO is a tool that can make your day-to-day life as a VMware administrator easier. It does this by enabling you to take some common tasks that are likely manual in your environment and automate them. In addition, you can make these workflows as simple or as complex as you want, using drag-and-drop components and some more advanced scripting.

NOTE

Yes, I said *advanced scripting*. Yes, I am aware that scripting might scare some folks off. However, you do not want to confuse scripting with developing code. Also, vCO's choice of scripting language, JavaScript, even sounds similar to the programming language Java. I assure you that, as with most scripting, we will be working at a much higher level. This means that what we cover in those sections mostly shows you where to go if you need to delve deeper than we can go with the GUI.

To do these wonderful things, vCO uses the components shown in Figure 1.1.

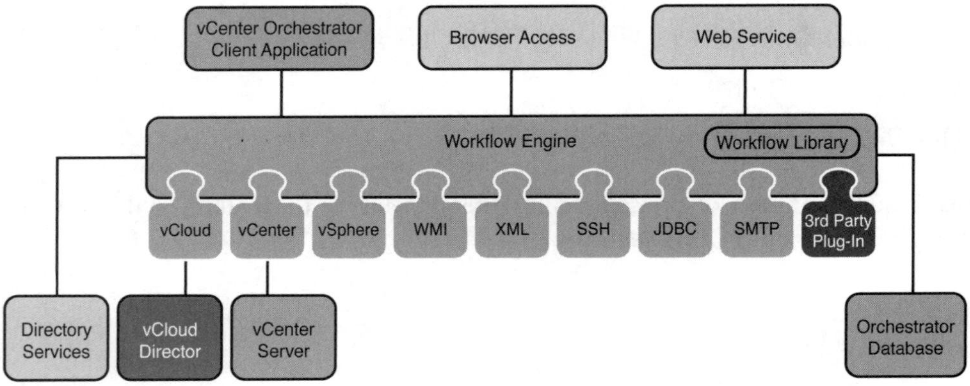

Figure 1.1 vCO components

> **NOTE**
>
> Figure 1.1 shows the WMI plug-in. By the time you are reading this, however, it will have been retired in favor of a PowerShell plug-in for Microsoft Windows operations.

As you can see, the vCO workflow engine is extensible and makes use of a number of both built-in and third-party components. Now that you know what vCO is, let's explore a bit of what vCO can do for you.

> **NOTE**
>
> What is a *workflow*? Chapter 6, "Introduction to Workflow-Fu," covers that topic. For now, conceptualize workflows as just that: a flow chart of actions taken to perform a task within your IT infrastructure.

What Can vCenter Orchestrator Do?

The purpose of vCO, and part of why I imagine VMware includes it with every single vCenter Server installation, is to reduce operational complexity and save you time (and perhaps money).

Save time and money? As touched on in this chapter and delved into later in the book, you'll begin to see where automating your day-to-day activities (better known as workflows in the vCO world) will deliver on those promises. However, with a promise like that, it had better do some awesome things, right? At a basic level, vCO enables you, as an administrator, to take some of your day-to-day workload and start to offload it to an intelligent automation platform.

Through the use of both VMware and third-party plug-ins, you can start to realize the promise of "private cloud," such as virtual machine (VM) provisioning and flexibility. As Figure 1.1 shows, the puzzle-like parts are the various plug-ins that make vCO both extensible and versatile. Take the vCenter plug-in, for example; it enables vCO to interface with vCenter Server for various aspects of virtual machine provisioning, maintenance, reporting, and management. In addition, VMware and the vCO team provide plug-ins for the VMware vCloud stack, to help further simplify working with your "cloud" environment.

You'll find this easier to conceptualize with an example, so how about a teaser screenshot for something that we build together later? Take a look at Figure 1.2, better known as the

"Nuke Virtual Machine from Orbit" workflow from Chapter 10, "Amazing Smoothies Day 4: VM Decommissioning."

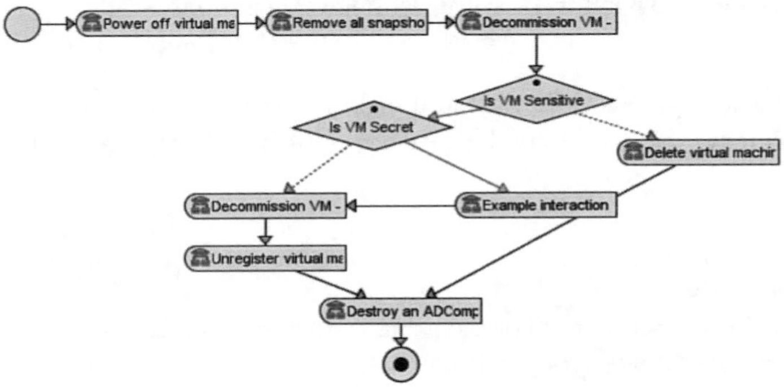

Figure 1.2 Schema for Nuke Virtual Machine from Orbit

So, now that your appetite is whetted for vCO by knowing some of what it is capable of, let's examine why you should use vCO.

Why Should You Use vCenter Orchestrator?

I could spend a number of pages enumerating why using vCO is a good idea. However, a few main reasons why you should use it should suffice:

- Do more with less
- Reduce the risk of human error
- Save time

Do More with Less

The news reports state that the economy might be heading in a positive direction again; however, that doesn't mean that management has approved your last request for headcount. Meanwhile, you have taken a look at the project work for this year, compared that to an increase in service calls and ongoing maintenance, and well, even if there were 3.14159 more hours in a day, you would still not be able to get it all done.

This is where vCenter Orchestrator starts to shine. Consider how many service calls could be solved with some basic self-service tools. Next, let's take the ongoing maintenance: same thing. At the end of the day, if you have a defined process for it in your vSphere infrastructure, you can likely automate it with vCO.

Once automated with vCO, you will save enough time to start conquering the other things demanded of your schedule.

Even with process in place, there will always be EBSAK, which stands for error between seat and keyboard. A process run manually may go right 99 out of 100 times, but it takes only one time to break the success of the other 99.

Reduce the Risk of Human Error

In an ever-increasing world of interruption, even the most repetitive task can fall victim to an instant message, SMS, or phone call. It is for these reasons that automation systems, and specifically vCO, came about: to do work on your behalf and let you know if things *don't* go according to plan.

Whenever humans teach other humans new skills, the opportunity for misinterpretation exists. A task automated with vCO becomes three things: standard, repeatable, and predictable. This allows the human component to move from reactive to proactive and to focus on improving the task itself. The automation of the task is easy, but the power of the automation itself is great.

Save Time

As mentioned previously, if you have a defined process, no matter how informal (more on that later), for a task within your vSphere infrastructure, you can likely automate it with vCO.

What do you gain from this automation? Time. As anyone involved in IT knows, the most valuable asset IT professionals have is their time. vCO helps you make the most effective use of that time. Take snapshot monitoring, for example:

> **NOTE**
>
> The assumption here is that you are doing each of these by hand in the vSphere Client. If you are using PowerCLI or another automation toolkit already, well, you're ahead of the game and should go have a congratulatory vBeer.

- **Logging in to the vSphere Client:** 30 seconds to 1 minute, depending on vSphere size
- **Locating all VMs with open snapshots:** Several minutes
- **Validating the age of the snapshot:** 5 seconds per snapshot

- **Validating size:** 5 seconds per snapshot
- **Filing an incident report for each:** 2 minutes (variable)

For a single snapshot hidden among 12 VMs, that likely isn't that painful. However, for more than a dozen VMs or snapshots, or if you have to look more often than once every few days, you can start to see where vCO can really help to save you some time. vCO even includes a workflow by default to perform this work. Chapter 8, "Amazing Smoothies Day 2: Dealing with Snapshots," covers this in detail, but for now, Figure 1.3 shows it in action.

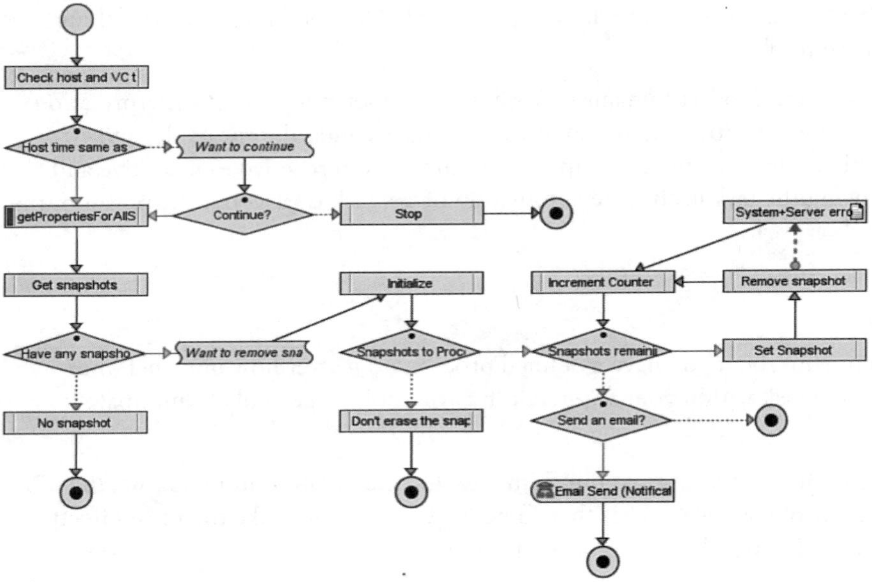

Figure 1.3 Schema to remove old snapshots

> **NOTE**
>
> Regarding incident reports, I'm not sure what your organization calls them. Some common terms are *tickets*, *service requests*, and *incident reports*. The point here is that depending on your process you should, at a minimum, identify that a specific VM has a snapshot running. You likely also want to notify the owner of said VM every few days.

Okay, so now that you are thoroughly sold on using vCenter Orchestrator, let's take a moment to think about who should use, or otherwise have access to, your vCO systems.

Who Should Use vCenter Orchestrator?

Rather than spend a lot of time in the front matter of the book explaining "who should read this book," I opted for this section. After all, if you have picked up a book on vCenter Orchestrator, you have already identified yourself as part of the target audience.

Who in your organization should be using vCO? I can't pretend to prescribe that to you because ultimately it depends on what you will be using vCO for. If you are striving for the "self-service portal" type of flexibility mentioned earlier, you will have any number of folks from across your organization logging in. These may include your IT administrators, managers, or delegates from other departments who request new VMs or VM maintenances. If you choose to expose less functionality to your end users, the cast of players changes again. At a minimum, however, you want at least your vSphere administrators to have access along with whoever is designing the workflows or business processes.

With this in mind, let's consider some common use cases for vCO and work from there into which organizational players might end up needing access.

NOTE

These are some of the use cases that we examine further in Part III, "Amazing Smoothies, Inc. (a.k.a. Real-World Use Cases)":

- Snapshot maintenance
- Virtual machine lifecycle

When returning to each of these later in this book, we consider in more detail the ins and outs of the processes and process owners. For now, let's simplify things a bit.

Snapshot Maintenance

Snapshot maintenance has a number of components to it. Each component potentially has its own process, as well. For the sake of this chapter, we go with snapshot monitoring as a subset.

Snapshot monitoring consists of the following basic steps:

1. Identify running snapshots.
2. Validate age.
3. Validate size.
4. Validate remaining space on the datastore.

NOTE

These will vary based on how your organization is structured.

As you can see, you can complete all of these tasks with a quick glance at the VMs running in your vSphere Client. Therefore, the process will likely fall to either a vSphere or VM administrator. Seems straightforward so far, right? Let's take a look at virtual machine lifecycle next to see how this might get more complex.

Virtual Machine Lifecycle

Like snapshot maintenance, the VM lifecycle topic can consist of any number of processes. Each process is as unique as the organization performing the tasks. With that said, we again pick a common one and break it down into some common steps. For this example, we use "VM birth" or "create a new VM." From there, our list of steps/tasks looks similar to the following:

1. A new VM request comes in.
2. The availability of resources is checked.
3. Management gives approval.
4. Change management approval is granted.
5. The configuration management database (CMDB) is updated.
6. The VM is built.

You can see right away the two or more steps that potentially require a step outside the vSphere administrator's realm. Some, like management approval, may even require a step outside the IT department. After all, who will approve the chargeback for "yet another VM?" Or in the case of change management approval, depending on how complex your change management process is, a designated member of the change management board may need access to approve the new VM.

In these cases, you need to provide either vCenter Orchestrator access to each of these groups or a functioning web portal for the respective groups to access. That web portal might additionally need to be integrated upstream into your existing processes or tools.

In these examples, you can start to see that depending on your organization's processes and workflows, the number of touch points for groups outside the vSphere administrators can grow significantly—so much so that the level of organizational buy-in will determine how far you can push the threads of workflow automation into your vSphere administration duties. Having that buy-in is just one of the many things that will help you in determining when to use vCO.

When Should You Use vCenter Orchestrator?

I suggest that you use vCenter Orchestrator *all the time*.

That, however, is not practical, and it is potentially dangerous. It is not practical in that not every task needs to be automated or have a workflow attached to it. Consider troubleshooting. Although you might have a methodology, no two cases are alike. This leaves you in the position of either having to write an extremely complex workflow or leaving this set of tasks not automated.

NOTE

Depending on your environment, it is possible to focus workflow development on troubleshooting and resolving the 20% of issues that eat the 80% of your administrators' time. That said, there is always a point of diminishing returns when you head down this path. Be aware of it and focus your automation and workflow development where it will have the biggest impact.

As far as potentially dangerous, that is where having defined processes or tasks comes into play. Therefore, the best times to use vCenter Orchestrator are the following:

- You have a repetitive task to complete.
- You have a time-consuming process.
- You have well-defined processes.
- You have repetitive tasks.

Now that we've about answered all the questions about vCenter Orchestrator, knowing where it fits, both in your processes and in overall vSphere management, is key.

Where Does vCenter Orchestrator Fit?

Where does vCO fit? Well, more specifically, where does vCO fit into your overall vSphere management strategy? To be honest, that is up to you as the master of your vSphere domain. vCO provides various integration points, with third-party infrastructure components and with the VMware product suite, that make it suitable about anywhere.

How's that? Consider some of your common tasks as a vSphere administrator and where either automation or a workflow engine could help, including the following:

- VM provisioning
- Managing virtual resources
- Hardware provisioning
- Handling hardware faults
- Day-to-day management

This list is not comprehensive, but it does give you a starting point to think on (although there are plenty of other places to start your thinking). Another way to see where vCO might fit is to imagine a typical day for yourself as a vSphere administrator. Mind you, I know that the only thing typical about most days is that they are not typical; however, the goal is to think about the tasks that you perform most often. Have you ever been annoyed by any of them? Well, that's a good place for vCO.

Still not seeing it? That's okay; it took me a while at first, too. Let me walk you through the example that made it click for me: VM provisioning. Simple, you say? Consider the component parts:

1. Identify VM requirements.
2. Confirm requirements meet available resources.
3. If requirements do not meet available resources, provision additional resources.
4. Build the VM.
5. Install the operating system.
6. Notify requestor of VM availability.

NOTE

The process (if you have one) for your organization will likely vary. The goal here was to outline some of the most common steps.

Depending on how formal this process is within your organization, you may perform some of these tasks via email, others using the vSphere Client, and yet others using storage or other tools. Where vCO shines is in taking all of these steps and enabling you to build them, using a drag-and-drop GUI, into a single workflow. Now think about that!

Excited yet? If so, you're likely thinking, "That's cool, I'll take two." Let's look at how to get there from here.

How to Get Started

This is the topic of the entire next chapter. You will see that it is easier than you might think. The next chapter covers basic installation and some more complex and scalable vCenter Orchestrator installation strategies.

Summary

This chapter answered some basic questions about what vCO is and what it is capable of. Additionally, the chapter gave examples of both when and why to use vCO. Finally, the chapter touched on how to get started with vCO.

Chapter 2

Installing vCenter Orchestrator

After reading Chapter 1, "Introducing VMware vCenter Orchestrator," you should have a good grasp of what vCO is and is capable of, and are likely ready to begin an installation. In this chapter, we build a vCO installation upon which the remainder of the examples in this book are built.

To be more specific, this chapter covers three things:

- vCO installation types

  You need to make a few different architecture and scale decisions when deploying vCO. This section covers each of the three types of vCO installation.

- vCO installation

  This section takes the architecture decisions from the preceding section and applies them to an actual installation.

- The vCO Client

  Finally, you are introduced to the vCO Client.

Before moving along, it is important to note that this chapter covers only installation. Chapter 3, "Configuring vCenter Orchestrator," covers configuration.

vCenter Orchestrator Installation Types

If you have purchased vSphere, it includes the license to run vCenter Server, and when you install vCenter Server, vCO is silently bundled right along at install time. However, this is not the only way to install vCO, and depending on your needs, be they scalability, geographic, or even organizational, your vCO installation can be tailored to fit. This section covers three basic installation types:

- Installing vCO alongside vCenter Server
- Installing vCO as a standalone server
- Separating vCO and the vCO Database

These install types should cover the majority of deployments. For each install type, we start with a basic description, logical diagram, and finish with the *why* behind each choice. With that in mind, let's take a closer look.

NOTE

This chapter does not discuss the virtues of physical versus virtual for a vCO deployment because that would not otherwise change much, if anything, in this discussion. Besides, everything should be a virtual machine (VM), shouldn't it?

NOTE

In most vCO deployments, you use the install types listed here or a variant of them. Some things not covered here include scaling vCO horizontally and having redundant vCO servers. These each have an associated rabbit hole of design decisions that are beyond the scope of this book.

Installing vCO Alongside vCenter Server

Installing vCO alongside or on the same server as you install VMware vCenter Server is the default method for deploying vCO. In fact, it is silently installed in a disabled state when you install vCenter Server onto a host, as shown in Figure 2.1.

VMware provides the vCO installation in this fashion so that when you are ready to begin automating and orchestrating your business processes there are fewer barriers to entry. Note that although it is installed at this point, some additional configuration is needed to make it functional (as covered in Chapter 3). From a logical perspective, your installation environment could be conceptualized as shown in Figure 2.2.

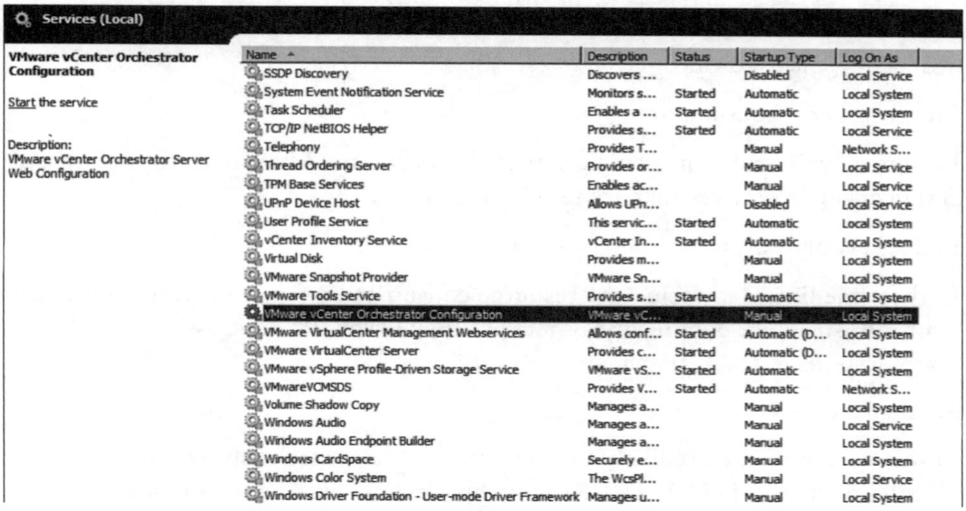

Figure 2.1 The vCO service installed with vCenter

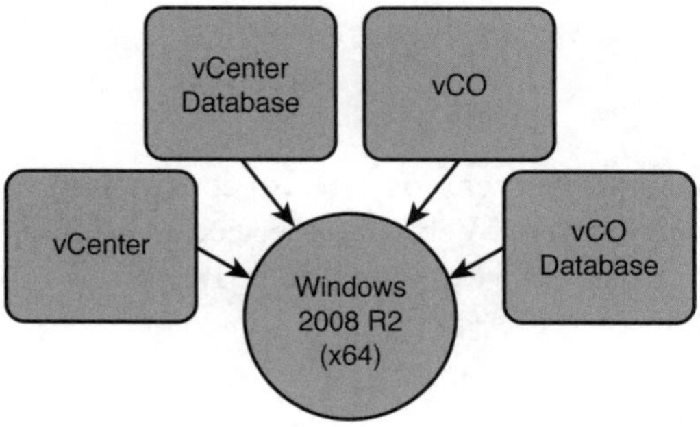

Figure 2.2 A typical single-server vCO installation

Now that you know what this install looks like from a logical perspective, and where to click to make it happen, why would you perform this install type? There are a few reasons, actually. Let's look at some of the pros and cons and some of the times when you would use this setup.

Pros

The pros include the following:

- Lower resource consumption

  Having all vCO roles on a single server allows you to reduce both the computing and licensing resources that are required to run it.

- Reduced complexity

  In the same line as lowering the resource consumption for vCO, you also reduce your infrastructure complexity. There are now fewer IPs to be assigned and fewer systems to track, patch, and secure.

- Maintenance

  In this situation, you are likely to have a one-to-one relationship between vCenter Server and vCO. Therefore, in any given maintenance situation, vCO cannot perform actions if vCenter is otherwise unavailable.

Cons

The cons include the following:

- Scalability

  When installed on the same server as vCenter Server, you are also constrained by the same set of resources. Further, the vSphere WebAccess service associated with vCenter Server can and will use all the memory assigned to it. If not managed properly, it could affect vCO.

- Security

  Having all vCO and vCenter Server roles installed on a single host would allow an attacker who compromises one service ready access into another.

- Maintenance

  Having multiple services on the same server is a great way to reduce cost. After all, isn't that one of the fundamental benefits of virtualization? However, having vCO and vCenter Server reside on the same VM, you now have to account for both services in any maintenance scenario.

- Reliability

  When running vCO, the vCO Database, and vCenter Server with the vCenter Server Database on the same host or VM, you put both services at risk of failure.

Most notably, if you haven't sized resources appropriately, if either vCenter or vCO becomes a resource hog, it will affect the stability and performance of the other service. In addition, if there is an unexpected bug in vCO, it could also cause vCenter to crash.

- Flexibility

  Having both vCenter and vCO together limits your ability to test and upgrade the individual components separately. If a vCO upgrade requires a system reboot, vCenter would experience downtime, as well.

Use Cases

This particular installation type is best suited for smaller deployments, such as the following:

- Small business

  This install type is excellent in smaller or cost-conscious IT environments.

- Proof of concept

  If you are setting up a proof-of-concept environment, this particular install type enables you to spend less time during the installation and configuration of vCO and more time focusing on your automation workflows.

- Lab environments

  This install type is also well suited to the lab. In fact, outside of the installation covered later in this chapter, it is the method I use in my own lab and on which much of this book is built. This is because I have rather limited lab resources that I need to make the most of, so reducing the footprint and resource consumption is key.

Installing vCenter Orchestrator as a Standalone Server

Next we consider the standalone, or self-contained, vCO model. That is to say, this installation type separates your vCO installation from vCenter Server. It is given its own server. This makes your environment slightly more complex because of the additional server instances that you must deal with. The additional servers mean additional servers to be patched, secured, and otherwise managed.

NOTE

When I say *server* here, it can be used to mean either physical server or virtual server. My recommendation is to install it as a VM. You may, however, have some organizational constraints that prevent this. As stated at the beginning of this chapter, the physical versus virtual machine discussion is beyond our scope.

Let's take a look at the standalone situation conceptually (see Figure 2.3).

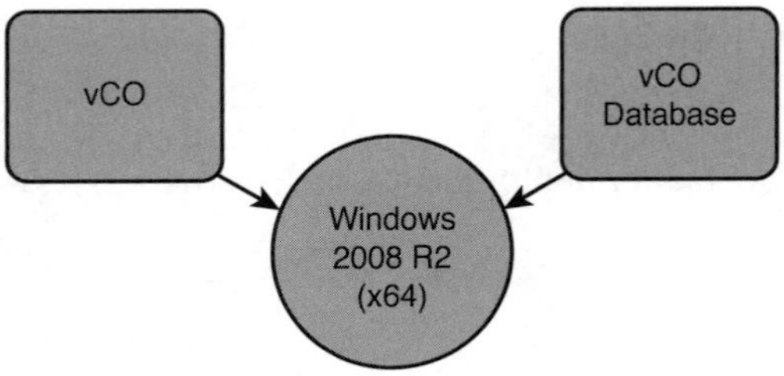

Figure 2.3 A "standalone" vCO installation

This path provides some benefits to offset the added complexities. These benefits are first realized in the reduced load on your vCenter Server because the vCO service is now running elsewhere. You will also notice that no longer having vCO and vCenter protects one against a failure of the other. The approach of installing both vCenter and vCO on the same server puts one service at the mercy of another. As critical as the vCenter Server service is, you do not want a stalled or crashed vCO instance to halt your operations.

Here are some of the pros and cons of this approach.

Pros

The pros include the following:

- Scalability

  Decoupling vCO from your vCenter Server instance allows you to dedicate resources to vCO without having it directly affect vCenter.

- Maintenance

  This approach lets you have a many-to-one relationship between vCenter Server instances and your vCO instance. In addition, you can reboot each vCenter Server and not affect the vCO instance, should it be currently executing tasks in another vCenter.

- Survivability

  Should a single vCenter Server crash and burn for whatever reason, you no longer have to worry about it also taking down vCO with it.

- Security

  Having fewer services on a single box to track and harden reduces the management overhead and reduces the likelihood of misconfiguration. In addition, an attacker attempting to compromise the box now has another step before attacking vCenter Server directly.

- Flexibility

  Whereas flexibility was listed as a con before, it is now a pro. This is because having a separate vCO server will enable you to test, upgrade, and reboot the two servers independently of one another.

Cons

The cons include the following:

- Management

  With this approach, it means at least one additional server in your environment to maintain. Patching, antivirus, backups, and any other systems policies now need to be applied to an additional box.

- Licensing

  One more server means one more Windows 2008 R2 Server licenses to buy. This applies mostly to smaller organizations without Microsoft enterprise licensing agreements in place.

Use Cases

This installation type is best suited for the following types of environments:

- Small or medium business

  As your small business grows, the availability of services starts to become more critical. Therefore, the enhanced survivability and ease of maintenance provided by this model are well suited to your needs without overly increasing the complexity of your environment.

- Multiple vCenter deployment

  Decoupling vCenter Server and vCO, as this installation type does, makes the management of multiple vCenter Server instances easier. This is primarily for two reasons: First, as you add additional vCenter Server instances for vCO to manage, it will require additional resources. Having vCO and vCenter separate enables you to scale these resources independently. Second, there is no longer a maintenance dependency between vCO and vCenter, allowing you to reboot a single vCenter without affecting the vCO server executing tasks on another.

Installing the vCO Virtual Appliance

The vCO virtual appliance is likely one of the most straightforward and easy ways to get started with vCO. That is, the vCO team has done a lot of work to provide a preinstalled, preconfigured vCO environment that is ready to go almost immediately after download. In addition, although it is self-contained, it can be broken out into its constituent parts and be made to work the same as the Windows installations.

This chapter does not cover the installation of the vCO vApp. If you can deploy a downloaded virtual machine, you can deploy the vCO vApp.

Separating the vCO from the vCO Database

This is likely one of the more complicated vCO setups you will end up performing, but it is not without its benefits. Breaking vCO out as a self-contained server brought you some additional scale; so, too, will you gain some scaling efficiencies by separating vCO from the vCO Database. So, what do I mean by breaking out vCO from the vCO Database? Figure 2.4 shows the different servers and their relationship.

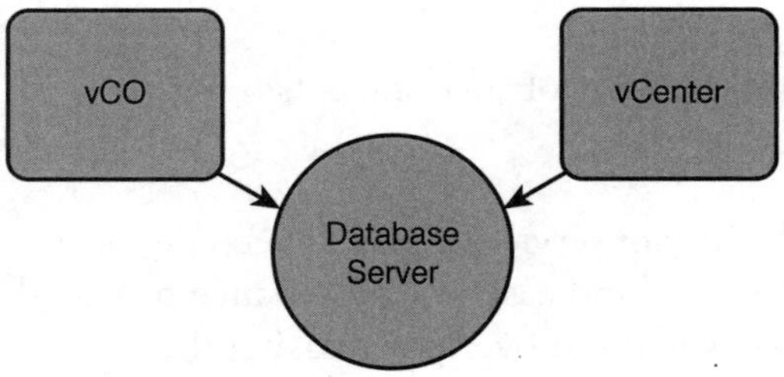

Figure 2.4 A vCO server with a separate database server

NOTE

It is not necessary to use the same database server or instance for the vCO Database. This can be located anywhere that the vCO server has access to.

Okay, so now that you've got an idea about what this looks like, we can consider the pros and cons of this method of deployment.

Pros

The pros include the following:

- Scalability

  In much the same way as separating vCenter and vCO improved scalability, removing the database server role from the vCO server allows you to continue to scale the vCO instance.

- Performance

  With all your roles broken out now, you can tune each of them individually for performance. Some examples might include putting the database on fast spindles and providing vCO a large amount of RAM and a fast CPU to process workflows.

- Security

  This follows on the security point from the last deployment method, in that you have removed yet another role from the server, thus reducing its attack surface.

- Survivability

  In this deployment scenario, you can now place the vCO Database onto a highly available Microsoft Clustering Service (MSCS) to provide application-level failover in addition to VMware High Availability for VM failover.

Cons

The cons include the following:

- Maintenance

  For this one, we could copy and paste the definition from the last deployment methodology. This is because having a separate database server, if one did not already exist, now adds YAB (yet another box) to your environment.

- Resources

  Now that all three roles (vCenter Server, vCO, and database) are broken out, you need to make sure you maintain at least the minimum resources required for each. Depending on your environment, these resources may be at a premium.

- Cost

  If you have to acquire additional resources to run in this methodology, these will add cost. You also need to ensure you are licensed appropriately for both your OS and the database server (also potentially adding cost to the solution).

Use Cases

The use cases for this last install type are logical expansions in size and scale from that of installing vCO on a standalone server.

Installation Type Comparison

Table 2.1 is a quick reference for the pros and cons discussed earlier.

Table 2.1 Pros and Cons

	Maintenance	Resources	Cost	Scalability	Security	Performance
With vCenter	Complicated	Low	Low	Small	X	Low
Standalone	Easy	Medium	Medium	Medium	✓	Medium
Separate DB	Easiest	High	High	Big	✓	Best

vCenter Orchestrator Installation

Now that you've selected the right installation type for your environment, it's time to cover the installation of vCO itself. In this section, we install vCO as a standalone server.

Only one, you say? Well, that's because vCO is installed at the time you install vCenter Server from the outset, only leaving us the configuration tasks to perform. The process for installing vCO as a standalone server is nearly identical to separating vCO from the database. As we come across differences, I call them out in the text.

Before we begin the installation, let's take a moment to look at the minimum requirements and some recommendations as to where to tweak these for better performance.

- 1 CPU or vCPU (recommended: 2)
- 4GB RAM (recommended: 6GB for vCO)
- 2GB Disk (recommended: 4GB or more)
- LDAP Directory Service
    - Active Directory (2003 or 2008)
    - Novell eDirectory
    - Sun Java Directory
    - OpenLDAP (unsupported)
- Static IP (recommended: both a static IP and a DNS entry)

NOTE

At the time of this writing, the vSphere documentation does not specify database compatibility. In addition, you want to revisit the documentation at vmware.com prior to installation to ensure you are up to date.

When calculating the total amount of RAM you need, you must add the recommendation here to the RAM required by other services on the server. For example, vCO sharing a server with vCenter Server would look similar to the following:

- **vCO:** 6GB
- **vCenter (< 100 hosts):** 1GB
- **Windows 2008:** 512MB
- **SQL Express:** 256MB

That leaves you with roughly 8GB of RAM required to run all these roles on a single server.

With that last bit out of the way, are you ready to go? I certainly am. The process for installing vCO is as follows:

1. Obtain the installation files.
2. Extract the install files and open .\vCenter-Server\vCO\.
3. Run vCenterOrchestrator.exe.

4. Agree to the license.
5. Choose an install directory.
6. Select the install type.
7. Select the location for shortcuts.
8. Install.

Obtain the Installation Files

The files we are looking for are either the ISO or .zip archive of the VMware vCenter Server installation. You can obtain these files from the Downloads section of the VMware website.

Extract the Install Files and Open .\vCenter-Server\vCO\

For this example, I've chosen the .zip file. However, the ISO also works if you have the appropriate tools to read the file. Figures 2.5 and 2.6 show the location of the installation files and the extracted vCO installer.

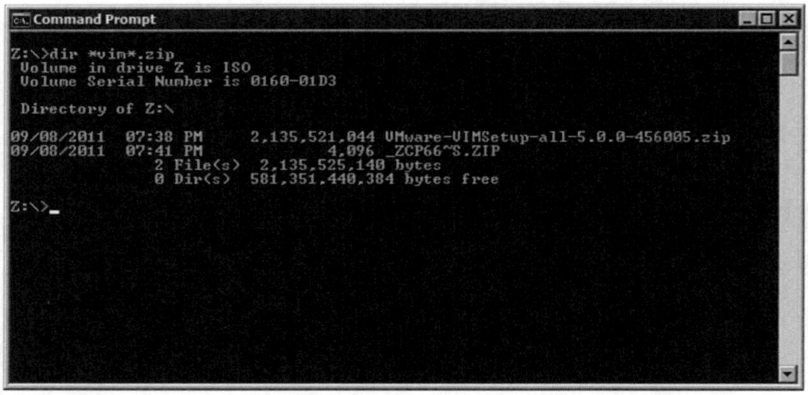

Figure 2.5 Locating the installation files

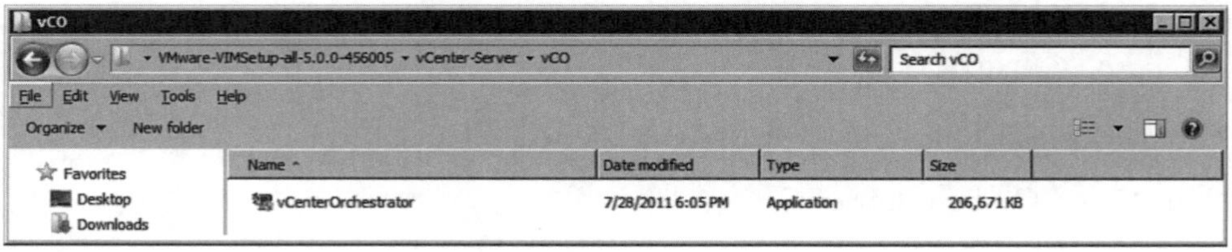

Figure 2.6 Extracted install files

Run vCenterOrchestrator.exe

Now that you have grabbed the files and found your way to where you need to be, it's time to get down to the actual business of installing. Run the file vCenterOrchestrator.exe. Figure 2.7 shows the welcome screen.

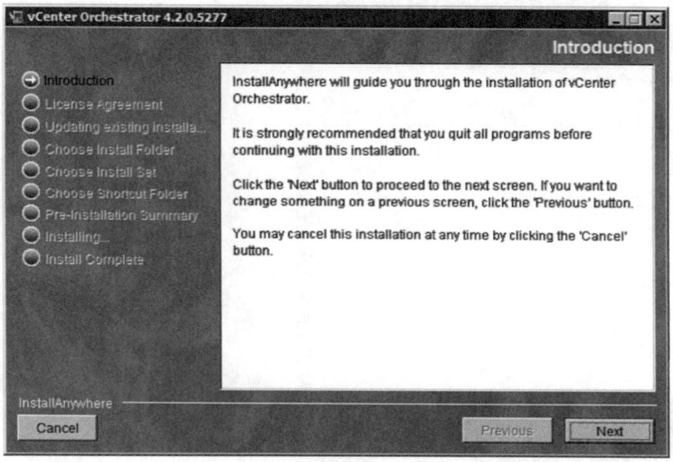

Figure 2.7 Installation welcome screen

Agree to the License

Every installation has them, as shown in Figure 2.8. Mostly, you click Accept and move on.

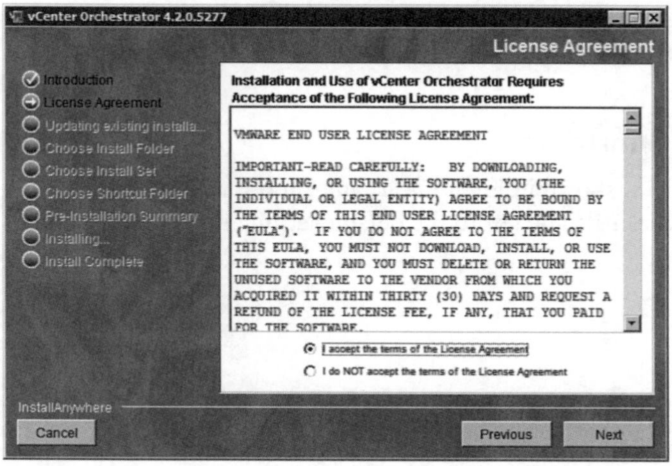

Figure 2.8 License agreement

Choose the Install Directory

Change the default as needed based on your system policies. In this example, we leave the default (see Figure 2.9).

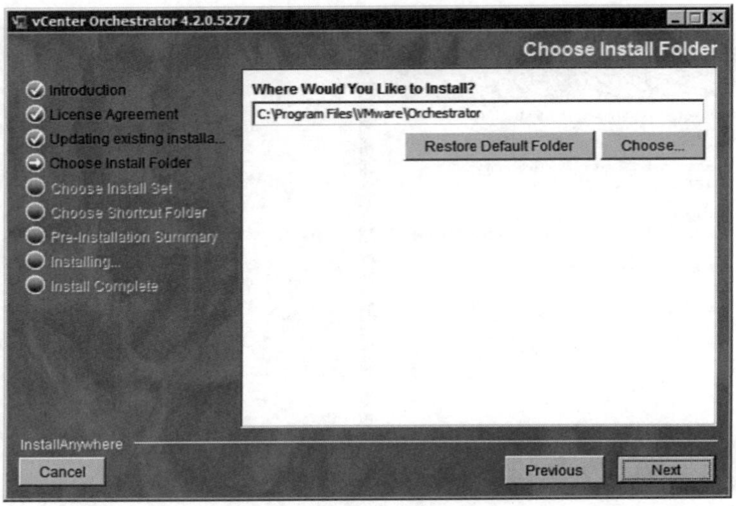

Figure 2.9 Choosing an installation folder

Select the Install Type

Your choice here varies based on where you will be managing the vCO server. In most cases, I recommend choosing both Client and Server, as shown in Figure 2.10. This way, you can test functionality local on the server in the absence of reliable networking.

Select the Location for Shortcuts

We're almost there. On this screen, shown in Figure 2.11, you choose where to place vCO shortcuts. In most instances, this can also be left to the default setting; it puts all the vCO tools at your fingertips.

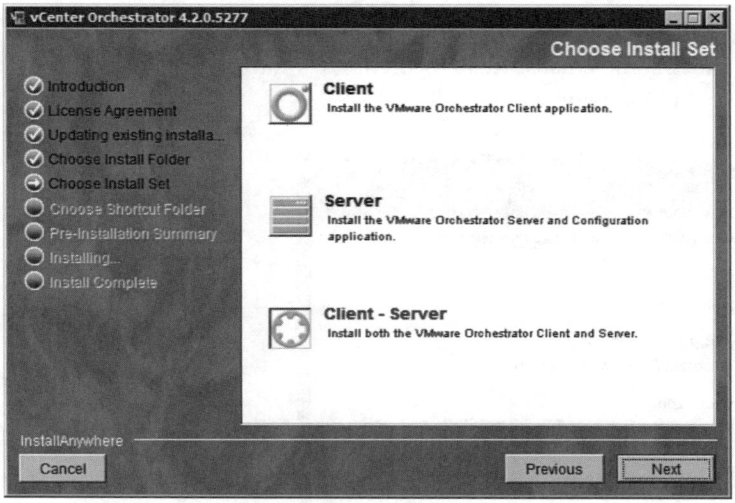

Figure 2.10 Choosing an installation type

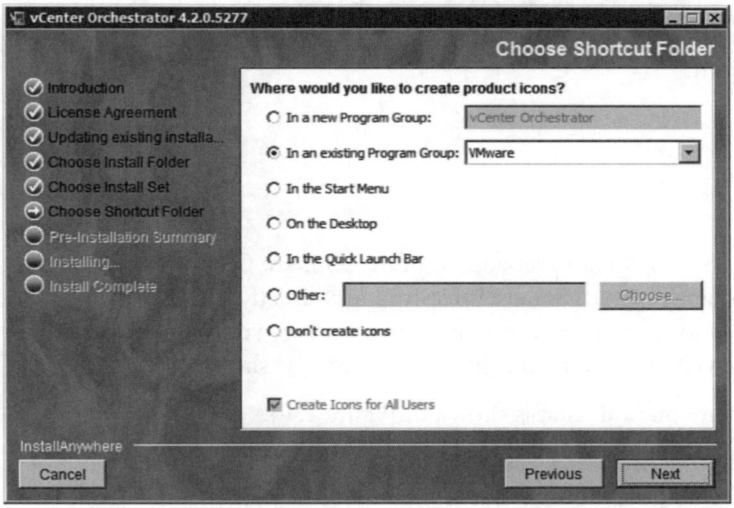

Figure 2.11 Choosing a location for shortcuts

Install

Sit back, grab a coffee, or check some emails. Really, you don't want to have to watch yet another blue bar work its way across your screen.

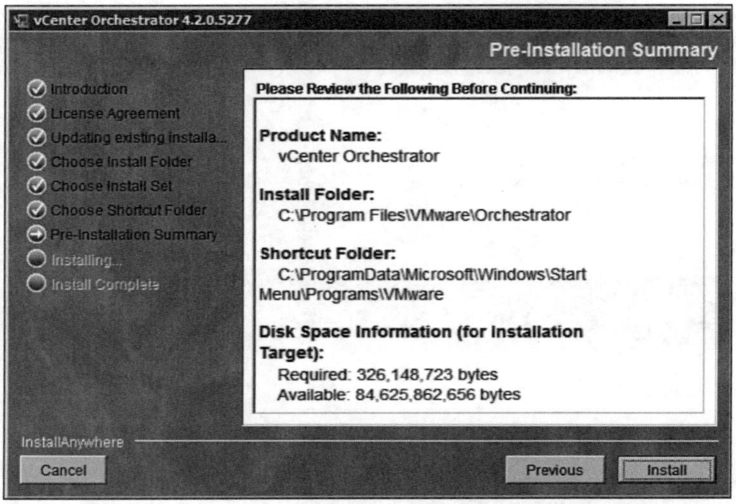

Figure 2.12 Installation summary

The vCO Client

vCenter Orchestrator has its own client independent of the vSphere Client. Whereas the vSphere Client is built to manage your vSphere infrastructure directly, the vCO Client is used to manage workflows and related features that in turn manage your vSphere infrastructure. You can find the vCO Client in your list of programs, as shown in Figure 2.13.

On opening the vCO Client, you find what is shown in Figure 2.14.

Note we have not yet configured the vCO server, which as you see here, results in us not being able to connect. Have no fear, though; that is what the next chapter is all about.

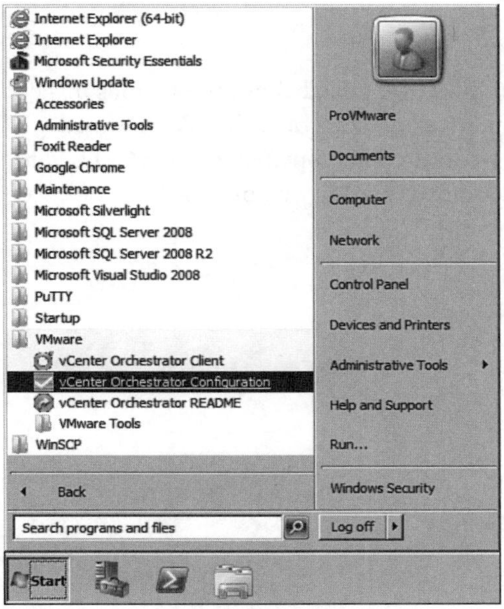

Figure 2.13 Locating the vCO Client

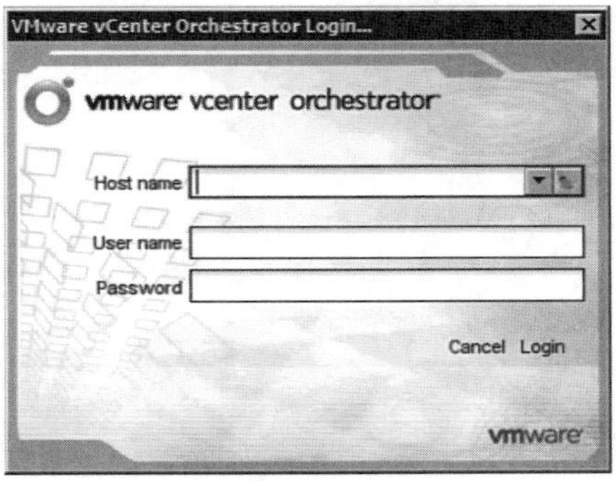

Figure 2.14 Opening the vCO Client

Summary

In this chapter, we covered quite a bit of ground. First, we talked about the various installation types you can use with vCO along with the pros and cons of each. We then walked through a vCO standalone installation. Finally, we located and opened up the vCO Client. Overall, this was a pretty quick and straightforward chapter, but one on which we build as we begin to configure vCO in the next chapter.

Chapter 3

Configuring vCenter Orchestrator

As you saw in Chapter 2, "Installing vCenter Orchestrator," vCO will not even let you log in before it is configured. So, configure it we must. There is no shortage of configuration options for vCO, either. The basic configuration we walk through in this chapter leaves you with a working configuration on which we build the remainder of our workflows. Our basic configuration covers the following areas:

- Starting the vCO Web Configuration service
- Changing the default vCO configuration service password
- Configuring networking
- Configuring LDAP
- Database configuration
- Configuring SSL
- Licensing the vCO server
- Plug-in configuration
- Installing vCO as a service
- Backing up the configuration

It might not look complicated, but if this is your first time configuring vCO, some of these items can be a bit obtuse when you begin to configure them. With that, here we go.

Starting the vCO Web Configuration Service

This step is needed only if you are using the vCO service that was installed when you installed vCenter Server. This is because when installed alongside vCenter Server, the vCO service is set to manual. Here is the procedure to start this service:

1. Click Start.
2. Click Run.
3. Type **services.msc.**
4. Locate vCenter Orchestrator Web Configuration Service.
5. Click Start.

Figure 3.1 shows what the service looks like in the services list once started.

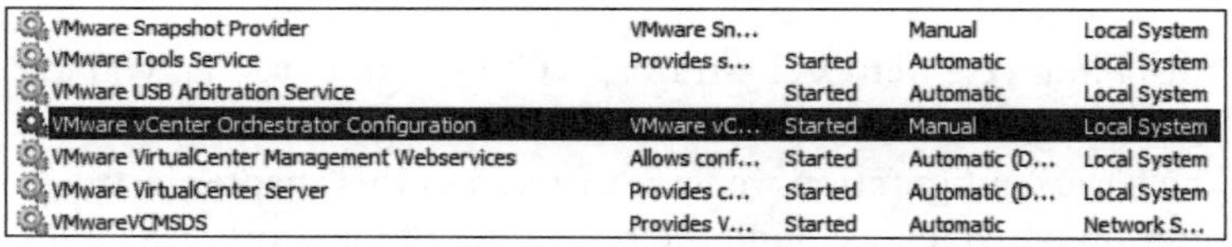

VMware Snapshot Provider VMware Sn... Manual Local System
VMware Tools Service Provides s... Started Automatic Local System
VMware USB Arbitration Service Started Automatic Local System
VMware vCenter Orchestrator Configuration VMware vC... Started Manual Local System
VMware VirtualCenter Management Webservices Allows conf... Started Automatic (D... Local System
VMware VirtualCenter Server Provides c... Started Automatic (D... Local System
VMwareVCMSDS Provides V... Started Automatic Network S...

Figure 3.1 Starting the vCO Web Configuration service

> **NOTE**
>
> Because you will not be logging in every day to configure the vCenter Ops service, I recommend leaving this set to Manual. This keeps the resources consumed by this service from affecting the remainder of your environment. More important, it also helps reduce the attack surface of the vCO server. You will, however, need to start it again should you need to make changes to vCO (perhaps to add a second vCenter Server or add a plug-in, for example).

Changing the Default vCO Configuration Service Password

Although you could skip this step, I strongly recommend against it and suggest instead that you pick a suitably long, random password for the vCO Web Configuration service. There are several web tools available to do this for you. Setting a long, random password helps reduce the attack surface of the box by having one less easily guessed password.

NOTE

The default username is vmware and cannot be changed. This makes it that much more important that you choose a strong password, as with a fixed username half of the battle for guessing is done for an attacker.

The procedure for changing the default configuration password is as follows:

1. Open a browser and browse to http://<vCO_Hostname>:8282.
2. Log in with vmware/vmware.
3. In the right pane, click Change Password.
4. Specify both the old password and new password.
5. Apply the changes.

Figures 3.2 through 3.4 show the password-reset process.

Figure 3.2 The vCO Web Configuration Login screen

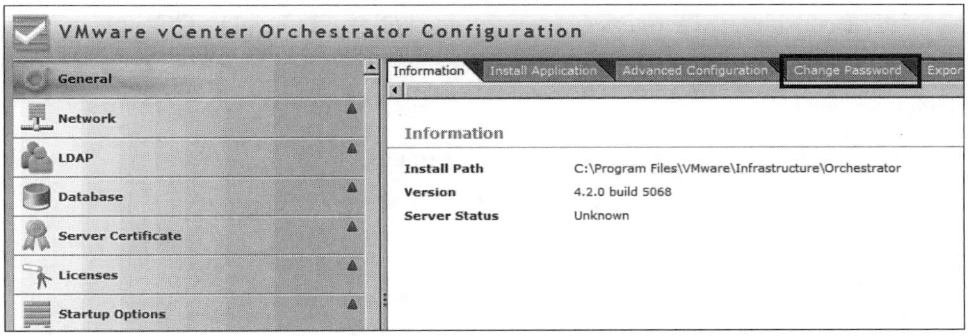

Figure 3.3 Click Change Password

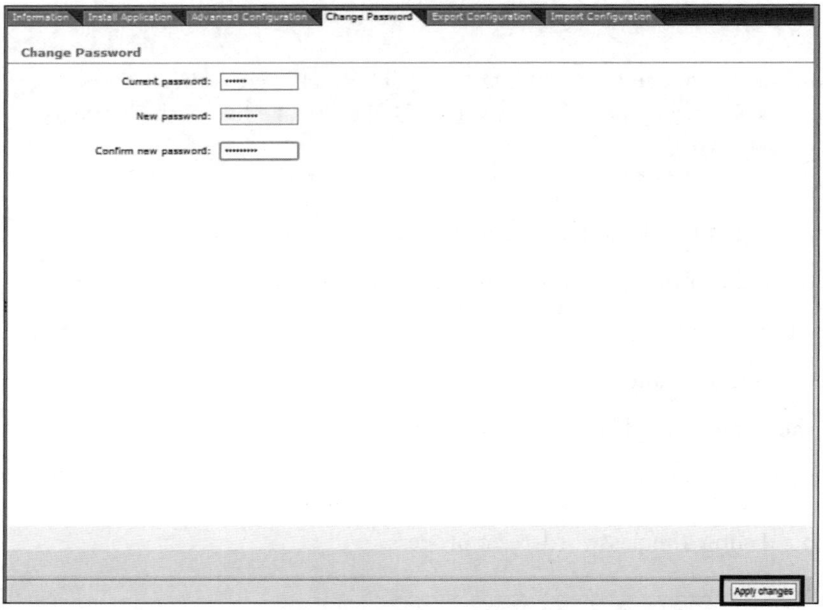

Figure 3.4 Specify passwords and click Apply Changes

Configuring Networking

In most instances, the server on which you run vCO will have multiple network interface cards (NICs) assigned to it. These include a management interface, a backup interface, and other networks vCO may need access to. Some common additional networks vCO might need access into would include things such as your storage network, management network, and Microsoft Active Directory network. In smaller environments, a number of these networks will be consolidated into one. However, you still need to make vCO aware of which network to bind to, or listen on. The steps needed to do this are as follows:

1. Select Network.
2. For the IP address, pick the network you want to use.
3. Confirm the communications ports.
4. Apply the changes.

In Chapter 2, as we were discussing the vCO requirements, we recommended both a static IP as well as a DNS entry. Now that we are configuring vCO, this becomes even more important because having these ensures you can consistently access vCO. It also makes administering vCO, and any required network access control lists, easier. vCO automatically enumerates the IP addresses assigned to the server for you to select in the drop-down, as shown in Figure 3.5.

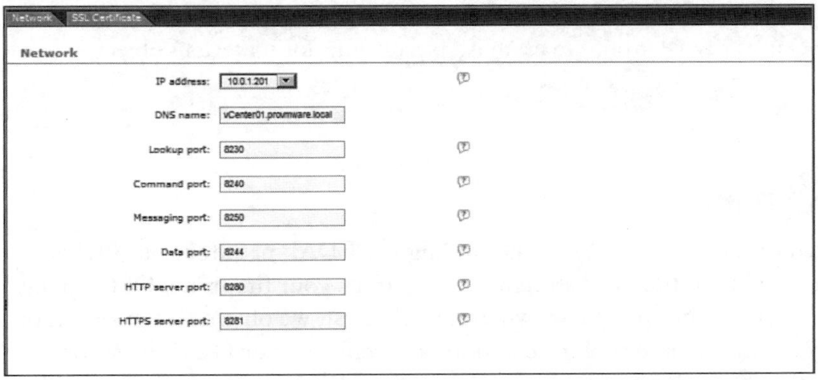

Figure 3.5 IP Address drop-down on the Network page

Also of note in this section are the default communications ports. Rather than list them all here, I refer you to the VMware-specific documentation for them. My recommendation is that unless you have specific organizational requirements to change these from non-default ports, or have a conflict with another application, you want to leave these as default.

Configuring LDAP

LDAP, or Lightweight Directory Access Protocol, is how vCO proxies user authentication back into your existing environment. Be that Microsoft Active Directory, or Novell eDirectory, vCO relies on a third-party authentication source. To perform this configuration step, you need the LDAP path for the OU, or organizational unit, that contains your users. Lost? Well, I show you how to get that path for Microsoft's Active Directory. The procedure to configure vCO to use LDAP is as follows:

1. Find your LDAP path.
2. Fill in the form.
3. Click Apply.

As part of your LDAP configuration, you need to provide vCO with an LDAP group to identify which users are members of the vCO Admins group. In the example, I created a specific group for this. You want to configure this as is appropriate for your environment and its security requirements.

NOTE

A working LDAP configuration is critical to the operation of your vCO environment. This is because vCO uses LDAP groups to establish permissions for its various objects and workflows.

Find Your LDAP Path

Of the tasks required to set up LDAP for vCO, finding the LDAP path for your OU is going to be the one that is not the most straightforward if it's your first time. Of the many ways to obtain this information, we review two examples. First, we obtain this information using the DSQuery command-line tool to search for a specific user or OU. The second example uses the search boxes built in to the vCO interface. For these examples, we will use the AD hierarchy in Figure 3.6.

NOTE

In some cases, if you have multiple LDAP servers and one is not accessible, the configuration will time out and yet still display as if it's correctly configured even though it is not.

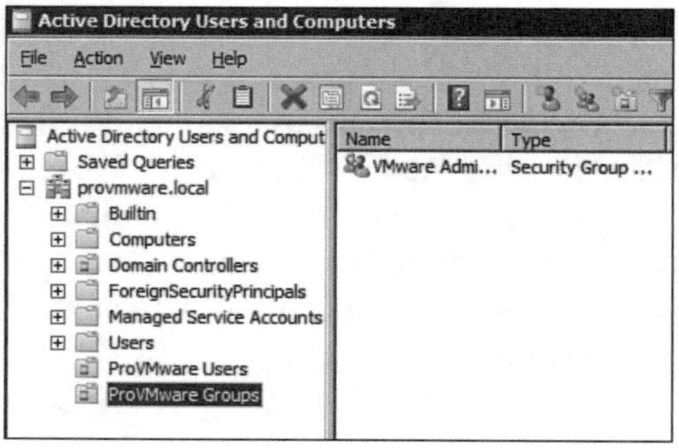

Figure 3.6 Active Directory hierarchy

DSQuery

In this example, there are two OUs in which the users and groups are kept: ProVMware Users and ProVMware Groups. These correlate to the User lookup base and Group lookup base in vCO. We also need to identify the location of VMware Administrators group to use as the vCO Admin group in vCO. To do that, we use the following DSQuery commands:

```
PS C:\> DSquery OU -name "ProVMware Users"
"OU=ProVMware Users,DC=provmware,DC=local"

PS C:\> DSquery group -name "VMware Administrators"
"CN=VMware Administrators,OU=ProVMware Groups,DC=provmware,DC=local"
```

This method gives you information that can be copied and pasted right back into the LDAP configuration page. The next method performs a search directly within the interface.

> **NOTE**
>
> The DSQuery tool is only installed by default on Windows 2008 servers that also have the AD Domain Services role installed. To obtain this tool on a server that does not have this role installed, you can download it from the Microsoft website.

vCO Interface LDAP Search

Using the same AD hierarchy from Figure 3.6, we use the vCO interface to fill the remaining values (see Figure 3.7).

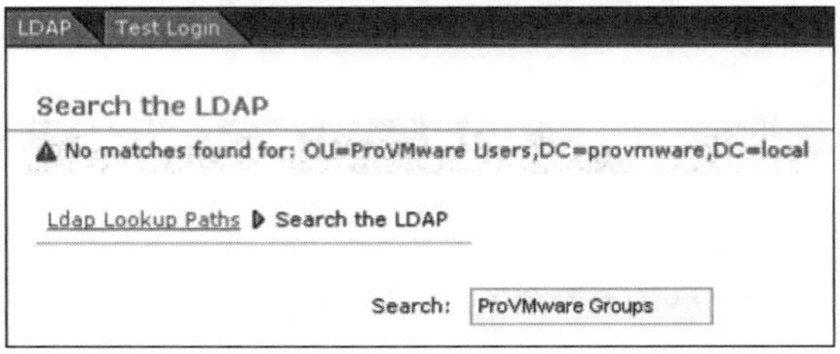

Figure 3.7 The Search dialog

When your search is complete, it should only be a click away from populating the field you searched for.

Fill In the Form

Rather than call out each specific field in the form (because most of them are straightforward), I note some specific fields that warrant some special attention, as follows:

- Root
- Use SSL
- Use Global Catalog
- User/Password

The Root section is called out because this field is also expecting an LDAP path. To obtain this LDAP path, you want to grab the DC= components from your other LDAP fields. This provides vCO a root location from which to start its searching.

Called out next is Use SSL. My recommendation here is to use this setting because it provides SSL encryption for LDAP traffic between vCO and your LDAP server. This additional layer of security further hardens your vCO instance and helps reduce the attack surface by preventing potential information leakage. You cannot set this field, however, until you import the SSL certificate on the Network SSL tab. We cover this in the "Configure SSL" section, later in this chapter.

Next on our list of special fields is Use Global Catalog. Checking this option helps vCO in its lookups of Active Directory objects. This brings us to the final field, User/Password. My recommendation for this field is to use a specially created AD account for the vCO service, with a suitably long password.

Figure 3.8 summarizes the options chosen and the entries in the fields.

When you have finished filling out the form, click Apply Changes at the bottom of the page. vCO then runs a validation and calls out any errors in the log pane at the bottom of your window.

There are a few other things to note when configuring vCO to use LDAP that will save you some headaches down the road:

- Use an LDAP server that is physically close to your vCO installation. This reduces the latency of the queries that vCO must make and keeps performance snappy.
- Set the user and group lookups to the narrowest LDAP path possible. As in, don't target your entire directory because doing so will result in huge queries and slow down the entire vCO system.

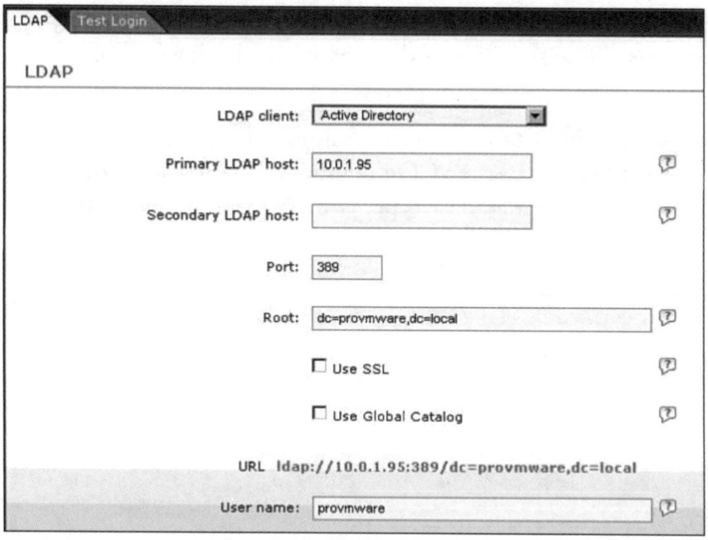

Figure 3.8 Screenshot of the options chosen and the filled-in fields

Database Configuration

Another critical component of vCO is the vCO Database. The vCO Database is used to maintain job or workflow execution state among other items. Thus, the database is key to vCO operating successfully. To configure a database for use with vCO, you must perform the following steps:

1. Create a database service account.
2. Create the database.
3. Select the database type.
4. Fill in the form.
5. Install the database.

The first two tasks are done on servers other than where your vCO server is. In fact, they may need to be done by another group or individual within your organization. If you are the domain admin, you first need to create an AD user, with a suitably secure password. This is used as a service account to connect from the vCO server to your database server. You then need to set this login up on your database server, as well, and grant it permissions to your specific database. The specifics of these activities are beyond our scope, however.

Next up, we fill in the form and create the database. In this example, we use the SQLServer database type. You want to refer to the vCO documentation for additional supported database types. After selecting the database type, you are presented with the form in Figure 3.9.

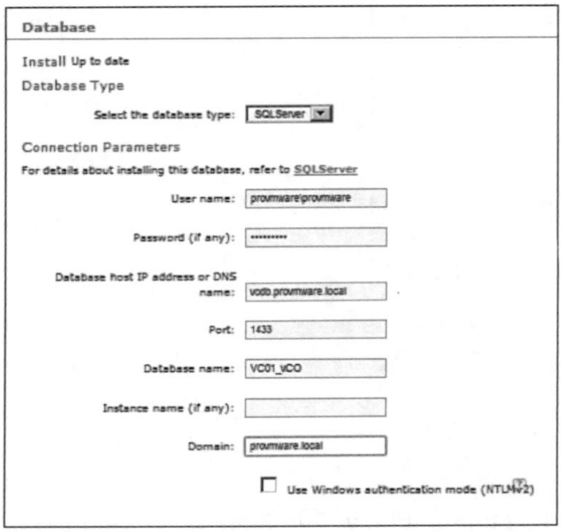

Figure 3.9 Configure database form

There are a couple of "gotchas" to look out for here. The first is to make sure that DNS is working and that the server name you are using is actually in DNS. The second is to ensure that your SQL server is configured for Windows Authentication; otherwise, you receive an error that looks like this:

```
Cannot connect to jdbc:jtds:sqlserver://vcdb.provmware.local:1433/VC01_
vCO;domain=provmware.local. Connection error was: Login failed. The login
is from an untrusted domain and cannot be used with Windows authentication.
```

After you've filled in the form, click Apply and vCO validates your inputs. Once you've corrected any errors, you are presented with the dialog shown in Figure 3.10.

When it's finished, the resulting window looks like Figure 3.11.

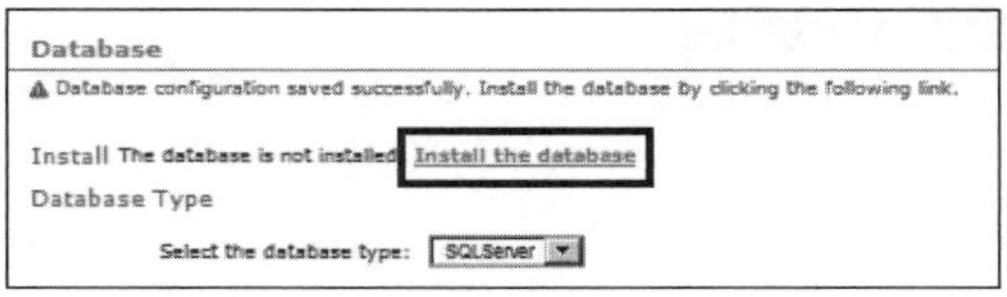

Figure 3.10 Install the database tables

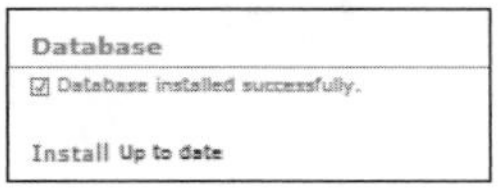

Figure 3.11 vCO tables installed

Configuring SSL

vCO uses SSL in two different ways. First, vCO uses SSL to secure communications between vCO and vCenter Server instances. The second way vCO uses SSL is to digitally sign exports from your vCO server. We break this section then into the following two parts:

- Secure vCenter communications
- Configure the vCO host certificate

Secure vCenter Communications

Configuring vCO to use SSL communications with vCenter Server consists of the following steps:

1. Open the Networking control panel.
2. Select the SSL tab.
3. Provide an address and select Import from URL.
4. Click Import.
5. Under Startup Options, restart vCO.

Figure 3.12 shows the SSL Certificate tab and the Import from URL section. You need to repeat steps 2 and 3 for each vCenter Server that your vCO server will communicate with.

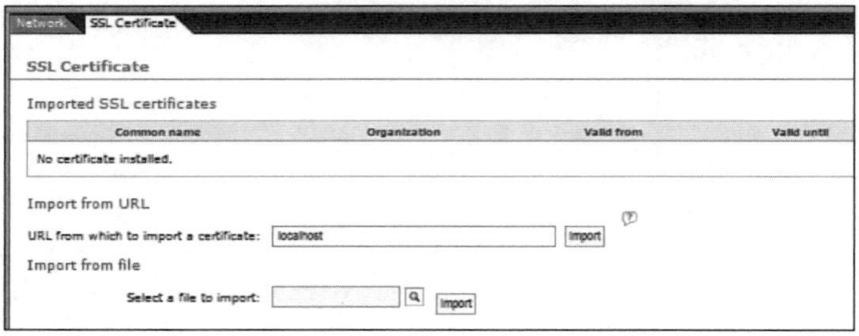

Figure 3.12 Import from URL

> **NOTE**
>
> In the URL dialog, you only need to use the server's name or IP address. In fact, at the time of this writing, using https:// causes the interface to error out.

Configure the vCO Host Certificate

As mentioned at the beginning of this section, vCO can use SSL to sign objects that you export from vCO. Most commonly, these are packages. However, before we can sign a package, we need to make sure vCO has an SSL certificate to sign them with. There are three methods for doing this:

- Import an existing certificate.
- Create a self-signed certificate.
- Obtain a third-party certificate.

This section covers the middle option, using the vCO interface to create a self-signed certificate. Self-signed certificates are a good option when you are either resource constrained or do not otherwise run your own PKI (Private Key Infrastructure).

To create and install the self-signed certificate, you need to open the Server Certificate page of the vCO interface. Once on that page, fill in the relevant fields and click Create. Figure 3.13 shows a completed form.

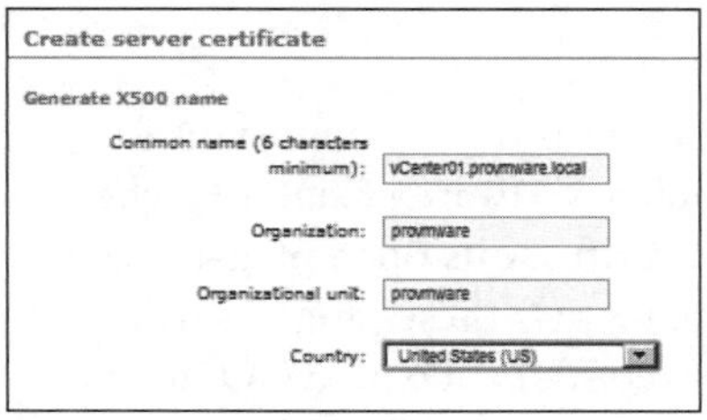

Figure 3.13 A completed server certificate form for a self-signed certificate

Licensing the vCO Server

Next on our list of configuration tasks is the licensing of the vCO server. vCenter Orchestrator, starting at version 4.0.x to the present, uses the same license as your vCenter Server. From this license, it establishes which edition of vCenter Server you have and configures itself accordingly. It is important at this stage to state that you need to have completed the vCenter SSL configuration in the preceding section before performing the configuration in this section.

On this screen, you have two options: have vCO retrieve the key from vCenter or enter the key by hand. Because this book is about automating things, we let vCO grab the license automatically, as shown in Figure 3.14.

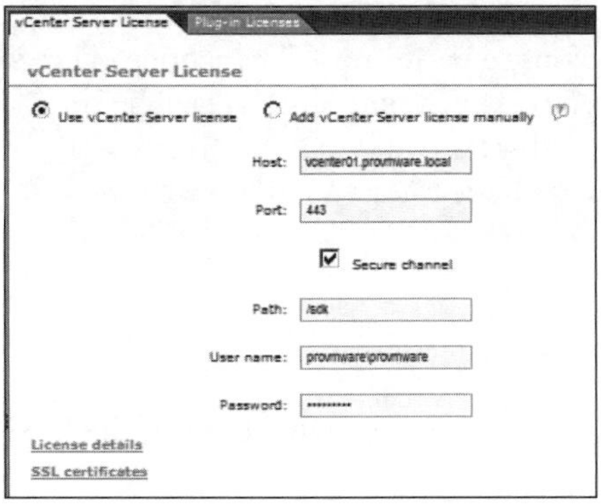

Figure 3.14 Licensing vCO from vCenter

Plug-In Configuration

This gets to be the second-to-last step in our configuration but is no less important for it. This is because, as we discussed in Chapter 1, "Introducing VMware vCenter Orchestrator," vCO is an orchestration engine that derives its power from its open plug-in architecture. Our job in this section is to configure both the credentials these plug-ins will use and which plug-ins will be enabled when the vCO service starts. To get vCO up and running, our configuration tasks are as follows:

- Provide plug-in credentials.
- Enable plug-ins for vCO startup.
- Install additional plug-ins.

Provide Plug-In Credentials

In providing the plug-in credentials, I recommend the same course of action as we took with the other required accounts in this chapter, and that is to create and provide credentials for a specific service account. This helps further harden vCO installation by providing an auditable user account for workflows, which have as few privileges as is needed to perform the actions defined for that plug-in. The user accounts you create for each plug-in must also be part of the vCO Admin group you specified when configuring LDAP.

NOTE

Each plug-in requires different vCenter Server permissions to perform various actions. The number and type of permissions required will vary based on which plug-ins you enable for your environment and therefore are beyond the scope of this book. However, you can seek guidance for role creation in the VMware Administrators Guide on the VMware website.

Enable Plug-Ins for vCO Startup

At the time of this writing, nine plug-ins that ship with vCO can be enabled out of the box:

- Database
- vCO Web Operator
- vCO Library
- vCO Enumerated Types

- Mail
- Net
- SSH
- XML
- vCenter Server

As you can see in Figure 3.15, each plug-in is enabled by default. For the installation used in this book, we stick with the defaults because doing so will help us work through our examples.

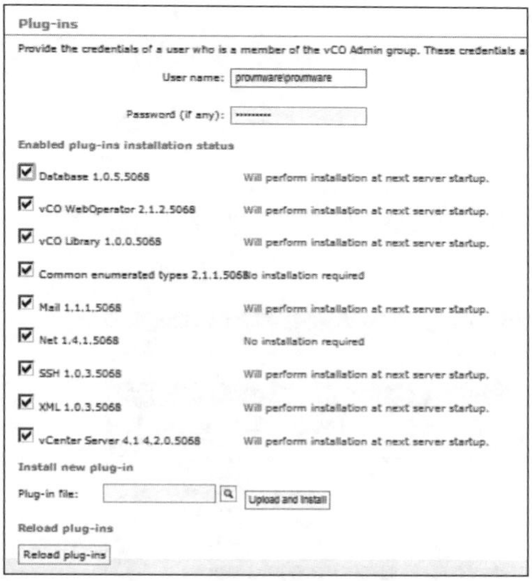

Figure 3.15 The vCO Plug-Ins Configuration page

Install Additional Plug-Ins

We have discussed a few times already that a good amount of vCenter Orchestrator comes from the plug-ins that are available for it. In addition to the base plug-ins, you can find more on the vCO Product page (www.vmware.com/products/vcenter-orchestrator/overview.html) and from individual vendors such as EMC and NetApp. At this time, we will not be installing any additional plug-ins.

To complete the installation and enabling of plug-ins, restart your vCO-related services.

Installing vCO as a Service

This particular step is singlehandedly just as critical as the rest of the steps because it configures the vCO server to run as a system service. This means vCO will be available to configure and execute workflows around the clock. After all, what good is orchestration engine if you cannot run disruptive workflows after hours? To install vCO as a service, select the Startup Options configuration item and then Install vCO Server as a Service, as shown in Figure 3.16.

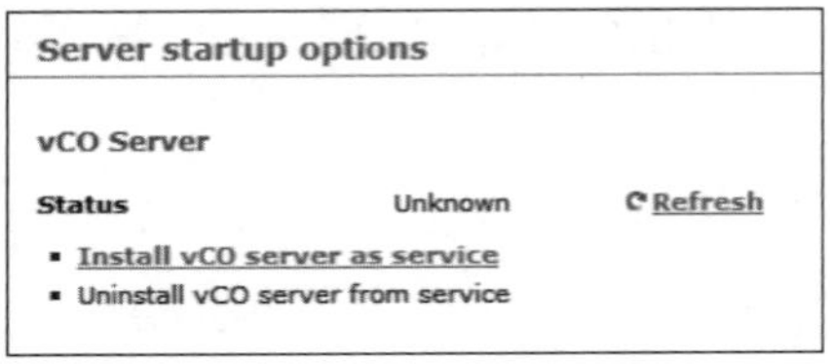

Figure 3.16 Choosing to install vCO as a service

You can also use this interface to monitor and control the vCO server status. Figure 3.17 shows the service now listed as a Windows service.

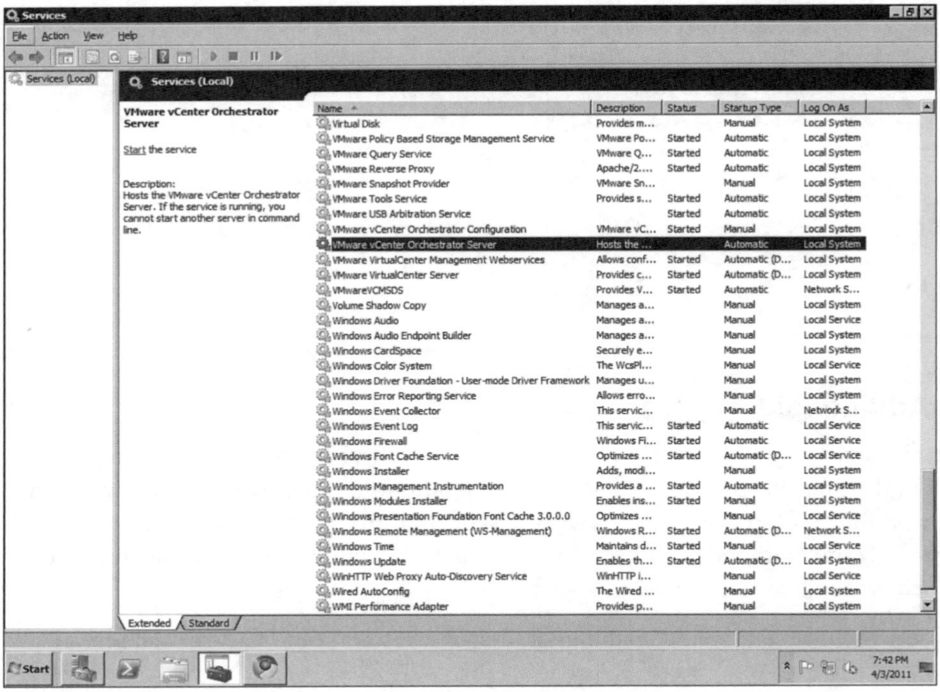

Figure 3.17 vCO installed as a Windows service

Backing Up the vCO Configuration

Now that you have vCO configured, it is a good thing to back up this configuration. This helps you get back to a working state should vCO become unusable in the future, with change control against future changes, and helps you deploy a new vCO engine later. To back up the vCO configuration, do the following:

1. Open the vCO configuration page at http://<vco server>:8282.
2. Log in.
3. Select Genera.
4. Click the Export Configuration tab.
5. Click the Export button.
6. Choose a location to save the file.

Figure 3.18 shows the Export Configuration page.

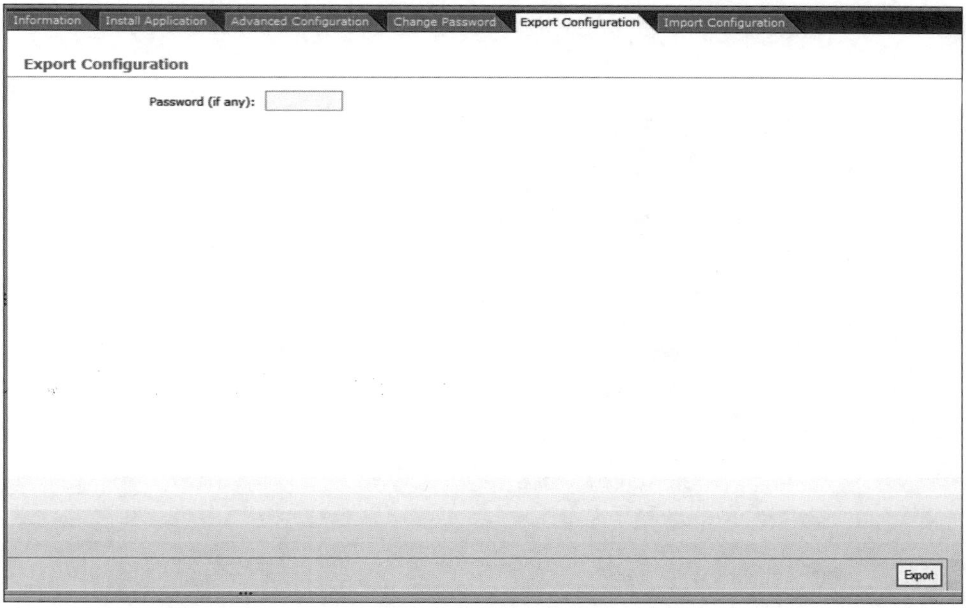

Figure 3.18 The Export Configuration page

Summary

In this chapter, we covered all the steps necessary to bring a freshly installed vCenter Orchestrator system to a functional status. This included setting a service password, configuring vCO networking, LDAP authentication, installing the vCO Database, vCenter SSL communication, SSL signing for vCO packages, licensing the vCO server, and finally configuring vCO to run as a system service. It is now with a working vCO installation that we move into Part II of this book, "Working with vCenter Orchestrator," and discuss the various vCO concepts.

Part II

Working with vCenter Orchestrator

Chapter 4

Identifying the Moving Parts

In this chapter, we investigate the various moving parts of a vCO installation. We do this by identifying each of the moving parts that make up our interactions with vCO. These parts include the following:

- Actions
- Packages
- Plug-ins
- Web views
- Resources
- Workflows

A few object types have been deprecated in this release of vCO (4.2), as follows:

- Authorizations
- OGNL expressions

Actions

After pulling back the drapes, we discover the first moving part within vCO: *actions*. In vCO, actions are objects that perform work. Although that might seem so simple it's stupid, let's consider it for a moment. vCO actions are JavaScript functions that take multiple inputs and produce a singular output. Because they are the "getting things done" component of vCO, actions are a fundamental building block for any workflows you may build.

Because actions are JavaScript based, they can communicate with the vCO API and any other API that you have installed using plug-ins. For me, it helps to think of vCO actions in the same way you would a library of "functions" or "methods" in a scripting or programming language. That is, after you define an action, you can recycle them in any workflow you build. This modularity has another advantage in that if you need to optimize or change the action, it gives you a single place to perform this change and have it affect all workflows.

Figure 4.1 shows a number of the actions that come built in to vCO.

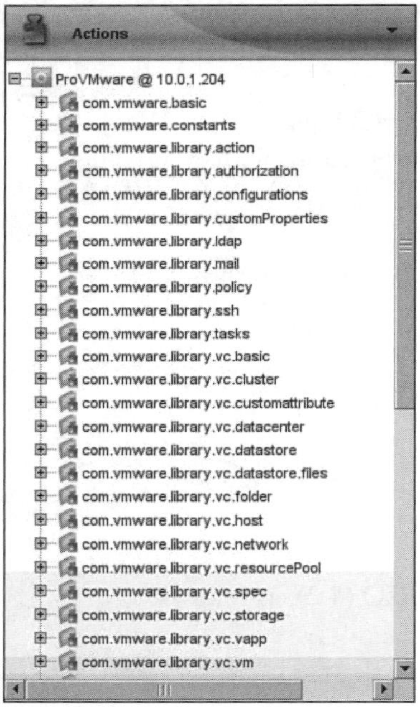

Figure 4.1 Built-in actions

Some of the more common tasks you will perform with the action object are as follows:

- Create an action
- Duplicate an action
- Import/export actions

Create an Action

There are a number of times when you would choose to create an action within vCO. As you learned in the previous section, an action works much like a function or method for those familiar with programming terminology. For those not, it gives you a way to create a step or process that is consistent and repeatable and can be used from many different workflows (for example, powering on a virtual machine). Although you might be able to do that with a single API call, having an action set for it allows you to drag and drop that step into any workflow that needs it without having to write the scripting.

To create an action object, follow these steps:

1. Right-click the top-level action, New Module.
2. Provide a name.
3. Right-click Module, Add Action.
4. Edit scripting as needed.

Figure 4.2 shows a newly created, empty action.

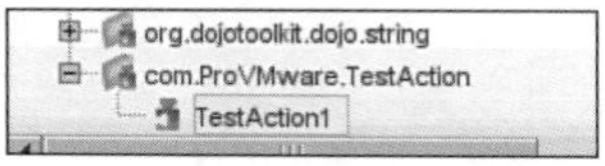

Figure 4.2 A newly created, empty action

> **NOTE**
>
> In Figure 4.2 notice that I have created a "folder" to contain custom actions. The reason for this is twofold: 1) Organization. Creating your own folder structure will help you locate custom actions with ease. It will also ease in assigning permissions and exporting actions. 2) Cleanliness/upgradeability. Not creating actions in the com.vmware or other vendor namespace helps prevent confusion and helps protect your custom actions against upgrades and the like.

Duplicate an Action

In addition to creating a brand-new action, you can duplicate actions. Duplicating an action is a great way to capitalize on work already done by VMware or another vendor, instead of starting from scratch.

To duplicate an action, follow these steps:

1. Right-click an action and choose Duplicate Action.
2. Choose a name.
3. Select an action module.
4. Copy the version history.

Figure 4.3 shows the Duplicate Action dialog box.

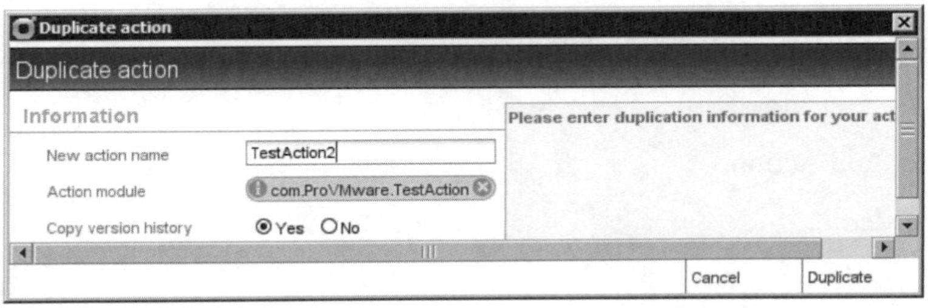

Figure 4.3 Duplicate Action dialog box

Import/Export Actions

To import and export actions, perform the steps presented in the following sections.

Import Action

Follow these steps to perform an import action:

1. Right-click a container and choose Import Action.
2. Choose Action Bundle.
3. If the action is a duplicate, choose whether to import.

Export Action

Follow these steps to perform an export action:

1. Right-click an action and choose Export Action.
2. Choose a location to save the file.
3. Add encryption and sign the file.
4. Click Save.

Figure 4.4 shows the Export Action dialog box.

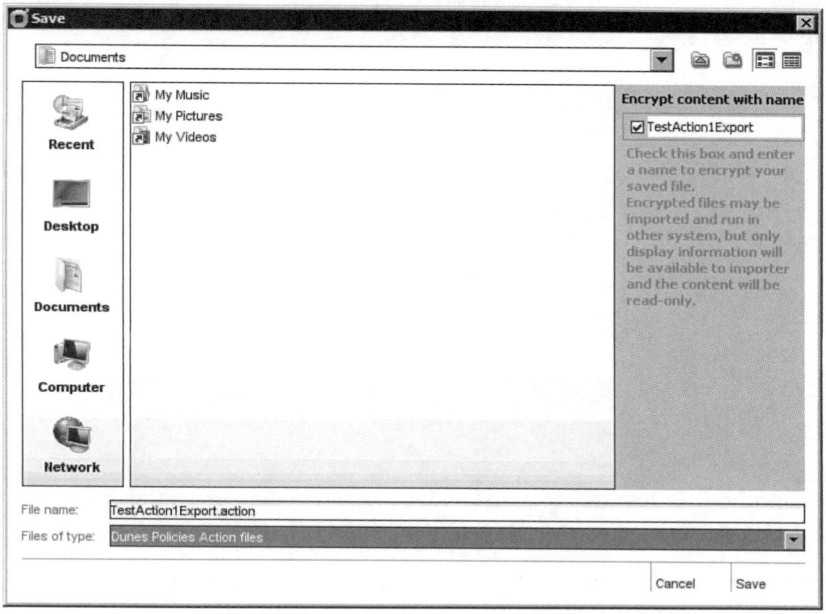

Figure 4.4 Export Action dialog box

Packages

Next on our list of curious things behind the vCO curtain are *packages*. In vCO, packages are the exportable and importable containers that you use to move various elements and objects from one vCO installation to another.

A vCO package can contain the following:

- Workflows
- Actions
- Policies
- Web views
- Configurations
- Resources

The packages included with vCO are presented in the following list. It's not specified, but these are all prefixed with com.vmware.

library.locking

library.webview

weboperator

library

library.xml

util

library.jdbc

library.ssh

library.mail

library.vcenter

vCO packages have a number of features to assist with security, dependency checking, and conflict resolution. These features allow for a great deal of flexibility.

Starting with security, knowing that the third-party package you are importing is coming from a trusted source can help give you piece of mind. It also allows you to encrypt sensitive information as it traverses between different vCO installs within your organization.

The vCO package system also has robust dependency checking. When you add an object to a package, vCO checks for any dependencies of that object and intelligently adds them to your package, too. If you have had to deal with a software packaging system before, say a Windows update that had a requirement for another, or a Linux package that required some others, you can see why this becomes important. Having these dependencies included in the package saves both you and anyone importing your package from having to spend time troubleshooting.

Another great feature for vCO packages is the built-in conflict resolution. When importing a vCO package into a vCO server, the vCO engine first performs a comparison of the objects contained within the package against those already in your vCO environment. If a conflict is detected, vCO shows the differences between the packaged version and the installed version and prompts the user. The user can then choose which elements to import or to import the entire package. Figure 4.5 shows this prompt.

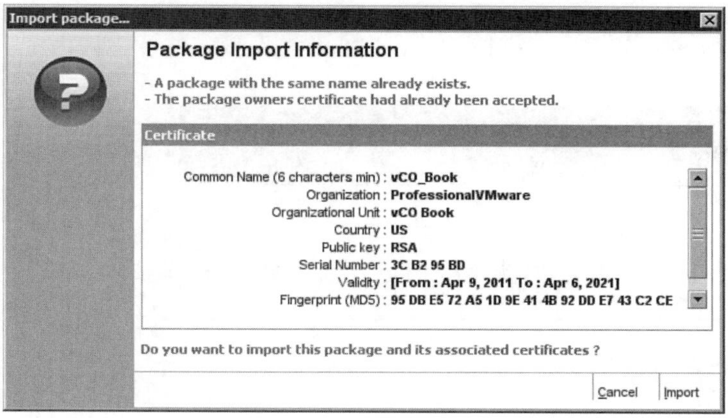

Figure 4.5 Package import conflict

The common actions you will experience with packages are as follows:

- Create a package
- Import/export a package
- Set permissions on packages
- Remove packages

Create a Package

To create a package, follow these steps:

1. Right-click in the white space below the Packages list and choose Add Package.
2. Choose a name.
3. Right-click the package and choose Edit.
4. Add objects (workflows, actions, and so on) to the package.
5. Click Save and close.

When naming the package, notice that all the current packages have a com.vmware type of name. This naming convention looks similar to an FQDN (fully qualified domain name), but backward, and like domain names, it works from general to more specific. For example, com.vmware.library.vcenter tells you that VMware wrote this package, that it is part of a library, and that the specific things contained within have to do with vCenter Server.

Figure 4.6 shows the Edit Package dialog. As you can see, the edit function is rather robust, enabling you to search for objects to add and providing version control.

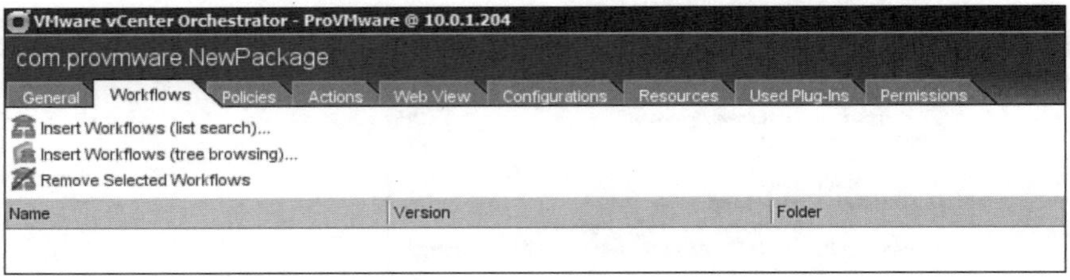

Figure 4.6 Edit Package dialog

Import/Export a Package

To import and export packages, follow the steps outlined in the following sections.

Import

To import a package, follow these steps:

1. Right-click in the white space below the Actions list and choose Import Package.
2. Select the package.
3. Resolve any conflicts (refer to Figure 4.5).

Export

To export a package, follow these steps:

1. Right-click a package, and choose Export Package.
2. Choose a location to save a package.
3. Assign permissions.
4. Check the Export Version History option.
5. Click Save.

Look at step 4 again. vCO gives you the option to export the version history of a package. This can be useful for tracking changes, working with VMware support, or co-developing the package with another vCO administrator.

Figure 4.7 shows the Export Package dialog box.

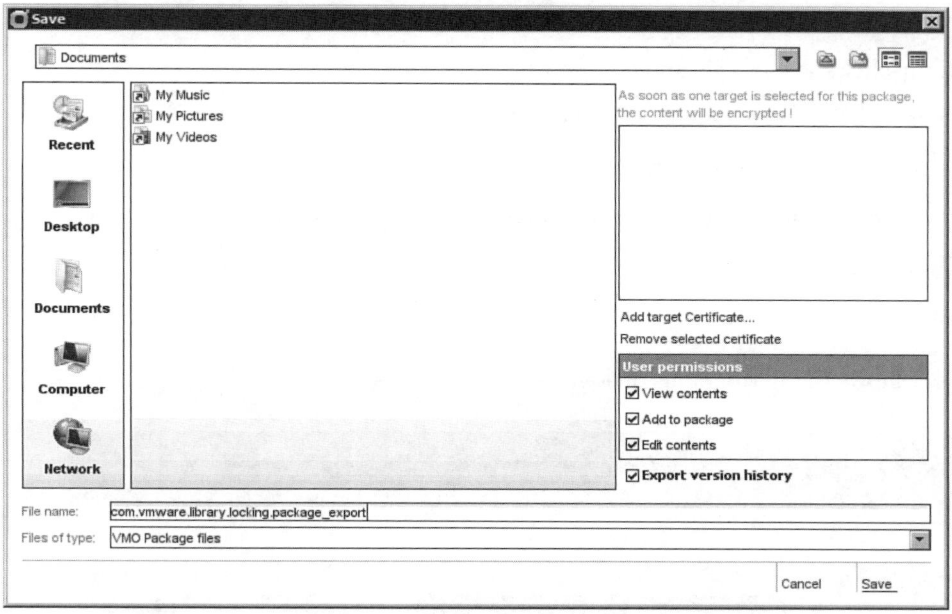

Figure 4.7 Export Package dialog box

Set Permissions on Packages

When working with packages, you have a few options available as far as permissions are concerned. Now is a good time to explain what these are:

- **View:** This is analogous to read-only in terms of permissions. That is, users with this permission will only be able to view the elements of the package, but not any of the scripting or schema.
- **Inspect:** When assigned Inspect, a user has a bit more in the way of rights than with just View but cannot make changes. At this level, the added permissions are to view the scripting and schema.
- **Edit:** With Edit rights, the user is not only able to view, but can now edit the elements in the package.
- **Admin:** When a user or group is assigned this permission, they get the whole kit and caboodle as far as permissions are concerned. In addition to the first three levels, the user can also assign permissions to the package.

To set permissions on a package, follow these steps:

1. Right-click the package, and choose Edit.
2. Select the Permissions tab, and choose Add Permission.
3. Select the permissions to grant.
4. Search for the user or group to which you want to grant permissions.
5. Click Select.
6. Save and close.

Figure 4.8 shows the Permissions dialog.

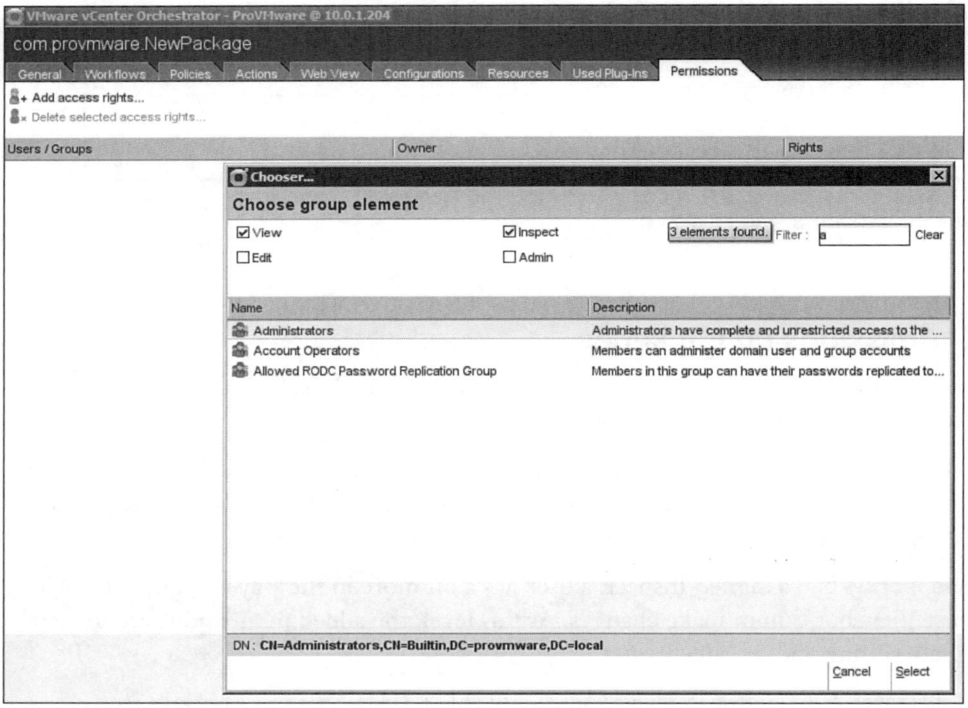

Figure 4.8 Permissions dialog

Remove Packages

To remove a package, follow these steps:

1. Right-click the package.
2. Choose the Delete option.
3. Confirm the deletion.

You have two options when deleting a package. The first is to delete just the package. The second is to delete the package and its contents. Deleting the package and contents is useful for cleaning up all the associated bits that you either created or imported with that package. Figure 4.9 shows the two options.

WARNING

A word of caution: You must understand deleting a package versus deleting its contents.

When you delete a package and its contents, you delete the markers and links to the actions, workflows, and other elements that may be used in workflows and packages that remain on the system.

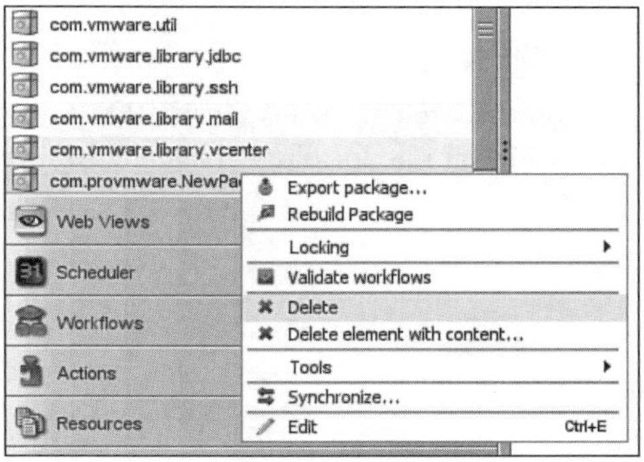

Figure 4.9 Delete or Delete Element with Content

Plug-Ins

Chapter 1, "Introducing VMware vCenter Orchestrator," talked about how the vCO workflow engine is plug-in based. In fact, vCO derives much of its power from its plug-in–based architecture. This applies to VMware technologies as well as third-party products such as the Cisco Unified Computing System (UCS).

Plug-ins provide vCO with new objects and methods to control various applications such as email, SSH, database, and other systems both inside and outside your vSphere environment. Because all the systems the vCO engine can manipulate are facilitated by plug-ins, VMware ships a default set of plug-ins with vCO. These plug-ins, as well as their use, are covered at length in Chapter 5, "vCenter Orchestrator Plug-Ins."

> **NOTE**
>
> Beyond the scope of this book, but worth mentioning, is that the vCO plug-in architecture is open. This means that if your vendor or custom in-house system does not provide a vCO plug-in, you can develop one. If developing your own plug-in doesn't suit you, you can engage VMware Professional Services to have one developed to meet your requirements. Included in the vCO documentation are directions on how to get started with plug-in development.

Notice that plug-ins are conspicuously missing from the vCO client. To work with plug-ins, we need to use a web browser to access the same interface we used when configuring vCO initially. Use the following URL to open the vCO configuration utility: http://<*Hostname / IP Address*>:8282. From there, you can install and configure additional plug-ins. For this example, we install the VMware VIX plug-in.

> **NOTE**
>
> The VMware VIX requires some additional configuration that we cover in Appendix D, "VMware VIX Plug-In." For now, we are just using it as an example for plug-in installation within vCO.

To install a plug-in, follow these steps:

1. Log in to the vCO configuration web interface.
2. Select Plug-Ins.
3. Under Install New Plug-In, use the search box to locate the plug-in file.
4. Click Upload and Install.
5. Restart the vCO Server service.

This is shown in Figure 4.10.

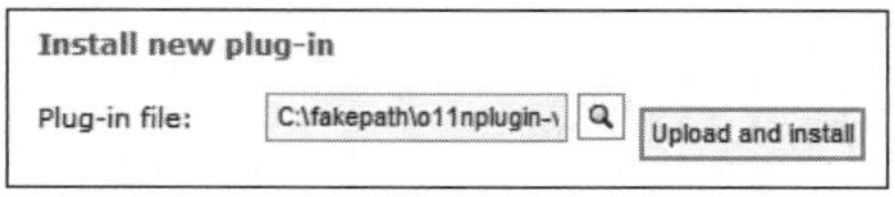

Figure 4.10 Installing the VMware VIX plug-in

Web Views

In addition to the vCenter Orchestrator Java (or fat) Client, vCO provides web views. Web views provide a great deal of flexibility in how you build and present vCO to your end users. This can be in the form of directly presenting them a web interface for self-service VM provisioning or in the form of integrating into an existing configuration management system.

Resources

Resources in vCenter Orchestrator are independent elements that allow the use of external elements within your vCO web views and workflows. Consider the case of sysprep: When you provision a new Windows VM from a template or a clone in vCenter, you can apply a "customization specification" to it. This customization is essentially a sysprep answer file for the specific flavor of Windows you happen to be installing. To enable your workflows to use these customizations, you want to import them as resources into vCO.

By importing your customization specifications as resources, you make it possible for a number of things to happen. First, you have a reusable element that you can add to any number of workflows and web views, without having to duplicate the effort. In addition, you now have a central, version-controlled resource on which you can make changes in one place and have them propagate automatically to all your workflows and web views.

For the present use, I show you how to perform the following actions with resources:

- View a resource
- Import an external resource

As we work on our use cases in Part III of this book, "Amazing Smoothies, Inc. (a.k.a. Real-World Use Case)," you will see plenty of examples where we integrate resources into workflows and web views.

View a Resource

To view a resource, you must do the following from the vCO Client:

1. Select Resources from the menu on the left.
2. Locate a resource.
3. Click the Viewer tab.

Figure 4.11 shows viewing of a resource in action.

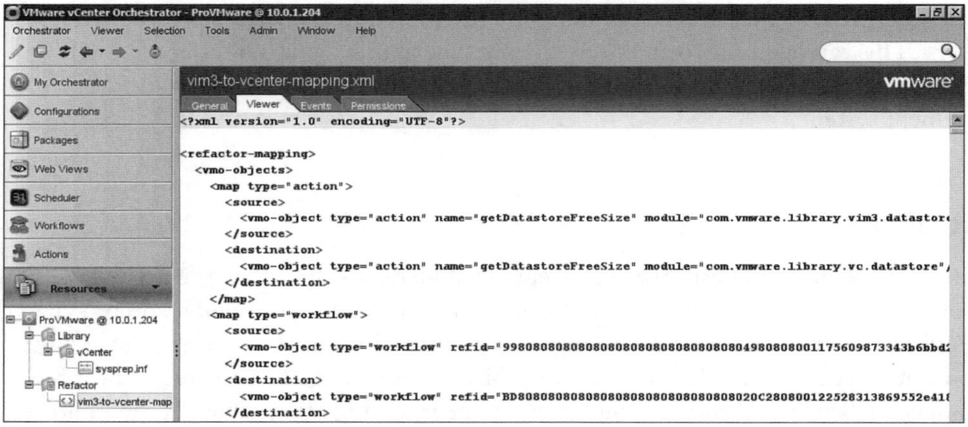

Figure 4.11 Viewing a resource

Import an External Resource

To import an external resource, you must do the following from the vCO Client:

1. Open the Resources tab.
2. Select a container/folder object.
3. Right-click the folder and choose Import Object.
4. Select the file to import.

Figure 4.12 shows the Import dialog.

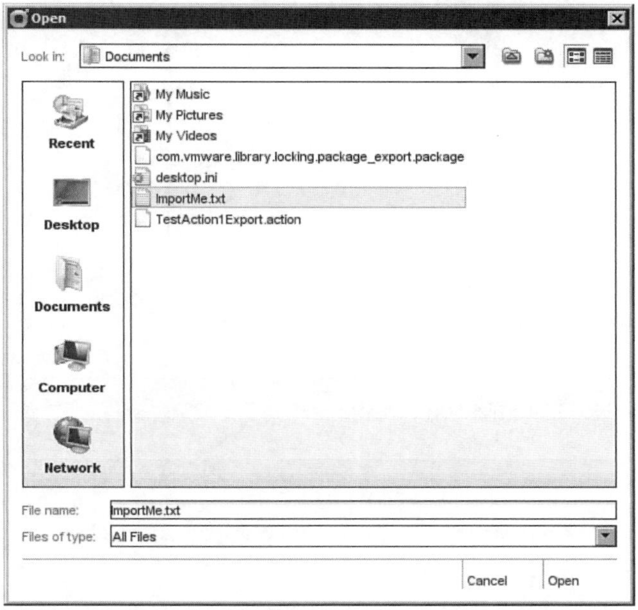

Figure 4.12 Importing an external object

Workflows

Workflows are made up of resources and actions and resemble a flow chart of the discreet steps you perform when working through a procedure within your environment. Put another way, when you provision a VM, you have a "preflight" checklist and set of tasks you take to bring the new VM online. That process from beginning to end is your workflow.

Let's take that a step further and look at the schema for the built-in "Provision VM from Clone, No Customization" workflow as shown in Figure 4.13.

We focus on the creation of workflows, actions, and resources for the remainder of this book. Workflows, specifically, are the subject of Chapter 6, "Introduction to Workflow-Fu."

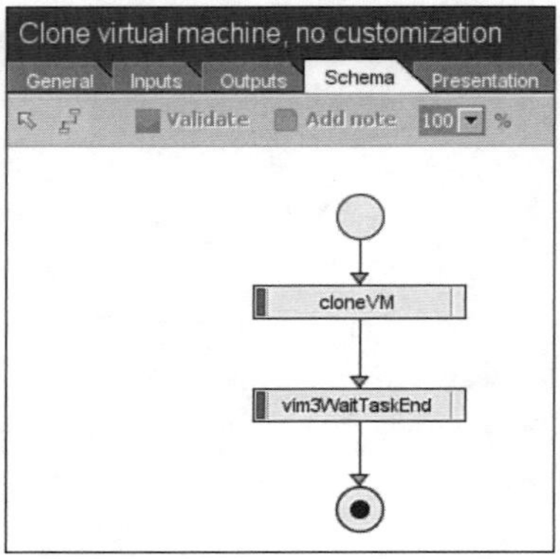

Figure 4.13 Provision VM from Clone, No Customization schema

Summary

In this chapter, we explored the many moving parts of a vCO installation. We did this by discussing each of its individual components and describing how they fit together. With this foundational knowledge of vCO, we dive deeper into both plug-ins and workflows in Chapter 5 and Chapter 6, respectively.

Chapter 5

vCenter Orchestrator Plug-Ins

Earlier chapters touched on vCenter Orchestrator's plug-in architecture and how plug-ins make vCO flexible enough to control infrastructure both within and surrounding your vSphere environment. In this chapter, we take a closer look at both the architecture and the plug-ins that ship with your vCO installation.

By the end of this chapter, you will be able do the following:

- Understand the vCO plug-in architecture
- List the default vCO plug-ins
- Configure the default plug-ins
- Use the default vCO plug-ins
- Use the vCO API Explorer

Understanding these items is critical to being able to work with vCO plug-ins and use them to build successful workflows.

The vCenter Orchestrator Plug-In Architecture

vCO itself is a workflow engine. Instead of building all the functionality you will ever need, for every device you will ever need to manage, vCO was written to provide workflow execution and scheduling services that act on objects. The objects I refer to are those that are "plugged-in" to vCO to support other technologies. This allows vCO to be extensible and provides a method for third parties to easily provide an orchestration interface for their devices.

Suppose, for example, you have recently made a large investment in a redundant firewall pair and some midrange storage. You now need to integrate these into your existing processes, be they for provisioning new servers or taking servers offline. Under normal circumstances, you accomplish this by logging in to each device and performing a similar configuration for each new virtual machine (VM) brought online. However, if your vendor has provided a vCO plug-in, you can add that component into your existing workflows with a few clicks.

Let's take a look at what this plug-in architecture looks like (see Figure 5.1).

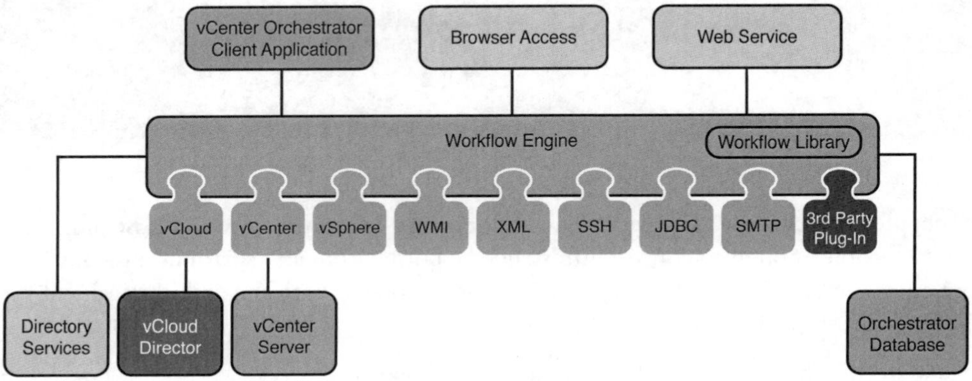

Figure 5.1 The vCO plug-in architecture

In Figure 5.1, you see the central workflow engine. In addition, you can see along the way the spots where each additional plug-in slots into that workflow engine to add new services. You also see pictured in Figure 5.1 the default plug-ins, which is our next topic.

vCenter Orchestrator Default Plug-Ins

As discussed so far, vCO is a plug-in–based workflow engine. Because vCO derives much of its power from plug-ins, it wouldn't make sense for VMware to provide you with vCO and no plug-ins to use it with. This section describes each of the default plug-ins and shows you how to use them, as follows:

- vCenter Server
- vCO Library
- Database
- SSH

- XML
- Mail
- Net
- Enumeration
- vCO Web Operator

vCenter Server

The vCenter Server plug-in provides communication with your vCenter Server(s) API. Further, it exposes all the inventory objects and management actions for you to use within your vCO workflows.

NOTE

At the time of this writing, the vCenter Server plug-in was only available for vCenter Server 4.1. However, the API calls it uses still appear to be present in the 5.x series and are what was used to build the examples later in the book.

Figure 5.2 depicts the default communication paths and firewall ports you need open between your vCO server and your vCenter Server to use the vCenter Server plug-in. If your environment requires these to run on different ports, these values can be changed within the vCO Configuration interface.

In addition to open ports between vCenter Server and your vCO server, you also need to configure your vCenter Server(s) within the plug-in configuration. To do this, follow these steps:

1. Open the vCO Configuration page, http://vcohost.domain:8282.
2. Log in using a vCO administrator account.
3. Under Plug-Ins, select vCenter Server.
4. Click the New vCenter Server tab.
5. Fill in the connection information.
6. Choose a connection strategy.
7. Click Apply Changes.

Figure 5.3 shows this information filled out. An important thing to note on this screen is the connection strategy. Your choice here is either Per User or Share a Unique Session.

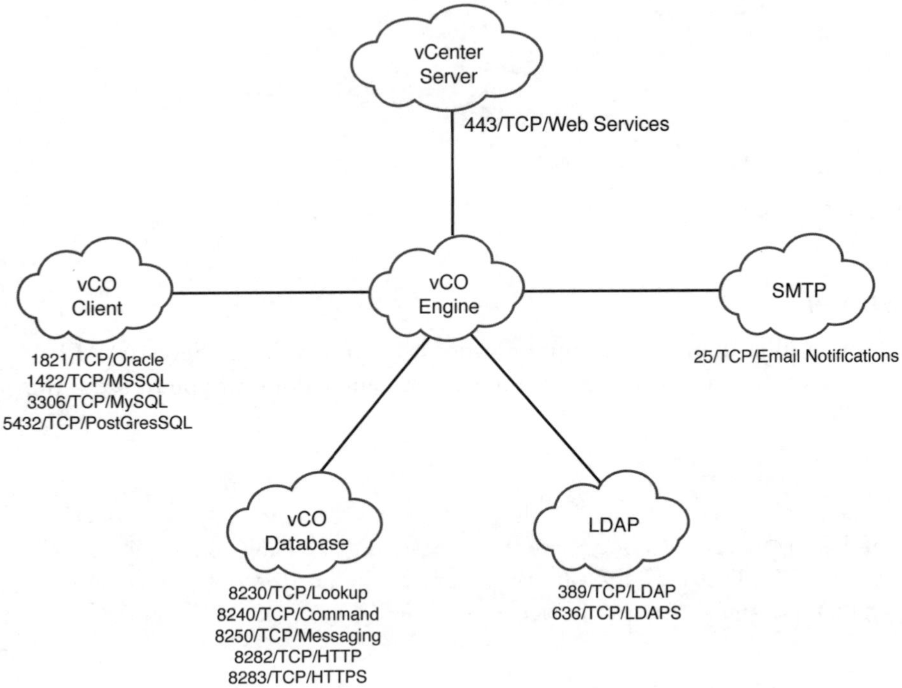

Figure 5.2 vCenter Server plug-in communication

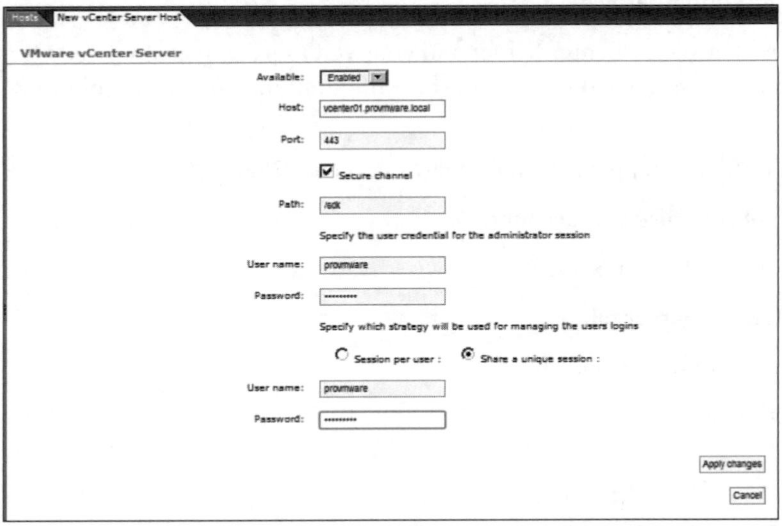

Figure 5.3 Adding a vCenter host to vCenter Orchestrator

Let's take a moment to understand the two connection methodologies:

- **Per User:** In the Per User model, vCO connects to vCenter Server with the credentials of the user who executed the workflow. From an auditing perspective, this enables you to see from which vCenter Server the user executed an action. On the flip side, Per User creates a new connection to vCenter Server for each running workflow, in turn consuming resources on your vCenter Server.
- **Share a Unique Session:** Using Share a Unique Session enables vCO to connect to vCenter Server using a single connection and single service account. This moves your point for auditing which user ran which actions back into the vCO Client. In addition, it can help reduce the operational overhead and resources used on the vCenter Server.

There are some additional features of the vCenter Server plug-in available, and those will be useful as we begin to develop and explore workflows. Those are the vCenter Server Plug-In Scripting Library and Workflow Library.

Scripting Library

When using vCO, you will find a lot of ready-to-use workflows that can immediately be applied to your environment. However, you will sometimes need to get under the hood and either modify the defaults or write your own. This is where the vCenter Server Plug-In Scripting Library comes in. It provides JavaScript functions, classes, methods, and other scripting resources to interface with the vSphere API. We cover parts of the Scripting Library in later chapters.

Workflow Library

In addition to access to all the managed objects and actions as provided by the Scripting Library, the Workflow Library provides a number of ready-to-run workflows for the most common administration tasks. The complete list of these workflows is a bit too long to include here, but here is a list of the categories:

- Batch
- Cluster and compute resources
- Custom attributes
- Datacenter
- Datastore and files
- Folder management

- Host management
- Resource pool
- Storage
- Virtual machine

> **NOTE**
> The categories here, as well as the workflows contained within, can be found under the Workflows section of the vCO Client.

Each of these workflow categories contains a number of individual workflows that can be either run as-is or customized to suit your needs. For example, the Virtual Machine Management category contains workflows to deal with snapshots. We explore these further in Part III, "Amazing Smoothies, Inc. (a.k.a. Real-World Use Case)."

vCO Library

The vCO library plug-in provides workflows for automating various aspects of vCenter Orchestrator itself. Automating the automation engine? In some senses, that is exactly what this does. There is no additional configuration to use this plug-in, and it provides the following categories of workflows:

- Locking
- Orchestrator
- Troubleshooting

The locking workflows work in conjunction with the vCO "locking" mechanism. The locking mechanism allows a workflow's schema to be protected from modification during runtime. The locking workflows then let you work with these locks en-masse.

The Orchestrator workflows break down into two subcategories: Tasks and Workflows. The Tasks category enables you to create either an individual or a recurring task. The workflows category is more interesting. The two workflows under this category change the vCO workflow execution to either execute a workflow several times in parallel with different parameters or to execute a workflow several different times in series, changing one parameter for each run. The number of properties you are working with determines the number of workflow runs for each of these. This functionality is useful when you are creating a large number of VMs. Kicking off each VM build in parallel can save time during the build process. However, if your storage or other resources are busy, executing the same set of VM build tasks in series will still get the work done while minimizing impact on resources that might not be able to handle a single parallel burst of execution.

Finally, you have the troubleshooting workflows. These enable you to export all the vCO logs to a .zip file. This is useful when you are troubleshooting the vCO service, troubleshooting a stubborn workflow, or are otherwise working with VMware support.

Database

The Database plug-in, like the vCenter Server plug-in, provides both a scripting API as well as workflows to manipulate SQL-based databases. Being able to connect vCO out to third-party SQL databases enables you to import various bits of information from your configuration management system or other databases and use it within your workflows. The workflows included with this plug-in are reference implementations of the Java Database Connectivity (JDBC) scripting API. Figure 5.4 shows these workflow examples.

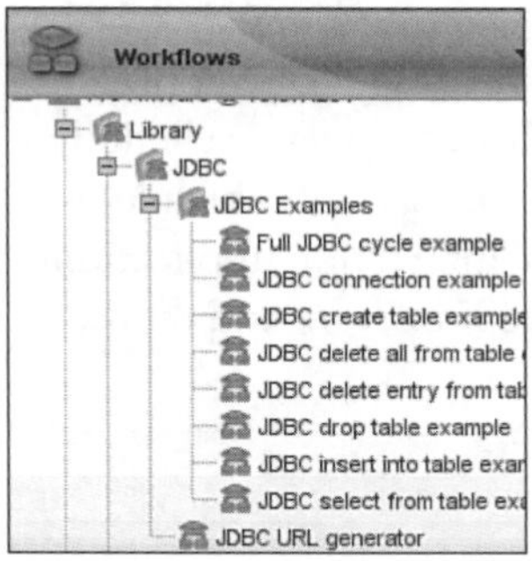

Figure 5.4 JDBC workflow examples

You can find more information about using the JDBC scripting API in the VMware documentation.

SSH

With the SSH plug-in, vCO can execute command-line interface (CLI) commands on remote systems from within a workflow over a Secure Shell (SSH) connection. This functionality is provided in much the same fashion as the Database plug-in, using a scripting API. In addition, you can use some sample workflows. Like the vCenter Server plug-in, the SSH plug-in needs some basic configuration. To do this, complete the following steps:

1. Open and log in to the vCO Configuration interface (http://<vcoserver>:8282).
2. Click SSH.
3. Choose New Connection.
4. Under Host Name, add the server to SSH into.
5. Apply the changes.

Figure 5.5 shows this screen.

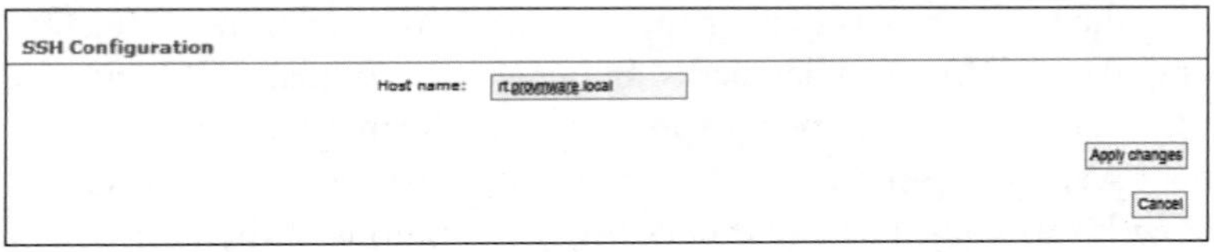

Figure 5.5 Adding an SSH host

Note that vCO did not ask for a username and password. This is because the SSH plug-in will use the credentials of the logged-in user executing the workflow. If you are scheduling the workflow to run later, or as a service account, you can use the run-as and schedule-as features to run the workflow in a different context. This has some interesting implications in that you need to maintain identical user accounts both in Active Directory and on the servers you are logging in to with SSH.

XML

Extensible Markup Language (XML) is beautiful, XML is fine, and if you like XML you can use it in vCO all the time. That is to say that vCO comes with a plug-in for creating, modifying, and otherwise working with XML documents. It provides this with both an XML scripting API and some basic workflows that can serve as examples.

Mail

Next up is the Mail, or Simple Mail Transfer Protocol (SMTP), plug-in. This plug-in provides you the capability to send emails from within a workflow. This is useful for notifying a user at various points of a workflow run, say if it were to fail or complete successfully. It is also useful for having your workflow send email into another system to initiate an action like generating a request ticket or similar action. Like the other built-in plug-ins, the Mail plug-in provides both a scripting API and workflow examples that can be used or modified for your own needs.

Figure 5.6 shows a listing of the included workflow examples.

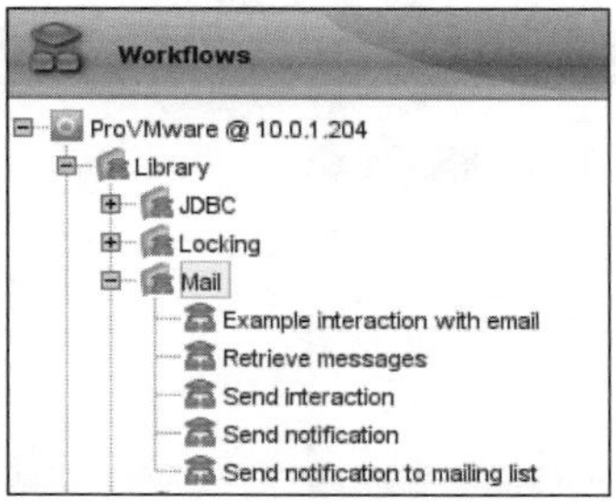

Figure 5.6 Mail plug-in workflow examples

The Mail plug-in requires some configuration before it can be used. During configuration, you'll note that you can only configure a single Default mail server to be used for all vCO email unless otherwise specified in a specific workflow. To configure the default email values, follow these steps:

1. Open the vCO Web Configuration interface.
2. Select the Mail plug-in.
3. Check the Define Default Values box.
4. Add the appropriate values.
5. Apply the changes.

Figure 5.7 shows the completed form.

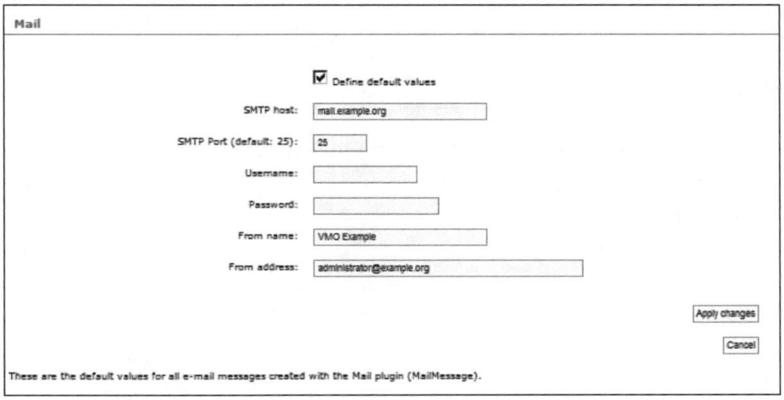

Figure 5.7 Mail plug-in configuration

Now that we've configured the Mail plug-in, we can test some of the workflow examples. Figure 5.8 shows the launching of the "Example Interaction with Email" workflow with the resulting email shown in Figure 5.9.

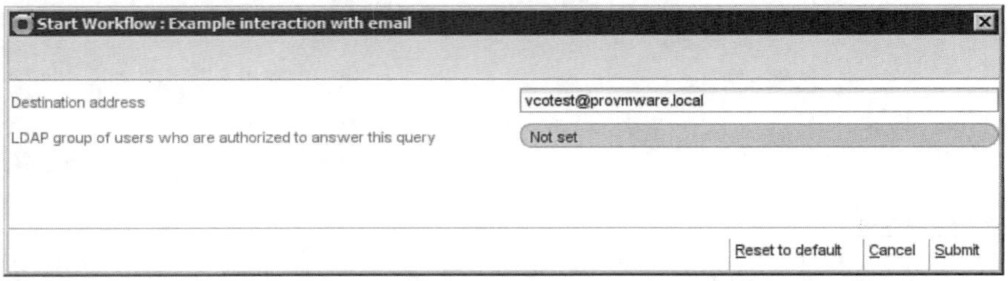

Figure 5.8 Launching the "Example Interaction with Email" workflow

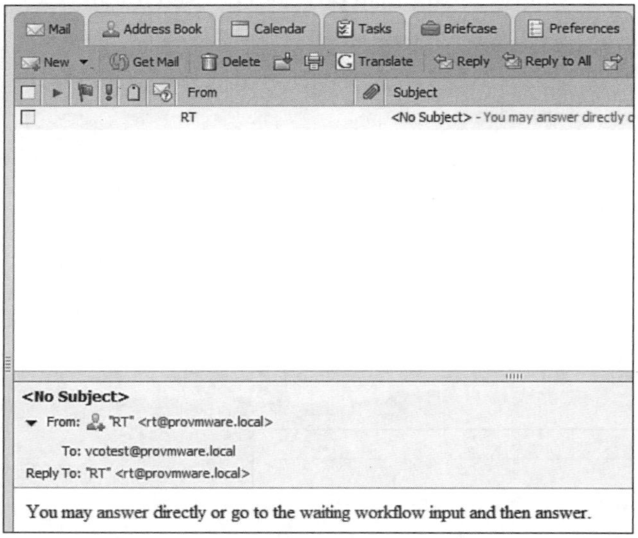

Figure 5.9 The email result after the "Example Interaction with Email" workflow run

Net

Next on the menu of default vCO plug-ins is the Net plug-in. The Net plug-in's job is to facilitate network communication over several additional protocols. "Isn't that what the SSH and Mail plug-ins do?" I hear you say. Well yes, but the Net plug-in provides several additional protocols, as follows:

- Telnet
- FTP
- POP3

With this plug-in, there are no usable workflows out of the box. You can, however, use the various scripting APIs provided to retrieve files, interact with devices that support Telnet, and retrieve email.

Enumeration

Next up is the Enumeration plug-in. This plug-in, like the Net plug-in, is available for use as a scripting API and has no usable workflows by default. The scripting API provides access to common enumeration types such as disk and RAM assignments as well as time zone, performance, and number of vCPUs assigned to a VM.

vCO Web Operator

This plug-in provides the web parts that enable your users to interact with vCO. There is nothing to configure here and no workflows by default. That said, in the vCO Client interface, there is an entire section for web views, as shown in Figure 5.10.

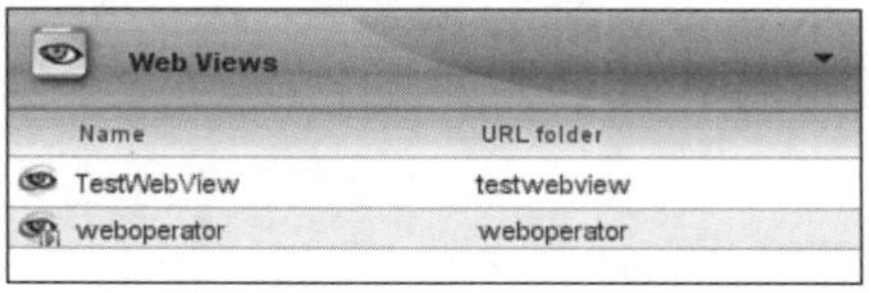

Figure 5.10 The Web Views section of the vCO Client

As you can see, I have selected the weboperator view and have published it; without doing this, the web views cannot be used. To see this view in action, you'll recall the test we did in the Mail section whereby we ran the "Example Interaction with Email" workflow. You can also access the WebViews by browsing to http://<vcoServer>:8280. After clicking the link that was shown in Figure 5.9, you will see the results shown in Figure 5.11.

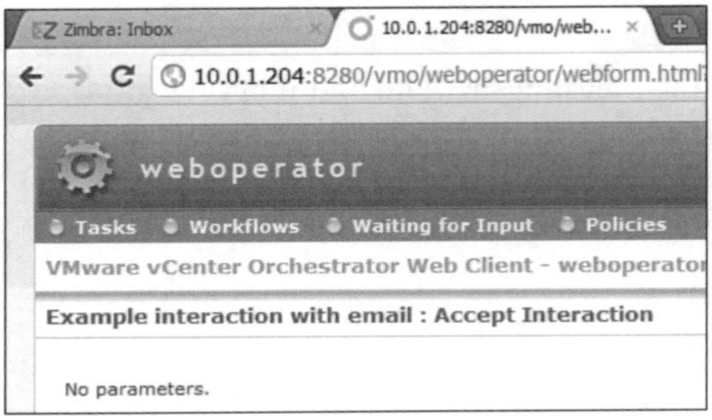

Figure 5.11 Interacting with vCO using email and web views

As shown in Figure 5.12, you can also interact with other workflows using the Weboperator web view.

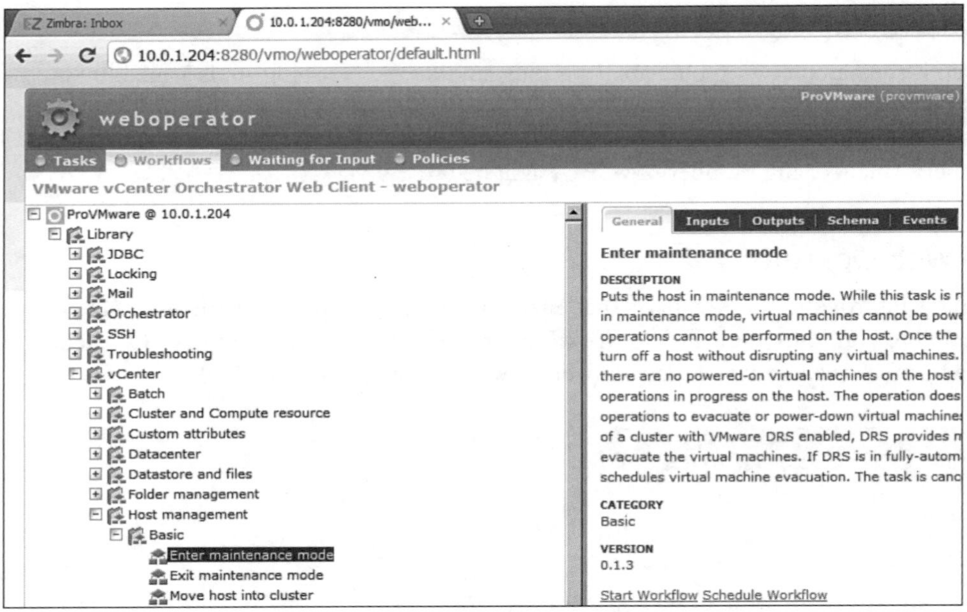

Figure 5.12 Interacting with workflows in web views

As we progress into our varying use cases in Part III of this book, you will see some additional examples of where this plug-in is useful for gathering approvals or self-service building of VMs.

Using the vCenter Orchestrator API Explorer

As we worked our way through configuring and using the various plug-ins included with vCO, you likely noticed that mentioned for several plug-ins is a scripting API. Because most of the default vCO plug-ins provide a scripting API, it makes sense to cover just one time how to access said APIs with the API Explorer rather than in each section.

The API Explorer, although self-descriptive, contains a lot of useful information and makes the life of nonprogrammers easier. That is, it contains a search function that enables you to find various objects and actions that can be used later in a scripting block.

> **NOTE**
>
> Objects and actions? Yeah, we touched on a bit of programmer-speak for a moment. *Objects* are simply things within your environment that vCO knows about, such as VMs or host systems. *Actions* or *methods* are the various things vCO knows how to do with these objects.

There are two ways to access the vCenter Orchestrator API Explorer: directly from the client or from the scripting tabs of the Workflows, Policy, or Actions section. To use the client, do the following:

1. Click Tools.
2. Choose API Explorer.

To access the API Explorer from the Scripting tab, open a workflow, policy, or action, for editing, then select the Scripting tab, and then search API.

Figures 5.13 and 5.14 show these, respectively.

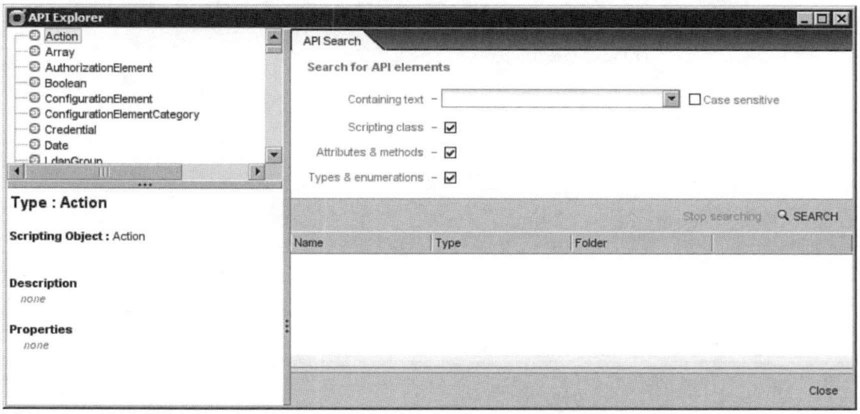

Figure 5.13 The vCO API Explorer

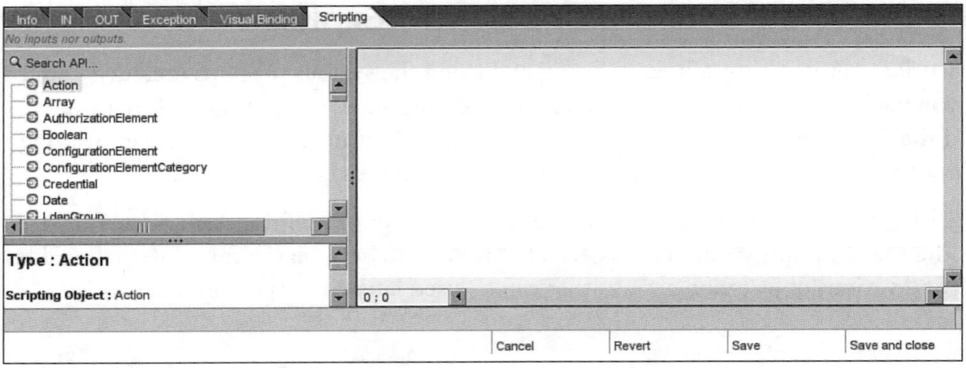

Figure 5.14 Scripting API search from the Workflows view

Summary

In this chapter, we examine vCO plug-in architecture. This included learning what the default plug-ins were, how to configure them, and how to use them. This also included a tour of the vCO API Explorer. Now that you have a good understanding of these tools, you can successfully implement vCO plug-ins within your own workflows.

Chapter 6

Introduction to Workflow-Fu

Welcome to the dojo of the workflow. Herein we uncover the core concepts and mysteries that are the workflow and show you how to become one with your inner workflow. That is, by the end of this chapter you will have taken the first steps in your journey to Workflow-Fu mastery. Specifically, you will have learned the following techniques of Workflow-Fu:

- Workflow organization
- Workflow concepts
- Workflow-editing process
- Modifying built-in workflows
- Creating new workflows
- Workflow scheduling

Take a moment to step back and become one with your inner workflow because here we go.

Workflow Organization

Before we begin getting too deep into workflows, it is important to step back for a moment to talk about organizing your workflows. There are a few reasons for organizing workflows and a few strategies behind the organization. First, we talk about a few reasons why it's important, and then we take a look at the approach that was adopted for the writing of this book.

NOTE

This section came up and got placed first, as during the course of writing this book I managed to lose a few workflows along the way. Starting over wasn't fun either, so I can't stress how important it is to pick some manner of organizational strategy and stick with it.

Beside the fact that I can't seem to keep my workflows straight, there are a few other reasons to keep your workflows organized. These include the obvious, easier to find and use again later use case. However, also consider you may not be the only person using vCO; therefore, having your workflows in a logical organization will reduce confusion and overhead in bringing other vCO users up to speed. Finally, consider the case where you enable users outside your vSphere management team with vCO web views. Having your workflows laid out well will help reduce confusion for this group of users, as well.

You can also choose to organize them by task, project, or system that the workflows interact with. Suppose, for example, you were creating workflows to tie in with a ticketing system. You would then create a folder specific to that system and then create subfolders and workflows underneath as needed.

You can also organize workflows by organizational roles and assign access rights to each top-level folder based on the role for each set of workflows. This is useful when you need to expose functionality to end users but don't necessarily want to give away the keys to the kingdom. Do you want everyone to be able to create virtual machines (VMs)? Probably not, at least not without some manner of control or adherence to change control processes. In this case, you can restrict those workflows to the users or groups who must have access.

The approach I've taken in the deployment and examples used for this book is to start with a vCO Book top-level folder. This way, I won't lose the workflows. I then created a subfolder for each use case from Part III, "Amazing Smoothies, Inc. (a.k.a. Real-World Use Case)," to make exporting them for use with the book simple. You can see this in Figure 6.1. When translated according to this description, it roughly maps to a top-level folder for the organization and subfolders for each project.

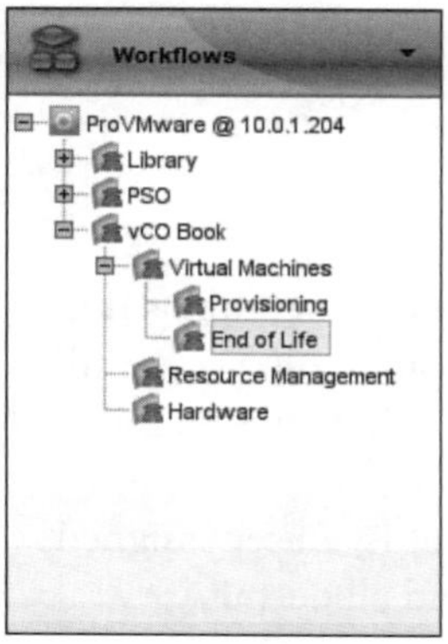

Figure 6.1 "vCO Book" workflow organization

Workflow Concepts

Before rushing headlong into workflow modification, it is crucial to understand some of the key workflow concepts:

- User permissions
- Credentials
- Attributes
- Parameters
- Schema
- Tokens
- Locking
- Presentation

The following sections each cover one of these key concepts.

User Permissions

Orchestrator has the capacity to restrict access to workflows to a specific set of users or groups. The permissions you can set on a workflow are as follows:

- **View:** View elements of the workflow except schema and scripting
- **Inspect:** Same as View, with the addition of scripting and schema

- **Execute:** Run the workflow
- **Edit:** Edit the workflow
- **Admin:** Set permissions on the workflow

The workflow permissions flow from the permissions set on the folder that contains it if you do not set any permissions on the workflow. In other words, if you do not set permissions, they are inherited. When you do set permissions on a workflow, it overrides the permissions of the upper-level folder, even if that folder is more restrictive. In addition, it is important to note that these permissions are not cumulative. That is, a user assigned Admin also needs to be assigned Edit to be able to edit workflows, and all permissions require the View permission. To edit the permissions to a folder or workflow, do the following:

1. Right-click the folder/workflow, and select Edit Access Rights.
2. Choose Add Access Rights.
3. In the chooser, specify the user and permissions.
4. Save and close.

Credentials

Being a techie, when unwrapping Orchestrator and starting to write the volume you are now holding, I decided, "Who needs manuals" and started rolling, that is until this particular property of workflows and the SSH plug-in. If you skipped that section of Chapter 5, "vCenter Orchestrator Plug-Ins," I'll spare you some page flipping: "…the SSH plug-in will use the credentials of the logged-in user executing the workflow."

Where this got me, is that vCO will use one of four ways to determine who the executing user is. These four ways are contained in Table 6.1.

Table 6.1 The Four Ways vCO Uses to Determine the Executing User

How Was the Workflow Started?	The Credential vCO Will Use
vCO web or GUI client	The logged-in user's credentials
Via policy	Credentials set up for the policy
Nested workflow	Can get credentials from parent
Web view	Credential of user logged in to web view

If none of these suit you, vCO also allows you to set the credential to run the workflow using either the Schedule Workflow As or Run Workflow As menu item.

Attributes

For those who are familiar with some basic programming concepts, attributes are roughly analogous to global variables and constants for a workflow. For those without a programming background, it can be helpful to think of attributes as being a reference to a value that can be accessed from anywhere within a given workflow.

Take, for example, our "Email Logs" workflow in the next section. The attributes we defined for the workflow were `zipFileName` and `emailAddress`. We were then able to access and manipulate these values later in the workflow as we needed.

Parameters

In the context of workflows and vCO, parameters are essentially the values a workflow will accept as inputs or generate as outputs. In our "Email Logs" example in the next section, this is the `localPath` parameter, or the path where the workflow will store its output. This enables the user executing the workflow to specify the location, making the file easier to find later.

Schema

The schema! When editing workflows, you will spend most of your time either scripting or in the schema editor. The schema editor is a Visio-like workflow diagram builder. As you'll see in Figure 6.7, the interface itself is straightforward and lets you link the various workflow objects into a flow chart.

Tokens

Workflow tokens are a depiction of the current state of a workflow's execution. Table 6.2 shows these states and their meanings.

Table 6.2 Workflow Tokens

State	What It Means
Running	Workflow is currently running.
Waiting for user interaction	Workflow is paused waiting on user-supplied input.
Waiting for event or timer	Workflow is paused waiting on either an external event or a timer to complete.
Canceled	Someone cancelled the workflow.
Failed	For one reason or another, the workflow failed to execute.
Completed	Well… you would hope they all got to this state.

Locking

Locking is a feature that disables your ability to edit a workflow while it is running. The ability to edit a running workflow is useful while developing workflows and interactive troubleshooting of a workflow. However, after you have determined that the workflow itself is "golden" or ready for production, it is best to lock the workflow to prevent accidental editing and unexpected results. It is also useful to lock a workflow if you will have more than one person editing or developing the workflow.

Presentation

Another key concept to consider during workflow development is the workflow presentation. That is, vCO gives you a large degree of flexibility in how the user is prompted for information at workflow execution time that covers both the vCO Java client and the web views, if you have them published. Why is presentation important? Well, consider that it helps with workflow usability and to ensure that you end up with valid inputs from the user. Along these lines there are two key points for presentation: constraints and decorators.

In terms of presentation, constraints enable you to set default, minimum, and maximum values. Constraints ensure those using your workflows are kept within the defined limits of your system. For example, when a user kicks off a workflow to build a new VM, you can set a default value for the OS, set a minimum (and maximum) for the disk size, and place constraints on memory. This has the benefit of allowing the user some customization while preventing an accidental denial of service because a VM was configured too large or too small.

In addition, workflow presentation enables the use of decorators. Decorators enable you to organize items in the interface and to show or hide elements or provide custom validation. For example, if you only want user darmok.jalad@tanagra.com to log in, you can add a custom validation to check the username.

Modifying the Built-In Workflows

Development of the mind can be achieved only when the body has been disciplined. To accomplish this the ancients have taught us to imitate nature.

—Kahn, Kung Fu

Like imitating nature in Kung Fu, Workflow-Fu is also best learned by imitating the workflows that come built in to vCO. We spend a good deal of time copying and modifying workflows in Part III of this book. However, there is a basic process to editing workflows that will make your workflow-building life much easier.

In our example, we modify the "Export Logs and Application Settings" workflow as shown in Figure 6.2 to send the resulting application logs via email to a defined user.

To do this, follow these steps:

1. Duplicate the workflow.
2. Edit the workflow.
3. Edit the schema.
4. Edit the user interaction.
5. Edit the script.
6. Validate the workflow.

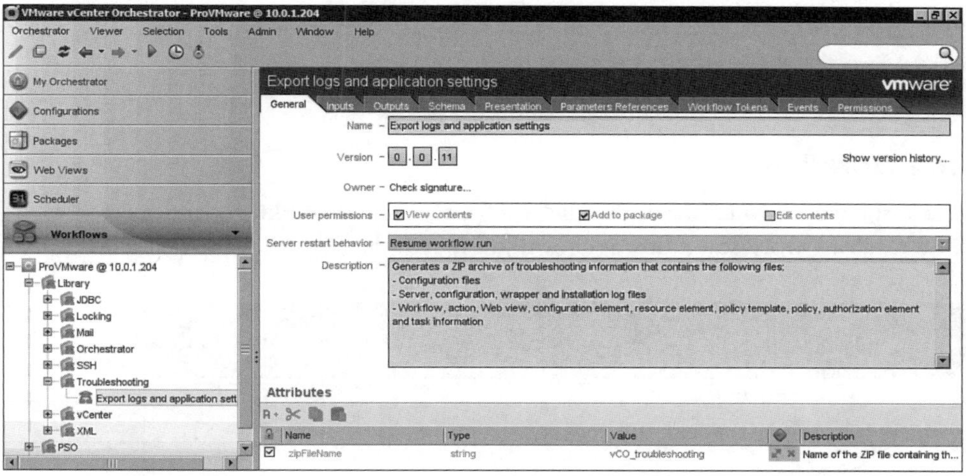

Figure 6.2 "Export Logs and Application Settings" workflow

Duplicate the Workflow

To duplicate the workflow, right-click the workflow from Figure 6.2 and select duplicate workflow. From there, choose a name and new location for this workflow, as shown in Figures 6.3 and 6.4, respectively.

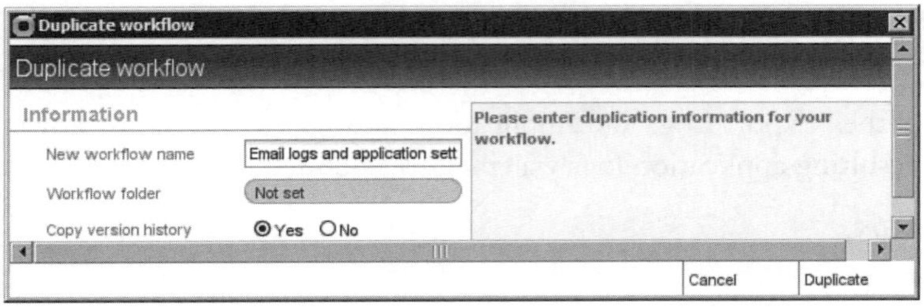

Figure 6.3 Duplicating the workflow

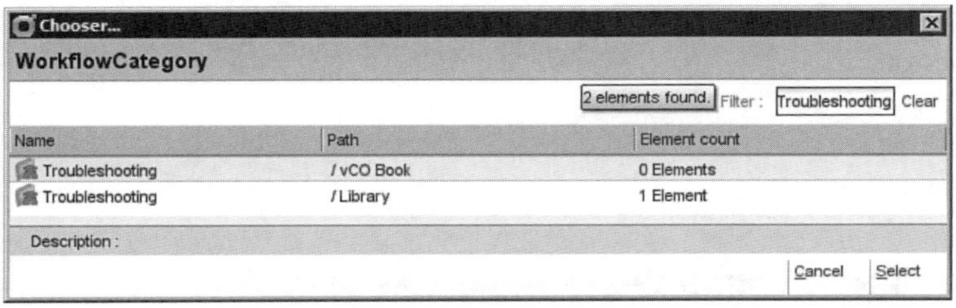

Figure 6.4 Selecting the workflow destination

Edit the Workflow

To get into the workflow editor, right-click the newly created workflow, and then click Edit. The resulting workflow editor is shown in Figure 6.5.

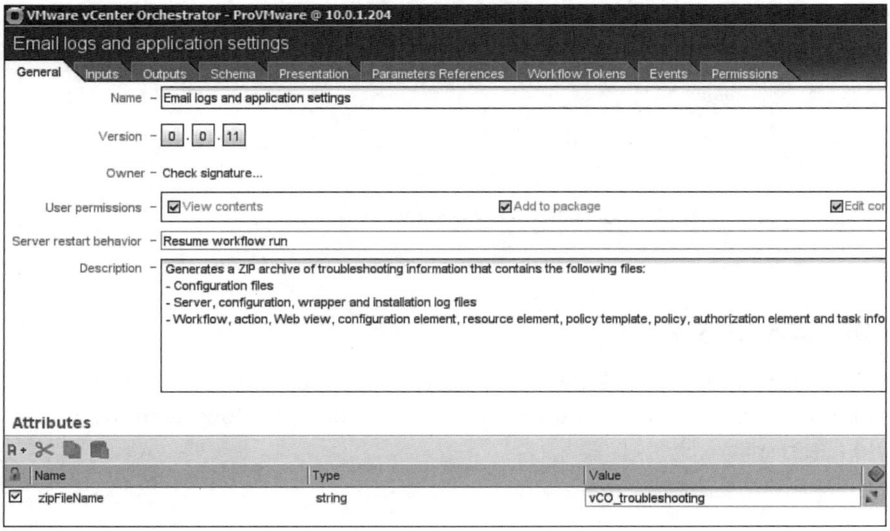

Figure 6.5 Workflow editor

Our first order of business is to edit the description to something that more closely reflects what our end result will be. Then, we must add an input to allow email to flow.

Edit Schema

Now we need to edit the schema of the workflow to add our extra email task. This requires a few steps:

1. Add user input.
2. Add a scriptable task.
3. Edit new elements.

Let's look at an actual example. Figure 6.6 shows the user inputs being added.

Figure 6.7 shows the schema editor.

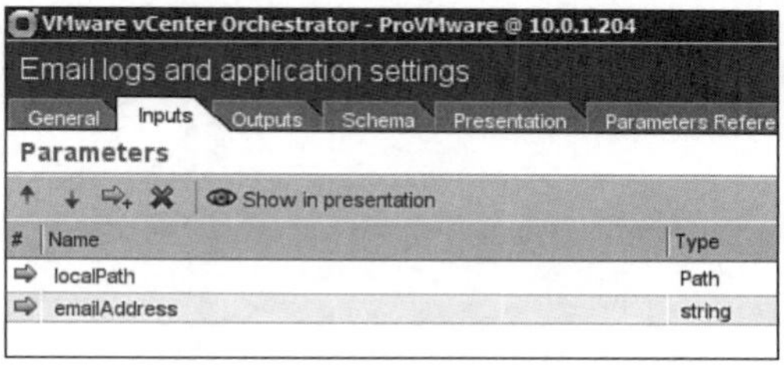

Figure 6.6 Adding inputs

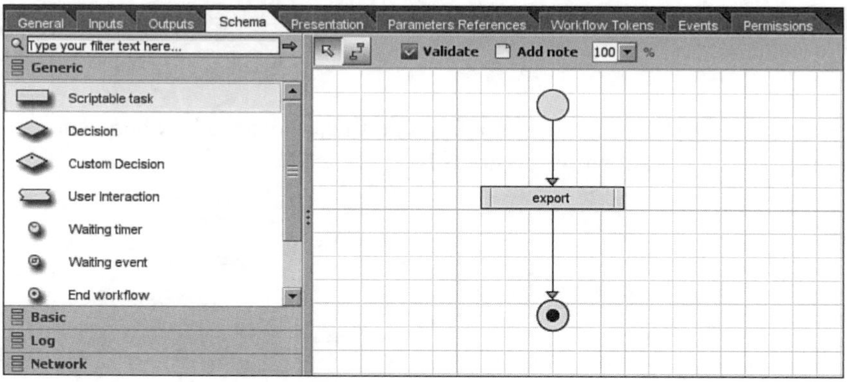

Figure 6.7 Schema Editor

Our first order of business is to add the user input task. To do this, select the link between the workflow start and the Export task, as shown in Figure 6.8.

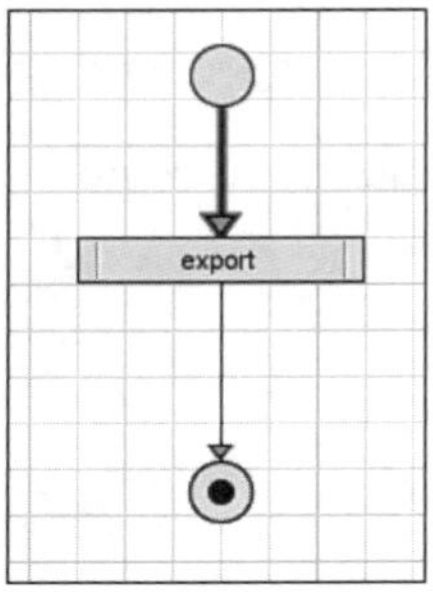

Figure 6.8 Link selected

Then, right-click and select Insert element, User Interaction Task, as shown in Figure 6.9.

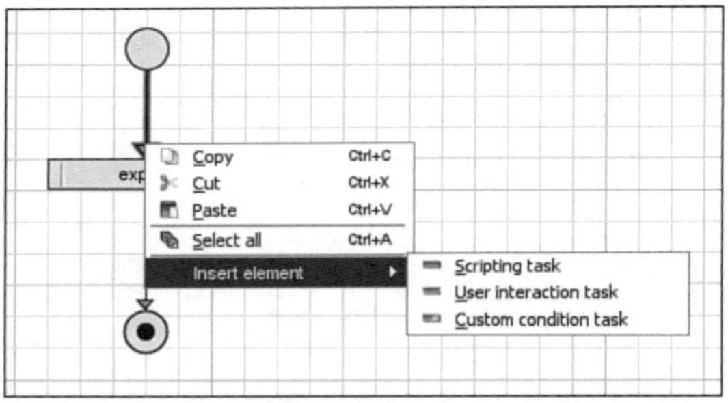

Figure 6.9 Insert user interaction

Then, we add in a scriptable task to send the email. To do this, select the link between Export and the workflow stop, as shown in Figure 6.10.

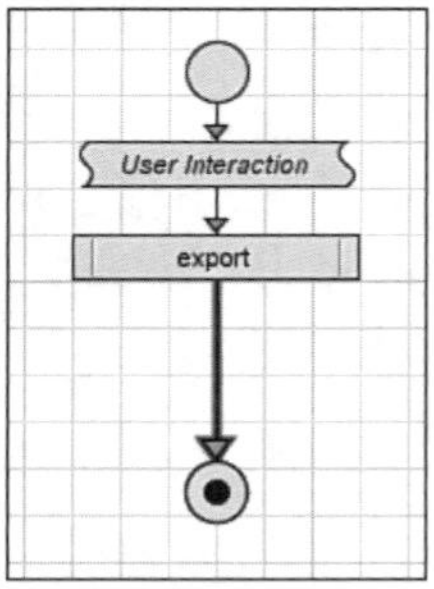

Figure 6.10 Link selected

With the link selected, right-click and select Insert Element, Scripting Task, as shown in Figure 6.11.

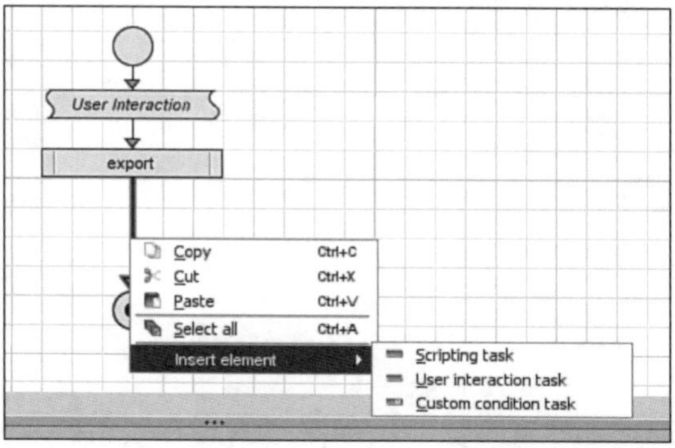

Figure 6.11 Inserting scripting task

Figure 6.12 shows the resulting workflow.

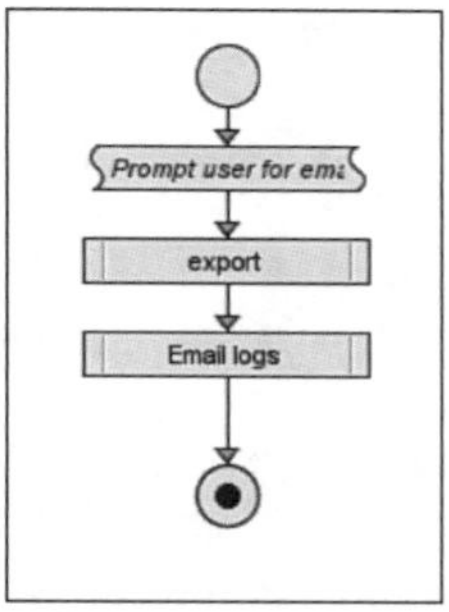

Figure 6.12 Final workflow

Edit the User Interaction

We need to edit the default input task to populate the `emailAddress` attribute that we will use in the scriptable task. To do this, select User Interaction; once that is selected, we work across the bottom tabs, starting with the Info tab, as shown in Figure 6.13.

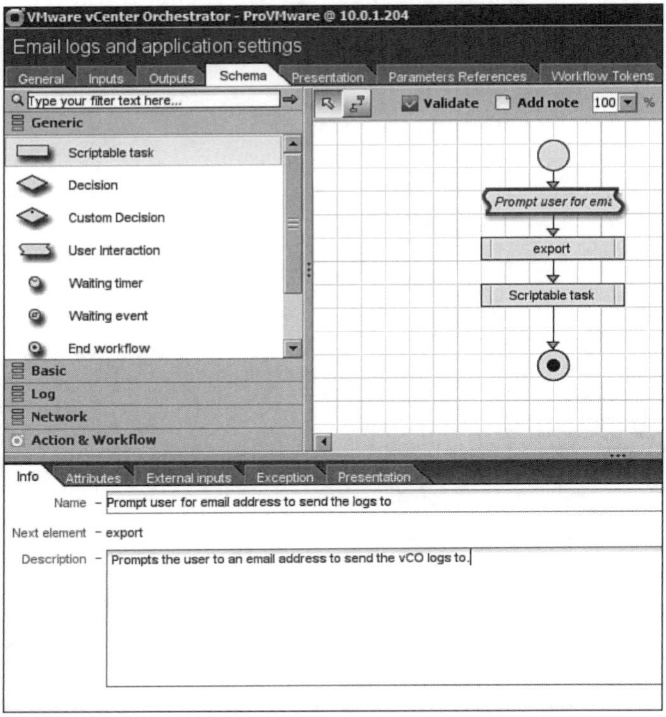

Figure 6.13 User Interaction, Info tab

NOTE

You want to save early and save often while editing workflows. Like editing a book in Microsoft Word, you don't want to miss a save and lose work. To make this faster, you can use Ctrl+S.

The next tab that we're interested in is External Inputs. In this tab, you want to press Ctrl+B to open the Chooser window. From there, select the Create parameter or attribute link to the right of the search box. Figure 6.14 shows the resulting window.

From there, click OK and save the workflow, and select the Scriptable Task task.

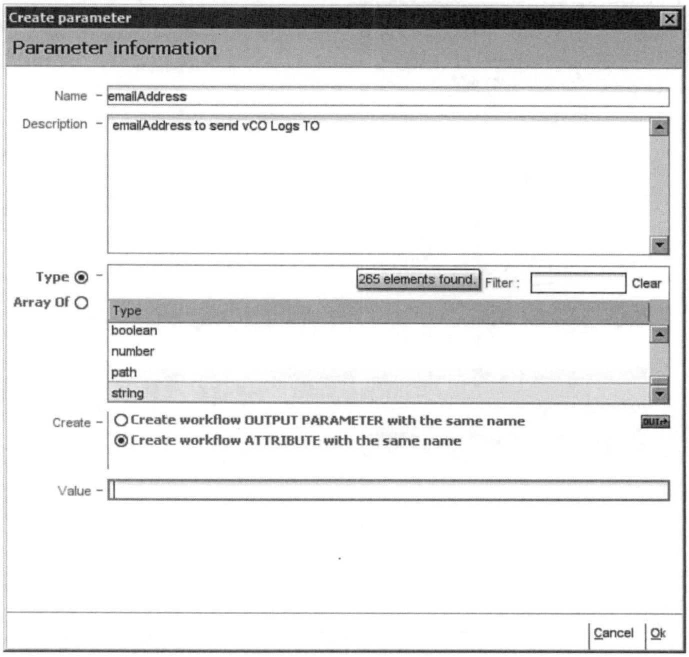

Figure 6.14 `emailAddress` attribute bound to user interaction task

Edit the Scriptable Task

Now comes the fun part, adding the email script. We have a few tasks to sort out before we get into the meat of the script, however. We'll work our way left to right using the tabs in the bottom window pane.

First, we rename the scriptable task to "Email Logs," as shown in Figure 6.15.

Next, we add parameters to the task. We add both `emailAddress` and `localPath` to the task, enabling us to get at both the file and the email address. To do this, select the In tab and press Ctrl+B. Figure 6.16 shows the results.

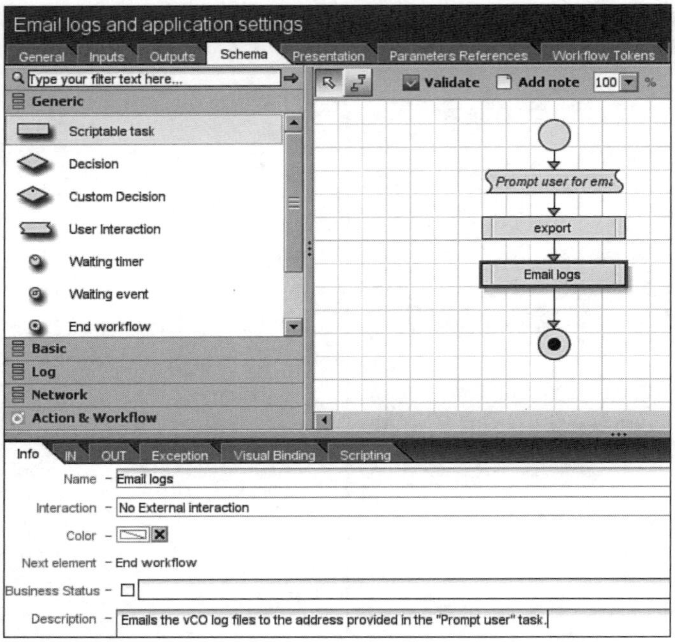

Figure 6.15 "Email Logs"

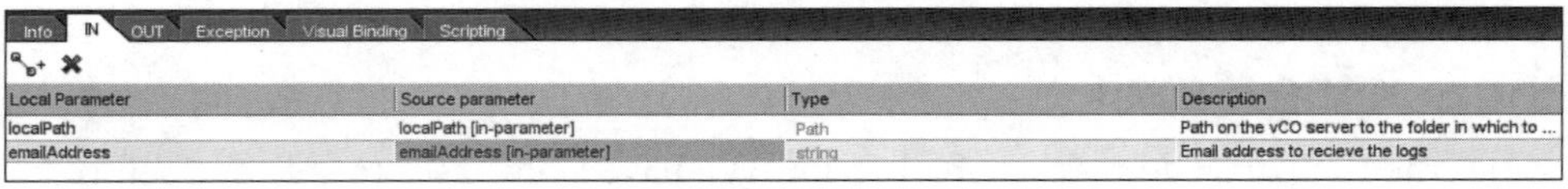

Local Parameter	Source parameter	Type	Description
localPath	localPath [in-parameter]	Path	Path on the vCO server to the folder in which to ...
emailAddress	emailAddress [in-parameter]	string	Email address to recieve the logs

Figure 6.16 `emailAddress` and `localPath` added to script task

Next, we select Scripting and add the following script:

```
var message = new EmailMessage();

var content = "vCO Logs Attached";

message.toAddress = emailAddress;
message.subject = "vCO System Logs";
message.addMimePart(content,"text/html; charset=UTF-8");
message.addMimePart(localPath,"application/zip");
```

```
System.log( "sending mail to host: " + message.smtpHost + ":" +
  message.smtpPort + " with user:" + message.username
                    + ", from:" + message.fromAddress + ", to:" +
  message.toAddress );

message.sendMessage();
```

This is the code to create and send email with vCO logs attached.

> **NOTE**
>
> The scripting language in vCO is JavaScript. As a vSphere and vCO administrator, you generally will not have to dive into it too often because VMware provides fairly robust out-of-the-box workflows.

The code creates an `EmailMessage` type scripting object, checks to see whether other email server parameters have been provided, and finally builds the message using our attributes as specified earlier.

Figure 6.17 shows starting the workflow, done by right-clicking the workflow and clicking Start Workflow. When launching the workflow, vCO automatically validates the workflow to ensure that it will run. Therefore, if you receive any errors when starting the workflow, it is because validation failed; so, you need to go back and correct something within the workflow.

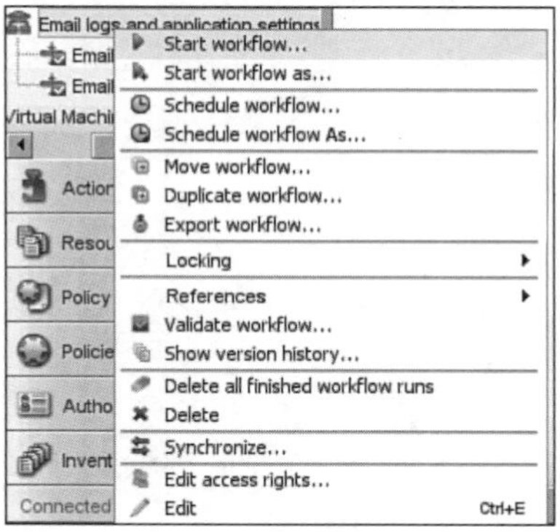

Figure 6.17 Email with vCO logs attached

Creating New Workflows

In a way, the modification of built-in workflows done in the preceding section created new workflows for us. Although that is true and helped identify the common components of a workflow, the process for creating a new workflow is subtly different and generally has the following order of events:

1. Determine what the workflow should do.
2. Create inputs.
3. Create the logical flow in the schema editor.
4. Bind input and output parameters.
5. Write scripts for scriptable or decision elements.
6. Edit the layout of dialogs.
7. Validate the workflow.

Other than the order having changed, the organization and editing steps from the edit existing workflow section still apply.

NOTE

With regard to binding, every variable (input, output, attribute, and so on) should be bound to something, even if that something is `NULL`. Besides being good practice, this prevents workflow validation from throwing errors and helps you ensure that every value has a use.

Workflow Scheduling

This section covers the following:

- Starting a workflow
- Basic scheduling
- Scheduling using different credentials
- Recurring workflows

There will be times, say during workflow development or with workflows tied into web views, that you will want to start a workflow manually. Do this by drilling down to the workflow you want to execute and right-clicking it. You can do this and select Start Workflow, as shown in Figure 6.17.

For most maintenance tasks, you will work with scheduled workflows. This will enable you to execute the maintenance without having to be awake during the maintenance window. Unless you want to be, that is. To schedule a workflow, you have two options: Schedule Workflow, which stores the credentials of the user scheduling said workflow, or Schedule Workflow As, which enables you to supply the credentials of a service account. We are going to work with Schedule Workflow As to schedule the "Email vCO Logs" workflow we created earlier to run once a week. To do this, follow these steps:

1. Right-click the workflow and select Schedule Workflow As.
2. In the resulting window, provide credentials.
3. Under Run Date and Time, select Tuesday at 11 a.m.
4. Set the recurrence to Tuesdays at 11 a.m.
5. Submit the workflow.

Figure 6.18 shows the Scheduling window filled out with these options. After you submit the workflow, it shows up under the Scheduler section in the vCO Client, as shown in Figure 6.19.

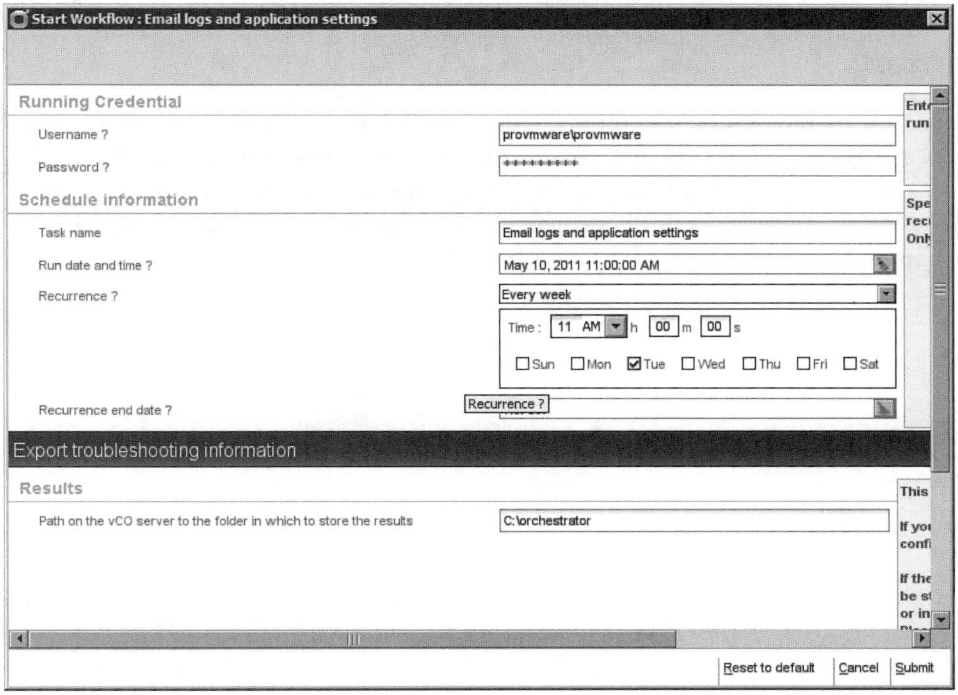

Figure 6.18 Workflow Scheduler window

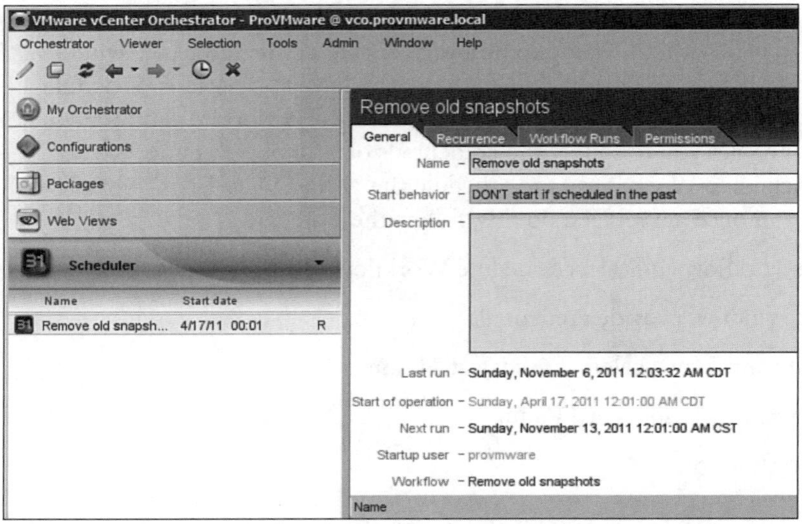

Figure 6.19 Scheduled workflow

Summary

Congrats! You are now a master in the ways of the workflow. We began with organization, covered some key concepts, worked through creation and modification, and finished with workflow scheduling. As you will see over the course of our scenarios and corresponding workflows in the remainder of this book, you will make good use of the knowledge gained in this chapter.

Part III

Amazing Smoothies, Inc. (a.k.a. Real-World Use Case)

Chapter 7

Your First Day at Amazing Smoothies, Inc.: Network Orientation

In this chapter, we flesh out the basics of Amazing Smoothies, a fictional company that we use in all of our use cases from this point forward. This includes a bit of the Amazing Smoothies history and how the company makes money. From there, we dive headfirst into the network layout and critical applications that run at Amazing Smoothies. Finally, we touch on some of the current pain points Amazing Smoothies is having. In this chapter, we cover the following aspects of Amazing Smoothies, Inc.:

- A brief history and tour of Amazing Smoothies
- The network layout
- Amazing applications
- Systems integration
- Growing pains

Ready to start your first day at Amazing Smoothies? We certainly think you are, so grab yourself a chair and prepare for your indoctrination into our flavor of corporate Kool-Aid.

A Brief History and Tour of Amazing Smoothies

Amazing Smoothies is as amazing as it is made up to facilitate the use cases later in the book. This is because I've always found it easier to show folks technical concepts within a real-world framework. Thus, Amazing Smoothies has come to our aide to allow us to demonstrate how the many and varied concepts of vCO talked about earlier in this book can and will apply to companies like yours. For this specific example, Amazing Smoothies is a fictitious smoothie stand company. Why? Because this gives us a number of interesting use cases to which we can apply vCO.

NOTE

You need to allow the sample company some artistic leeway. (In fact, I use the word *artistic* in the very loosest sense.) Amazing Smoothies is meant to be illustrative rather than prescriptive, so the examples are kept general enough for application in most cases. In others, they'll need some slight (or not-so-slight) modifications to run in your environment.

At a high level, Amazing Smoothies is a U.S.-based chain of smoothie shops that is rapidly expanding, so much so that there have been requests to start international franchises.

Now that you have a handle on what Amazing Smoothies does, let's take a look at their current IT systems.

The Network Layout

Being that this is the age of virtualization and Amazing Smoothies wants to keep its infrastructure costs low so that they can focus on their core business, 100% of their server footprint is virtualized using VMware vSphere. Because they are a start-up, and to keep costs low, their systems are hosted in a co-located datacenter. This has some of its own unique challenges, such as handling Amazing Smoothies retail branches, business, and warehouse/logistics systems. We cover these in Figures 7.1, 7.2, and 7.3.

You'll notice that in most cases I've left out both print and telephony services. This is not because Amazing Smoothies doesn't have them, but rather because they are not relevant to the tasks we cover and therefore a bit beyond our scope.

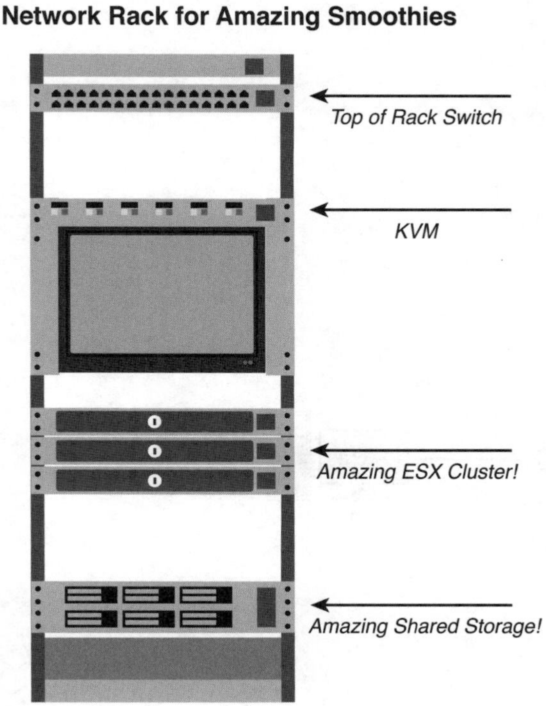

Figure 7.1 Amazing Smoothies co-location facility layout

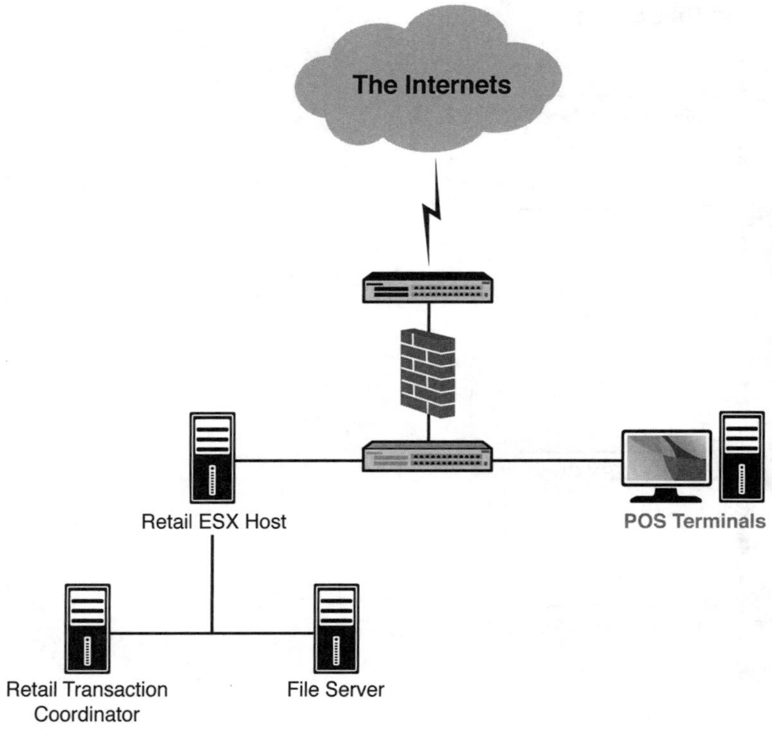

Figure 7.2 Amazing Smoothies retail layout

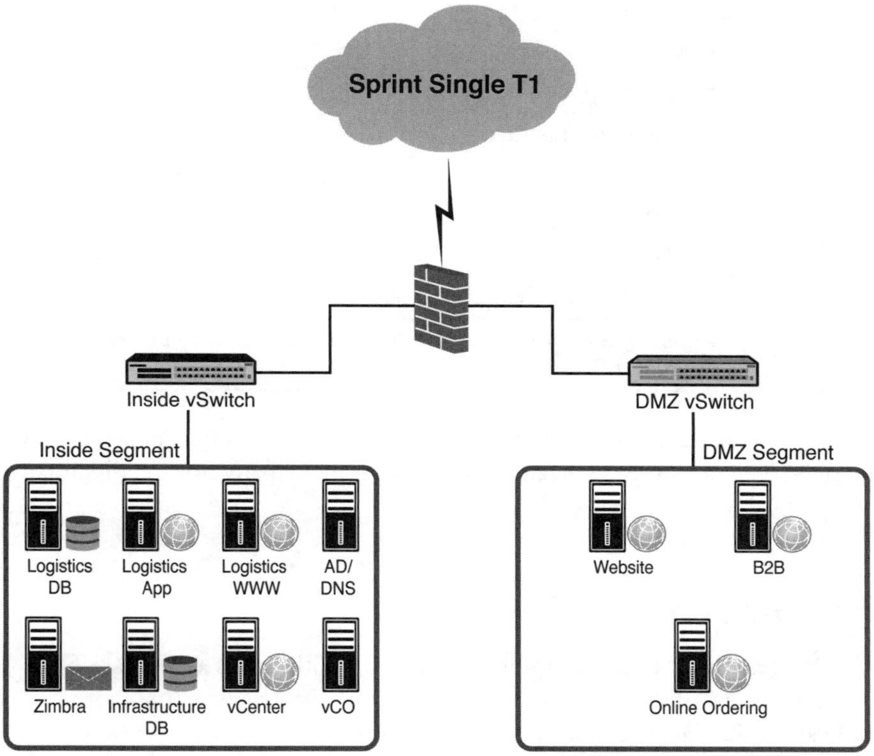

Figure 7.3 Amazing Smoothies business and logistics systems

Amazing Applications

As an amazing smoothie company and having to compete with some of the other retail smoothie giants in our industry, Amazing Smoothies not only differentiates ourselves with our proprietary Amazing Blend Smoothies, but also leverage various amazing applications to help us differentiate on customer service.

Amazing Smoothies runs a number of applications, and you will have seen some of these in the diagrams in the preceding section, but it's best to list them here, as well. Table 7.1 lists these applications and their uses.

Table 7.1 Amazing Smoothies Amazing Applications

Application	Use
VMware Zimbra	Email and shared calendaring
vCenter Server	vSphere administration
Amazing Logistics	Making sure the smoothie syrup arrives where and when Amazing Smoothies needs it
Request Tracker (RT)	Trouble tickets
Active Directory	Single Sign-On and LDAP
Amazing PoS	Amazing Smoothies custom point-of-sale solution based on Microsoft Dynamics POS

Some additional applications are in use around the Amazing Smoothies headquarters, but the list here should serve. As you see, Amazing Smoothies is a company not too dissimilar from most others.

Systems Integration

As you saw in the figures earlier in this chapter, Amazing Smoothies has a number of systems that function as part of the business. As with any complex business, the more systems and applications in play, the more varied and complex the manual processes and workflows will be. Fortunately, vCO has a number of plug-ins that provide for an incredible amount of flexibility when creating workflows that work across systems, including the following:

- SSH
- Mail
- Active Directory
- vCloud Director
- REST/SOAP

NOTE

This list is not comprehensive. As discussed several times in earlier chapters, one of the things that gives vCO its extensibility is that it is plug-in based and therefore easily adapted to new systems and integration points as your business grows.

Growing Pains

In your interview with Amazing Smoothies, you spoke with the head of IT to discuss some of their current pain points and some of their concerns for growth. The following concerns were laid out for you:

- Cleaning up snapshots
- VM provisioning
- VM decommissioning
- Resource management
- New hardware

In addition to these concerns, it was expressed that Amazing Smoothies is currently experiencing a hyper-growth phase and needs to have processes and systems that will scale as the company continues to expand and add new branches.

As the concerns have been laid out to you (the new Amazing Smoothies engineer), we will address these in the remaining chapters in this section.

Summary

Congratulations on finishing your orientation as a newly minted Amazing Smoothies employee! We hope you'll enjoy your free smoothies as you work through the problems outlined for you.

In this chapter, we covered the who and what behind Amazing Smoothies and their associated IT systems. We also briefly touched on the current pain points that Amazing Smoothies wants you to help solve through the application of vCenter Orchestrator. Finally, we talked about their choice in an IT ticketing system. Understanding the scenario described in this chapter will help you better apply the use cases in the chapters to come.

Chapter 8

Amazing Smoothies Day 2: Dealing with Snapshots

In this chapter, we extend the case study by tackling snapshots. Specifically, this chapter covers the following:

- Identifying our current snapshot processes
- Improving the snapshot processes
- Turning our processes into workflows
- Creating snapshots
- Committing snapshots

It's a pretty big task we have at hand, so let's get right to it.

NOTE

Because this book is covering vCenter Orchestrator (vCO), this discussion assumes your basic familiarity with the vSphere environment. Furthermore, your familiarity with the concept of snapshotting as seen by VMware is assumed, so this chapter does not cover what they are so much as how to handle them.

The Current Processes

At Amazing Smoothies, two actions are preformed with snapshots: creating them and removing them. Each of these has an associated set of steps to ensure consistency within the environment, as covered individually in the following sections.

> **NOTE**
>
> In VMware vSphere, you can take three actions with snapshots: create, delete, and revert. In the context of our Amazing Smoothies story, however, we do not automatically revert snapshots against our production environment (although you could use this feature in a lab or development environment to automate the build/test processes).

Creating Snapshots

Of the many use cases for VMware snapshots, the typical uses at Amazing Smoothie are as follows:

- Operating system updates
- Smoothie logistics software updates
- Troubleshooting/configuration testing

Each of these targets a specific virtual machine (VM) or set of VMs, but the process for each is the same. Figure 8.1 shows how to create a snapshot within the Amazing Smoothie vSphere environment.

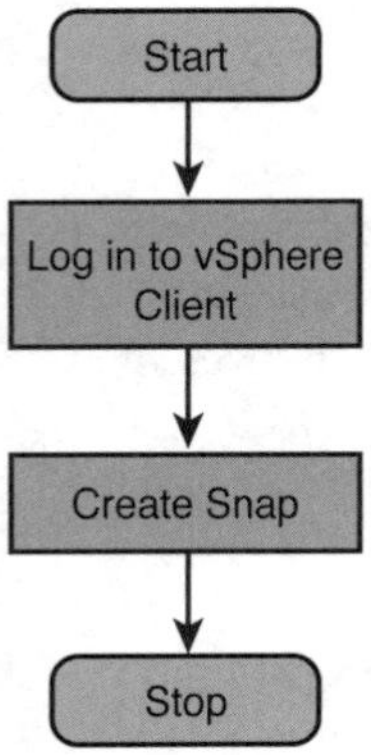

Figure 8.1 Amazing Smoothies snapshot-creation process

As you see, the process consists of three steps:

1. Log in to vSphere.
2. Select the VM to be the snapshot.
3. Create and name the snapshot.

This is quite straightforward. You will not find it this easy, however, if you need to snapshot more than a handful of VMs before maintenance. Consider, for example, the Smoothie Logistics Software stack shown in Figure 8.2. If the front-end web server clocks or transactions fall too far out of sync with the back-end databases, things can get interesting. Even though the admin staff is pretty quick with the clicking and keeping this sane for the existing four VMs, as Amazing Smoothies expands, this application needs to scale to 20 VMs in the near future.

NOTE

This is for the sake of example only. Other design/operational considerations apply to software patching the 20 VMs that make up the business-critical application for inventory delivery.

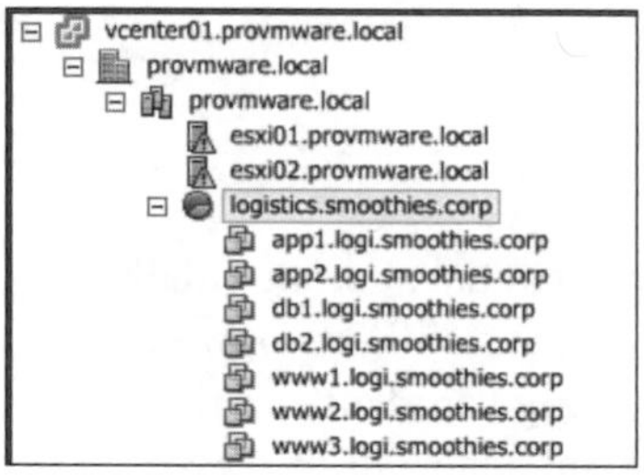

Figure 8.2 The Amazing Smoothie Logistics platform

So, the goal here with vCO is to snapshot large parts of the virtual infrastructure, which is relatively easy to do, as discussed in the following sections.

Committing Snapshots

Deleting or committing snapshots is the next item on our agenda. Amazing Smoothies, as described in "Creating Snapshots," also commits snapshots against the VM group that represents an application.

As with creating snapshots, committing them requires that you log in to the vSphere Client and progress manually from VM to VM on which you need to commit the snapshot.

> **NOTE**
>
> As you progress through this chapter, you will see references to both *deleting* and *committing* the snapshot. This is because in the VMware interface there is no commit, only delete. However, when reviewing how VMware actually handles snapshots, deleting the snapshot commits the changes contained within the snapshot file. For a more detailed explanation of snapshots and how VMware conceptualizes them, refer to the VMware website.

Problems with the Process

As you might surmise, even if you handle snapshots with care, issues can arise. The current manual process is error prone at best. After all, what happens if an administrator reverts all but one snapshot from an application? At the very least, Amazing Smoothies would be left with some data inconsistencies, which in turn can lead to misplaced or wrong-sized orders for supplies, or worse yet, inconsistencies in the accounting systems.

Have no fear, vCO is here, and it enables you to improve the process somewhat.

Improving the Process

As you read in the preceding section, snapshots are currently a manual and potentially error-prone process at Amazing Smoothie. However, all is not lost. With vCO, we can automatically create, revert, and commit snapshots. The following list identifies the improvements that we will make with the addition of vCO to our snapshot processes:

- Grouped-snapshot creation
- Grouped-snapshot deletion
- Scheduled creation and deletion

Before you start to improve the process and subsequently automate the handling of snapshots, you want to determine how best to handle this within the environment. There are two basic ways of looking at, or for, old snapshots: size and age.

Size

VMware snapshots, if left unchecked, can quickly grow to some pretty extreme sizes (size of the Virtual Machine Disks [VMDKs] on the VM + memory assigned). This can cause your datastore to fill, which can then lead to some angry users. In turn, the number of snapshots in the tree can exacerbate the size because each requires its own space.

Although we cannot prescribe the optimal size for a snapshot, it should certainly be kept less than the total amount of free space on your volume. To monitor this, you can set alarms in vSphere along with scripted actions. One of the biggest contributors to the size of snapshots is age.

Age

As just mentioned, age is one of the biggest contributing factors to snapshot size, mostly because of the natural data change over time in a server. Even an unused server generates logs or other blocks of data that change.

You want to consider a number of things other than size when deciding how long to keep snapshots. Consider, for example, why the snapshot was taken: Operating system updates? New version of an application? New developer release? Each has its own testing periods, necessitating different snapshot ages. Your decision should take this into account, as well.

Decision

After careful analysis of the typical growth rate of snapshots and a review of the standard use of snapshots before you joined Amazing Smoothies, you have determined the optimal age for a snapshot is about 7 days.

> **NOTE**
>
> You will still need to use vCenter or other alerting to notify you of snapshot growth beyond 7 days. However, the process that follows should ensure this particular alert will be used only for true emergencies.

Process

Now that you have reviewed the current process and have decided how you want to handle snapshots, it's time to build some workflows, as discussed next.

Turning the Process into a Workflow

Here we are, where the proverbial rubber meets the road in the chapter: the selection of the workflows to use or modify to do our bidding. Of the numerous ways to approach this, I want to highlight a few and explain why we're taking a particular route.

Net New Workflow

Ah! The feeling of starting with a fresh workflow is much like an artist with a blank canvas on which to create. In our case, we might be able to reduce a bit of complexity when compared to the workflows that ship with vCO. However, we're all about saving some time, and given that the vCO product team has already invested a large amount of time into making sure these workflows fit most use cases, starting from scratch might not make the most sense.

Modify the Existing Workflows

Herein lies a good tradeoff between flexibility and time investment, if you are careful. That is to say, not all the built-in workflows are easy to modify, and you can easily overwhelm yourself trying to figure it out. However, you also need to weigh the potential complexity against the potential time investment in creating a brand-new workflow. In the case of Amazing Smoothies, the built-in workflows match our use close enough that we do not need to modify the existing workflows.

Use the Existing Workflow

Included with the built-in vCenter Plugin Library are three workflows that enable us to accomplish our task:

- "Create a Snapshot [for all virtual machines]"
- "Remove Old Snapshots"
- "Revert to Current Snapshot [and wait]"

Note that the first and third workflows have [bracketed] terms in them. That is because a secondary workflow starts the same. The examples in this chapter use both.

You can find these workflows in the vCO Client under Library, vCenter, Virtual Machine Management, Snapshots.

> **NOTE**
>
> All workflows covered in the book are identified as being a part of the default VMware packages or custom. Custom workflows will be provided on the author's website for download shortly after publication of this book.

Remember reading that these workflows handle our needs? Well, let's take a closer look at some of their components. As we review the workflows, we look at the following aspects:

- Schema
- Scripting
- Scheduling

Creating Snapshots

First on the list is creating snapshots. As mentioned previously, two different workflows are included with vCO: "Create a Snapshot" and "Create Snapshots of All Virtual Machines in a Resource Pool." For the specific use case with Amazing Smoothies, we use the latter.

> **NOTE**
>
> Sometimes within your own organization, you will find that using the other workflow is appropriate, but I will leave investigating this workflow as an exercise for you.

Schema

Figure 8.3 shows the "Create Snapshots of All Virtual Machines in a Resource Pool" schema.

The first interesting point here is the first scriptable block: Initialize. This scripting block takes the resource pool and child resource pool elements as input and enumerates a list of VMs to work with. The output forming this block is used to determine how many times the workflow needs to loop and what VM it is operating on.

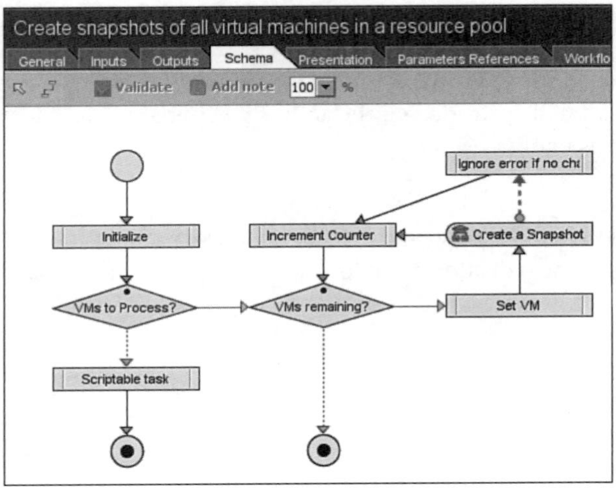

Figure 8.3 "Create Snapshots of All Virtual Machines in a Resource Pool" schema

The second interesting point in this workflow schema is the processing loop. This starts and loops at the custom decision block labeled VMs Remaining. The custom decision block checks the workflow's current place in the list of VMs to see whether it is at the end of the list. If it is not, it changes the current VM to be worked on and creates a snapshot. This happens in the Set VM and Create a Snapshot blocks, respectively.

Scripting

Now that you understand a bit more about the schema of the workflow, let's look at scripting. Why are we looking at the scripting? After all, we're not writing any code, are we? You are right; we are not writing a single line of code. Instead, even though the workflow does everything we are looking for, it is still a good idea to review the code, for a few reasons. Primarily, you want to take a brief look at the script as a quick sanity check. Yes, VMware wrote it, but it is always good to verify it meets your expectations. In addition, you might want to look at the script to familiarize yourself with the JavaScript used (and you might want to borrow some of the code for use in later workflows).

Instead of analyzing each block independently, this discussion covers the same blocks identified as *interesting* earlier in this chapter.

NOTE

Note that the scripting language used in vCO is JavaScript. You do not have to look at it too often, but some familiarity will go a long way in your workflow development.

Initialize

As stated earlier, the Initialize block takes a resource pool element as input and provides a few things as output:

- `allVMs`: Array containing all VM objects in the resource pool
- `vmCount`: Total number of VMs contained in all VMs
- `currentVM`: The current counter position

It does this using the following code:

```
01 // Retrieve an array of vms contained in the specified resource pool
02 if(childResourcePool){
03         allVMs = System.getModule("com.vmware.library.vc.resourcePool")
   .getAllVMsOfResourcePool(resourcePool) ;
04 }else{
05         allVMs = resourcePool.vm;
06 }
07 vmCount = allVMs.length;
08 currentVM = 0;
```

Note the following:

- Line 2 checks whether a child resource pool is available. If so, it proceeds to line 3, and otherwise skips to line 5.
- Line 3 is an example of calling the vCenter Server plug-in API. Specifically, we are using the `getAllVMsOfResourecePool` method to set the `allVMs` variable. As discussed in Chapter 6, "Introduction to Workflow-Fu," you can use the Search API functionality of the vCO Client to find almost any method or object you are looking for.
- Line 5: If there is no child resource pool, use the VM property of the current resource pool to obtain a list of all VMs. As with line 3, you can use the API Explorer or the vSphere Managed Object Browser to find more information about this property, or to find a more fitting property for your use case.

VMs Remaining

The VMs Remaining block is a custom decision block that takes both `currentVM` and `vmCount` as input and decides whether one is larger than the other. Notice the `System.Sleep` command prior to the decision. This is to give vCenter Server some time to actually execute the snapshot:

```
System.sleep(2000);
if (currentVM < vmCount){
       return true;
}else{
       return false;
}
```

If one or the other of `currentVM` and `vmCount` is larger, the workflow proceeds down the "true" path (the green line when viewing the schema). Otherwise, we exit the workflow.

Set VM

Set VM is another block like Initialize in that it changes some variables around and gets us ready for the next step in the path. Set VM takes `allVMs`, `currentVM`, and `snapNamePrefix` as input and returns `activeVM` and `snapName`, which are used in the next step. The code for this block is as follows:

```
01 // Set our activeVM object:
02 var activeVM = allVMs[currentVM];
03
04 var date = new Date();
05 snapName = snapNamePrefix + " " + date.toGMTString();
```

Not much magic here: Line 2 changes `activeVM` from the last VM processed to the next one in the list. Lines 4 and 5 get the current date and add it to the end of the snapshot name. This is useful for tracking when the snapshots were taken.

Create a Snapshot

The Create a Snapshot block is not like the others we've looked at, in that it's not a scripting block. Rather, it is a block that calls the "Create a Snapshot" workflow. Note that although no specific code is associated with this block, some configurable parameters are worth calling out. Figure 8.4 shows the parameters, and Table 8.1 describes the significant parameters.

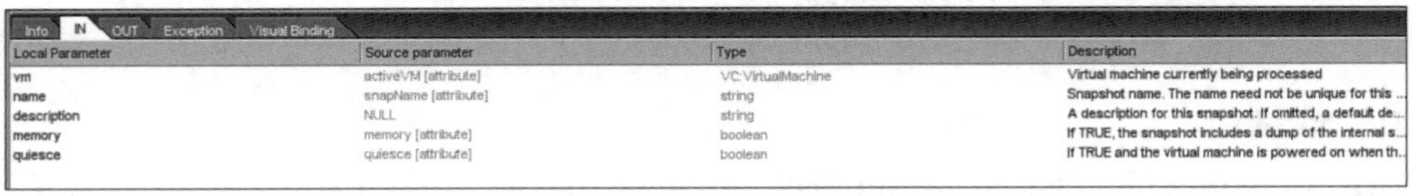
Info
IN
OUT
Exception
Visual Binding
Local Parameter
Source parameter
Type
Description
vm
activeVM [attribute]
VC:VirtualMachine
Virtual machine currently being processed
name
snapName [attribute]
string
Snapshot name. The name need not be unique for this ...
description
NULL
string
A description for this snapshot. If omitted, a default de...
memory
memory [attribute]
boolean
If TRUE, the snapshot includes a dump of the internal s...
quiesce
quiesce [attribute]
boolean
If TRUE and the virtual machine is powered on when th...

Figure 8.4 Parameters of the Create a Snapshot block

Table 8.1 Significant Parameters of the Create a Snapshot Block

Name	Source Value	Description
`vm`	`activeVM`	The current VM being processed
`Name`	`snapName`	The name of the snapshot
`Description`	`NULL`	Optional snapshot description
`Memory`	`Memory`	`True` or `False` value that determines whether memory will be snapshot
`Quiesce`	`Quiesce`	`True` or `False` value that determines whether the disk should be silenced before the snapshot

Scheduling

Now that you know how this workflow operates and have a good idea of what it looks like inside, we can schedule it. Chapter 6 covered scheduling, but it's worth noting a few of the specifics about scheduling this workflow. Figure 8.5 shows the Scheduling dialog.

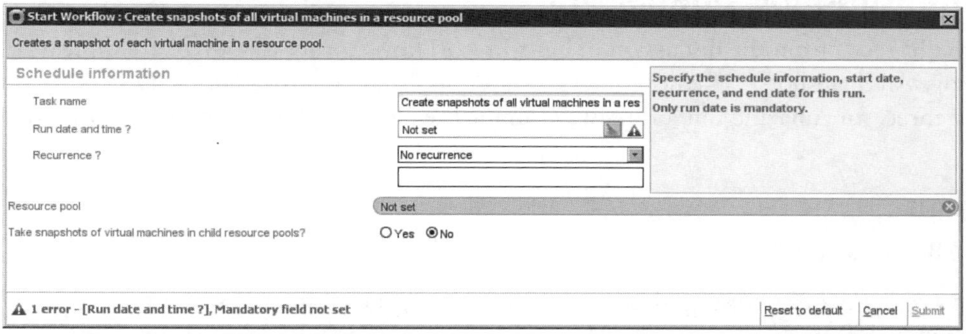

Figure 8.5 Scheduling the "Create Snapshot of All Virtual Machines in a Resource Pool" workflow

In addition to the basic scheduling bits, there are two other questions: Resource Pool and Take Snapshots of Virtual Machines in Child Resource Pools. For Amazing Smoothies, we schedule this workflow to start on 5/31/2011 and run monthly against the logistics.smoothie.corp resource pool. Figure 8.6 shows the resulting dialog.

NOTE

This is not the final schedule; instead, it is an example. We schedule this to align with the needs and processes of Amazing Smoothies in the "Real-World Application: Patch Cycles" section, later in this chapter.

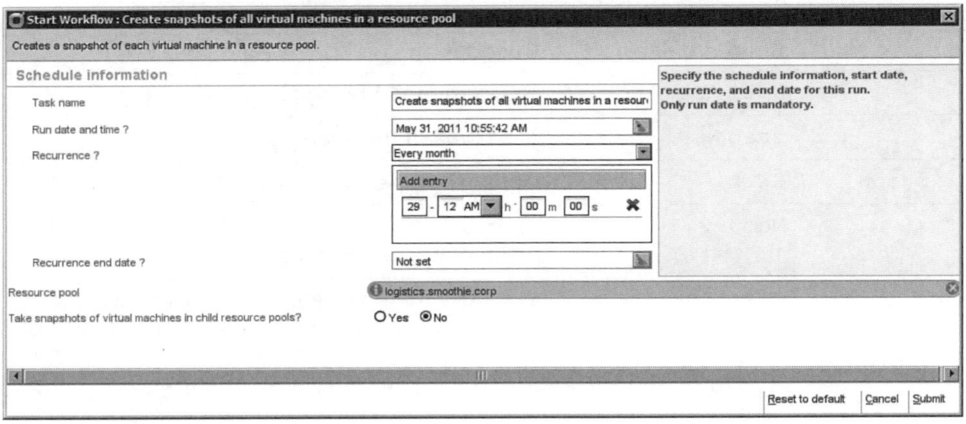

Figure 8.6 Scheduled

Committing the Snapshots

You might recall from the discussion of built-in workflows earlier that there are three: "Remove All Snapshots," "Remove Excess Snapshots," and "Remove Old Snapshots." Of the three, for Amazing Smoothies we examine the "Remove Old Snapshots" workflow.

Schema

Figure 8.7 shows the "Remove Old Snapshots" schema.

There are plenty of interesting things in this workflow, and as you can see, it is suitably more complex than the "Create Snapshots of All Virtual Machines in a Resource Pool" workflow previously discussed. To begin, working from the start of the workflow and including all elements until "Get Snapshots" has the workflow checking the current time on the vCenter Server against the host time to determine whether they are too far out of sync. If this is true, it prompts the user to continue. Checking the time synchronization between the host and the vCenter Server ensures that the workflow does not identify and delete the wrong snapshot.

From "Get Snapshots" until the end of the workflow, the workflow begins to process each workflow in turn, using the same type of loop we experienced in the last workflow. That is, take my list; check my position in the count; and if there are still snapshots left, change to the current snapshot, remove it, and loop.

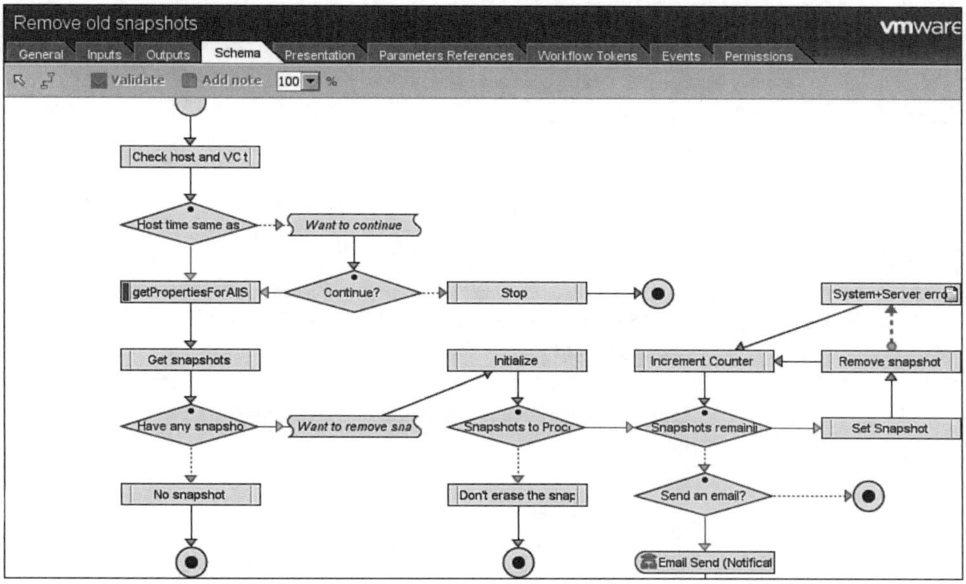

Figure 8.7 "Remove Old Snapshots" schema

Finally, the workflow ends with the opportunity to send email. The ticketing system at Amazing Smoothies makes it possible to open tickets via SMTP (email), thus enabling us to track which snapshots were deleted and when.

Scripting

Instead of covering all the individual "initialize" elements like we did before, this discussion focuses on "Get Snapshots" and "Remove Snapshot."

Get Snapshots

The "Get Snapshots" code is rather long. So, instead of reproducing the entire thing, here are the interesting parts:

```
snapshots = new Array();

var searchResults = Sytem.getModule("com.vmware.library.vc.vm.snapshot")
   .getAllSnapshotResultInDatastoreBrowser(false,false,false,true) ;

for (var i in searchResults) {
```

```
06          var files = searchResults[i].file;
07          for (var j in files) {
08                 ss = snapshotProperties.get(searchResults[i]
   .folderPath+files[j].path);
09                 if(ss){
10                        if(instanceObject==null){
11                               instanceObject =
   VcPlugin.convertToVimManagedObject(ss , instance);
12                        }
13                        dateNow = instanceObject.currentTime();
14                        timeForDateNow = dateNow.getTime();
15                        timeForDateModif = files[j].modification.getTime();
16                        diff = timeForDateNow-timeForDateModif;
17                        days = diff/86400000;
18
19                        if(days>numbrOfDay){
20                               snapshots.push(ss);
21                               System.log("The snapshot
   "+searchResults[i].folderPath +files[j].path+" of the VM
   "+ss.config.name+"
   had "+Math.floor(days)+" days");
22                        snapshotProperties.remove(searchResults[i]
   .folderPath+files[j].path);
```

If you pull up the scripting tab for this element, you'll see that I left out a good portion of the variable definitions and the structures that make the `for` loop work. This brevity allows us to focus on the interesting parts of the script. As before, here are the interesting lines:

- **Line 3:** There's that vCenter Server API again, this time with `getAllSnapshotResultInDatastoreBrowser`. This returns an object on which we can check the date the snapshot was created against the current date and determine the delta.
- **Lines 13 through 17:** Find the current time, the time the snapshot file was modified, determine the delta, and convert that to days.
- **Lines 19 through 21:** If the number of days old is greater than the number of days specified when the workflow was launched, add the snapshot to the list of snapshots to be deleted. Also, log it.

Remove Snapshot

Also worth noting is the method used to remove the snapshot. This block takes the active snapshot as input and removes it with the following code:

```
01        var vmName = activeSnapshot.config.name;
02        var snapshotID = activeSnapshot.id;
03        var task = activeSnapshot.removeSnapshot_Task(removeChildren);
04        var actionResult =
System.getModule("com.vmware.library.vc.basic").vim3WaitTaskEnd(task) ;
```

- Line 1 grabs the VM name from the `config` property of the snapshot. `activeSnapshot` is a variable of type `VcVirtualMachineSnapshot`. This means it contains a number of properties related to the current snapshot the workflow is processing. Of them, `config` represents the configuration, or the VMX file at the time the snapshot was taken.
- Line 3 removes the snapshot using the `removeSnapshot_Task` method, which is also part of the `VcVirtualMachineSnapshot` object.
- Line 4 waits for the task to finish before moving on.

Scheduling

Figure 8.8 shows the unique bits required to schedule this workflow.

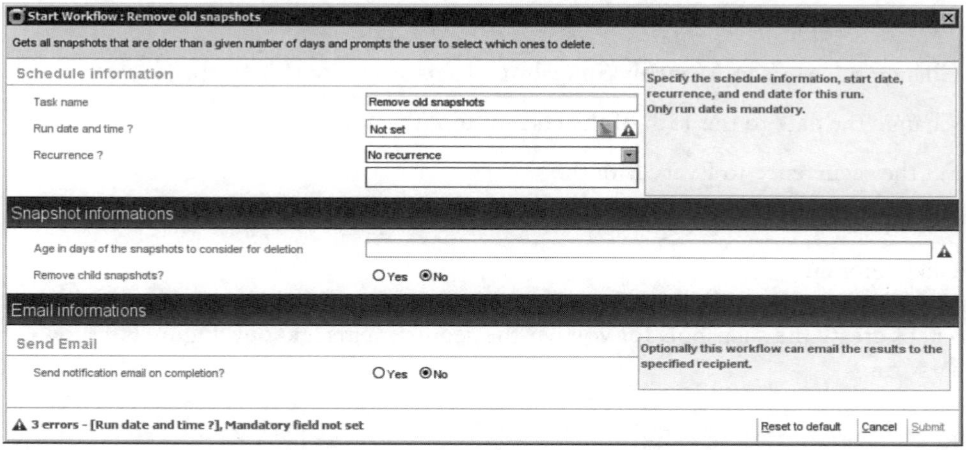

Figure 8.8 Scheduling "Remove Old Snapshots"

The important things to note here are that you need to specify the maximum age for a snapshot, if you want to delete all child snapshots, and the email information.

Real-World Application: Patch Cycles

Now that you know how each workflow behaves, let's schedule the "Create" and "Commit" workflows to handle the monthly patch cycle of Amazing Smoothies.

The requirements for the logistics vApp (collection of VMs) include the following:

- Snapshot taken 1 day before patching
- Patching performed on the 15th of every month
- Snapshot deleted after 7 days if not reverted

To schedule this within vCenter Orchestrator, open your vCO Client; drill down to the snapshot workflows under the Library, vCenter; and perform the steps listed in the following section.

Taking the Snapshots

To schedule the taking of snapshots, follow these steps:

1. Right-click Create Snapshots of All Virtual Machines in a Resource Pool.
2. Click Schedule.
3. Change the name to **Monthly Snapshot - logistics.smoothie.corp**.
4. Change the date to the 15th of the current month.
5. Set the recurrence to Every Month.
6. Change the resource pool to logistics.smoothie.corp.
7. Click Submit.

These steps create the snapshots for you per the requirements laid out. Figure 8.9 shows the final form.

NOTE

Notice that step 6 mentions the use of resource pools. Although this is true in the Amazing Smoothies environment, you will need to adjust as needed for your environment.

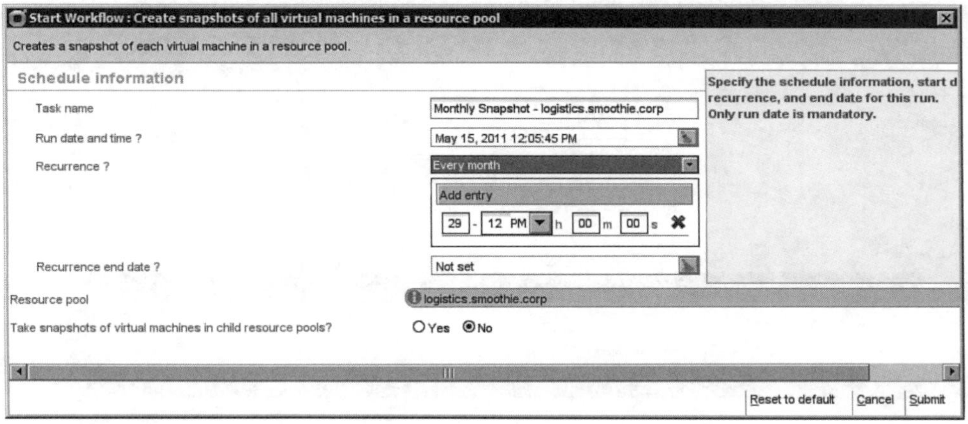

Figure 8.9 Completed scheduling for Monthly Snapshot – logistics.smoothie.corp

Deleting the Snapshots

To schedule deletion of snapshots, follow these steps:

1. Right-click Remove Old Snapshots.
2. Click Schedule.
3. Change name to **Remove snapshots – 7 Days +**.
4. Change the date to the 22nd of the current month.
5. Set the recurrence to Every Month.
6. Change the age in days to consider for deletion to 7.
7. Change Send E-Mail Notification to Yes.
8. Change the email address to **rt@provmware.local**.

These steps remove 7-day-old snapshots once a month, beginning 7 days after the patching snapshots are taken. Figure 8.10 shows the completed form.

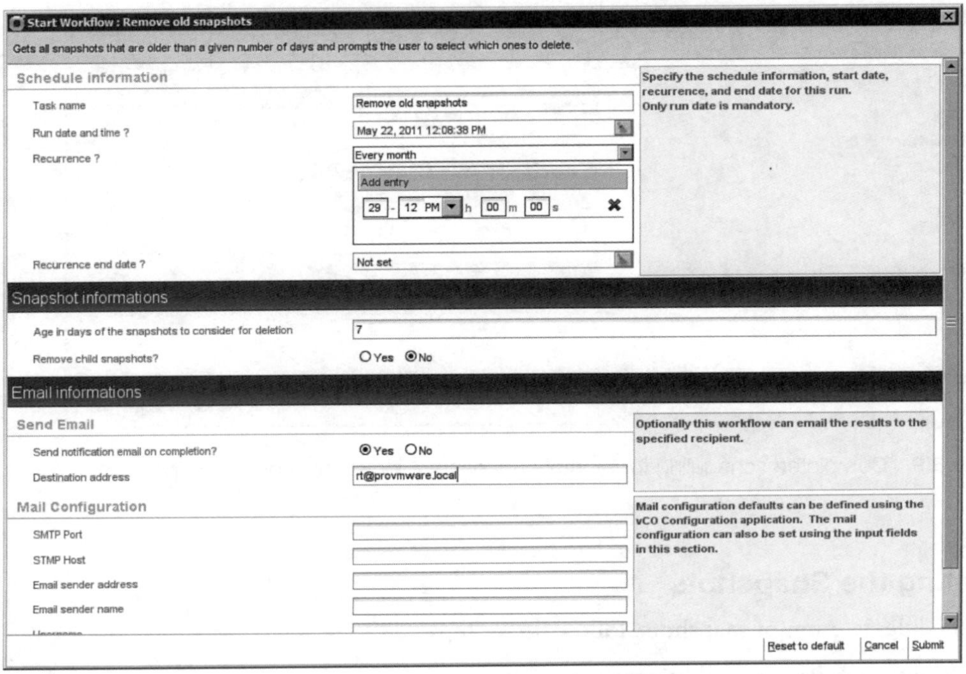

Figure 8.10 Completed scheduling for Remove snapshots – 7 Days +

Summary

At the beginning of the chapter (and the beginning of your second day at Amazing Smoothies), you were confronted with what looked like an insurmountable issue with the current state of snapshots. However, with a little bit of ingenuity and some vCO workflow magic, you tackled this problem and still have time for an extended lunch. Specifically, this chapter covered the current snapshot process and some improvements that you might make to the process. From there, the discussion turned to the workflows that vCO ships with to handle snapshots and finished with a real-world example of handling snapshots for monthly patch cycles.

Chapter 9

Amazing Smoothies Day 3: VM Provisioning

You might be wondering why this one was saved for later in our chapters on virtual machine (VM) management. You have been at Amazing Smoothies for 3 days and still have not built a VM? Well, there are a few reasons for that. First, you needed to relieve the pain that was being caused by the other issues. Second, it wasn't until today that you discovered that VM provisioning was being handled by nearly everyone and their brothers with a user account. Talk about VM sprawl!

As the preceding paragraph indicates, in this chapter we handle the building of VMs with vCenter Orchestrator. We talk about a number of things, including the following:

- The current VM provisioning method
- Building a VM with vCO
- Using "gold" images
- Customization with the VMware VIX plug-in

The Current VM Provisioning Process

As Amazing Smoothie has been in hyper-growth mode, early on the single administrator could no longer keep up with the workload. Because of this, lots of "savvy" users ended up with the VI Client and VM administrator rights within vCenter Server. Basically, everyone and then some could create VMs. In turn, the lack of process led to VM sprawl, resource contention issues, and supportability issues with the number and variants of installed operating systems. Let's take a deeper look at each of these problems. Once we have the problems identified and scoped properly, we look at how to solve them with vCO.

Too Many Cooks in the Kitchen

As described earlier, you can begin to see that it made sense during the hyper-growth for the administrator to get help where he could. However, you can also see where this might cause some issues. The issues that Amazing Smoothies has specifically run into with having too many cooks have been:

- Datastores out of storage
- VM sprawl and management
- Storage performance issues
- CPU contention
- Memory swapping
- Other performance issues

Each of these issues, although minor at first, has begun to cause considerable consternation among the users and management at Amazing Smoothies. So what to do? Some parts of the fix, such as restricted permissions, are beyond the scope of this book. As you'll discover in the next section, vCO has an interesting play in this area.

Too Many Templates

The next problem that was borne of the VM sprawl is the proliferation of "gold" templates. This is understandable because folks want to capitalize on the ability to rapidly spin up a duplicate of an existing install and get right to work. However, like the management issues presented earlier, there are additional space and image maintenance tasks that fall to the IT staff to manage, not to mention the addition of new and wondrous flavors of operating system, each with its own requirements that now need to be patched, tested, and otherwise maintained for rapid deployment.

At last count, there were no fewer than 35 image types at Amazing Smoothies. These run the gamut of OS types: Windows Server 2003, 2008, Red Hat Linux, Ubuntu Linux, both x86 and x64, and some even more exotic flavors of BSD-based systems. These were then broken into application servers, web servers, database images, and so on. As you can imagine, maintaining these can get out of hand pretty quick. Thankfully with vCO, we can reduce the total number of "gold" images under maintenance and build a workflow that can work in post-install customizations.

The vCO Way

There are multiple ways to skin this particular metaphorical cat. That said, the following are the areas you want vCO to address in building VMs:

- Consistent VM specifications
- "Gold" images
- Post-install customization/package installation
- Approval process

NOTE

In addition to these, there is still the problem of everyone having vCenter Server Client admin access. vCenter Server permissions are beyond the scope of the book, and you'll need to address these separately.

What follows in the next sections are breakdowns of the built-in vCO workflows to handle each of these specifically. After we look into each workflow, we tie them together with a workflow of workflows.

Consistent VM Specifications

Consistent VM specifications can be a battle of organizational policy in specifying which operating system or operating systems to use and what resources each type of server will use. Thankfully, vCO has a built-in workflow we can modify to facilitate this.

Create a Simple VM

Before we get too deep into VM types and customizing the workflow, we need to take a closer look at the workflow itself. In your vCO client, drill down to Library, vCenter, Virtual Machine Management, Basic. From there, select Create Simple Virtual Machine, and then select the Schema tab, as shown in Figure 9.1.

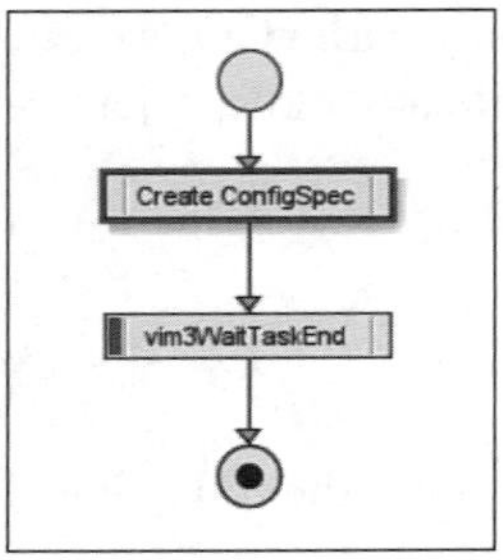

Figure 9.1 "Create Simple Virtual Machine" schema

On the surface, the workflow appears to be straightforward. However, lurking just beneath the surface is quite a bit of scripting magic that makes it all tick. We'll go over each bit, starting with the Create ConfigSpec scriptable task:

```
01 var configSpec = new VcVirtualMachineConfigSpec();
02 configSpec.name = vmName;
03 configSpec.guestId = vmGuestOs.name;
04 configSpec.memoryMB = vmMemorySize;
05 configSpec.numCPUs = vmNbOfCpus;
```

Note the following about the preceding code:

- Line 1 creates an instance of `VcVirtualMachineConfigSpec`. This is used to provide various values for customization to the create VM task.
- Lines 2 through 5 take values provided during the execution of the workflow and assign them to properties of the `configSpec` object.

The next bits of code assemble the actual path to the datastore on which the VM will be created:

```
01  // Compute vmxFilePath
02  var datastorePath = "[" + vmDatastore.info.name + "]";
03  System.log( "VMX file path : '" + datastorePath + "'" );
04  var files = new VcVirtualMachineFileInfo();
05  files.vmPathName = datastorePath;
06  configSpec.files = files;
```

- Lines 2 and 3 compute the datastore name and print it to the log (a useful trick for troubleshooting).

- Line 4 creates an instantiation of the `VcVirtualMachineFileInfo` object. This is used to provide the datastore file's location into the `configSpec` object that was created earlier.
- Line 5 takes the `datastorePath` from line 2 and sets the `vmPathName` property. This will be where the VMX (VM configuration) file lives.
- Line 6 takes all this work and stores it in the `configSpec` object that was created at the beginning of the script.

The next few sections deal with adding specific devices to the VM:

```
01 // Add Disk
02 deviceConfigSpec = System.getModule("com.vmware.library.vc.vm.spec.
config.device").createVirtualDiskFlatVer2ConfigSpec(
03        vmDiskSize, vmDatastore, 0, 0, VcVirtualDiskMode.persistent,
diskThinProvisioned );
04 deviceConfigSpecs[ii++] = deviceConfigSpec;
05
06 // Add Network
07 deviceConfigSpec = System.getModule("com.vmware.library.vc.vm.spec.
config.device").createVirtualEthernetCardNetworkConfigSpec( vmNetwork );
08 deviceConfigSpecs[ii++] = deviceConfigSpec;
```

There are a few more bits of code in this section, but rather than discuss all of them, I've grabbed two of the more interesting ones. These are interesting to us because they use variables provided on workflow startup to get going:

- Line 3 takes `vmDiskSize`, `vmDatastore`, and `vmThinProvisioned` and provides them as input to the `createVirtualDisk` method.
- Line 4 adds this to the list of specifications that will be added to `configSpec`.
- Line 7 adds a network interface card (NIC) to the VM and connects it to the network specified when the workflow was started.
- Line 8 does the same as line 4.

Finally, there is another interesting bit of script in this part of the workflow, and that is where the workflow actually submits the task to create the VM:

```
task = vmFolder.createVM_Task( configSpec, vmResourcePool, vmHost );
```

This takes the `configSpec` that was built in all of the prior lines, combines it with both the resource pool and ESX host specified when the workflow was launched, and submits it as a task to vCenter Server to complete.

This workflow also contains a scripting block to monitor the task once executed. In the schema, this is the `vim3WaitTaskEnd` block, and it contains the following code:

```
actionResult = System.getModule("com.vmware.library.vc.basic").
vim3WaitTaskEnd(task,progress,pollRate) ;
```

This line monitors the task created earlier until complete and causes the workflow to report success or failure based on the outcome of the task in vCenter Server. As you can see, we can modify this workflow in a few spots to suit our server type model, but before we get too deep into it, we should take a look at the Amazing Smoothies server type model.

Amazing Smoothies Server Type Model

In the case of Amazing Smoothies, we break down the "logistics" application into its OS and VM types (see Table 9.1).

Table 9.1 Amazing Smoothies Server Types

Type	OS	CPU	RAM (GB)	Disk (GB)
Web	Ubuntu x86	1	2	20
App	Ubuntu x64	2	6	20
Database	Windows 2008 R2	4	8	60

We have a bit of variety in both the server OS and specifications to work with, so let's set up three copies of the "Create Simple Virtual Machine" workflow for each of our server types.

> **TIP**
>
> These examples could be consolidated into a single workflow with a selector to provide the option of which server type to build. For this example, however, we make three copies and show you how to modify the one specifically.

I've made these copies in my vCO Book workflow folder shown in Figure 9.2. However, you will want to place these where it makes sense for your environment.

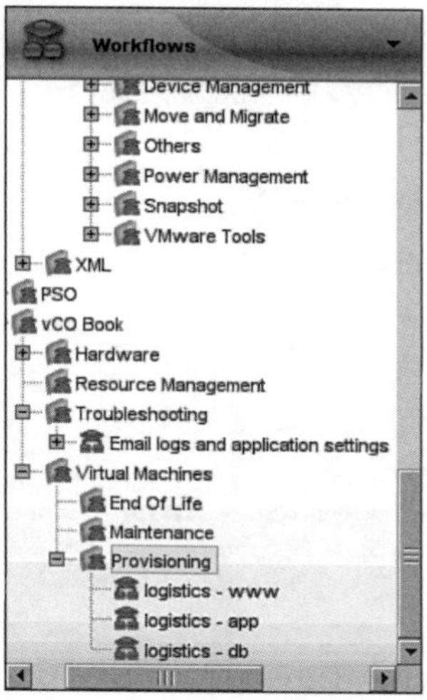

Figure 9.2 Server type–specific provisioning workflows

For this example, we dissect the changes made to "Logistics—WWW" to facilitate consistent image creation. To begin, open the workflow for editing by right-clicking and selecting Edit. By doing so, you open the Inputs screen shown in Figure 9.3.

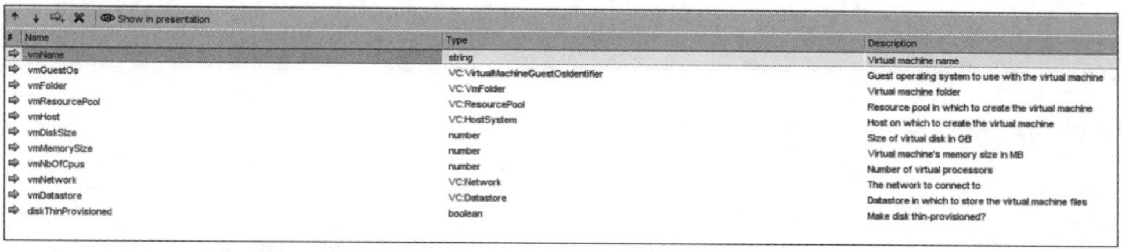

#	Name	Type	Description
	vmName	string	Virtual machine name
	vmGuestOs	VC:VirtualMachineGuestOsIdentifier	Guest operating system to use with the virtual machine
	vmFolder	VC:VmFolder	Virtual machine folder
	vmResourcePool	VC:ResourcePool	Resource pool in which to create the virtual machine
	vmHost	VC:HostSystem	Host on which to create the virtual machine
	vmDiskSize	number	Size of virtual disk in GB
	vmMemorySize	number	Virtual machine's memory size in MB
	vmNbOfCpus	number	Number of virtual processors
	vmNetwork	VC:Network	The network to connect to
	vmDatastore	VC:Datastore	Datastore in which to store the virtual machine files
	diskThinProvisioned	boolean	Make disk thin-provisioned?

Figure 9.3 Inputs for the "Logistics—WWW" workflow

Note that, when run, the workflow prompts for all the values in the Input section. This is a good Swiss army knife method for getting VMs provisioned, and there will be times when there is nothing wrong with that. However, our goal is to provide default values for the OS type, CPU count, and disk and memory size, so to do this we need to move these from inputs to attributes. To do this, follow these steps:

1. Select Input.
2. Right-click.
3. Select Move as Attribute.

You need to complete these steps for each of the following inputs:

- `vmGuestOs`
- `vmDiskSize`
- `vmMemorySize`
- `vmNbOfCpus`

> **NOTE**
> In workflow terms, an *input* is a value we are prompting the user for, whereas an *attribute* is a value we set at the beginning of the workflow.

Next, move to the General tab and create attributes according to the Table 9.2.

Table 9.2 Attributes for the "Logistics-WWW" Workflow

Attribute	Type	Value
`vmGuestOs`	`VC:VirtualMachineGuestOsIdentifier`	`ubuntuGuest`
`vmDiskSize`	`Number`	`20`
`vmMemorySize`	`Number`	`1024`
`vmNbOfCpus`	`Number`	`1`

The resulting window is shown in Figure 9.4.

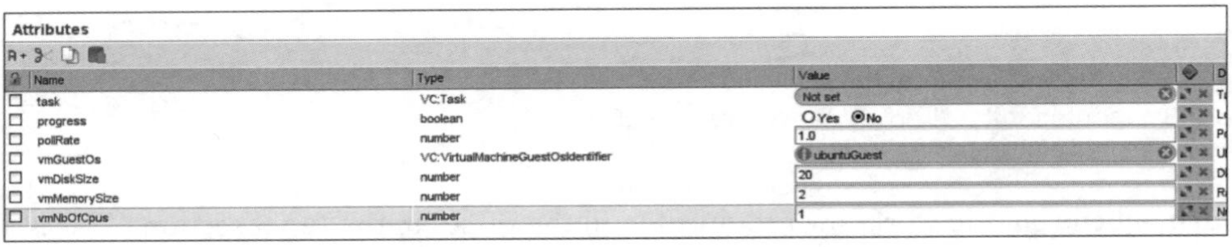

Figure 9.4 Attributes added to workflow

When you are executing the workflow, these fields will now be missing from the dialog box, and the results should look like Figure 9.5.

I will leave creating the other two as an exercise for you.

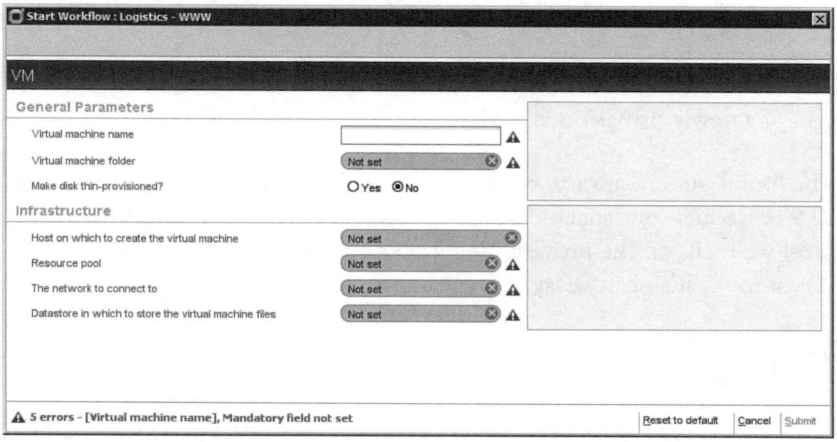

Figure 9.5 "Logistics—WWW" workflow execution after modification

> **TIP**
>
> It's worth the practice to modify these if you have not worked quite a bit with workflows in the past. However, if you need a quick start, the completed workflows are downloadable from the author's website.

Golden Images

Golden what? After your work in setting up a method for producing consistent VM builds and sizes, you found that this only helps you get so far down the path to simplicity of provisioning your VMs. So, the next step is to build out a "golden" base image onto which the rest of your configurations will be built. This way, instead of managing one base image for each server type and guest OS flavor, you can get into the business of maintaining a handful of base OS image types and supplying customizations after the fact.

As in the "Consistent VM Specifications" section, we attack this task on two fronts by first looking into the workflows that ship with vCO and then digging into some specifics for the Amazing Smoothie implementation.

vCO Built-In Workflows for Image Management

The vCenter plug-in for vCO provides a number of interesting workflows for image management. These cover the following areas:

- Image creation (clones and templates)
- Provisioning a VM from a clone and template
- Customization of a newly provisioned VM

Each of these can be found under Library, vCenter, Virtual Machine Management, Clone, as shown in Figure 9.6. Because our specific use at the moment is provisioning VMs from clones and templates, we focus on the provisioning aspect and leave image creation as an exercise for you. Trust me… it's pretty easy.

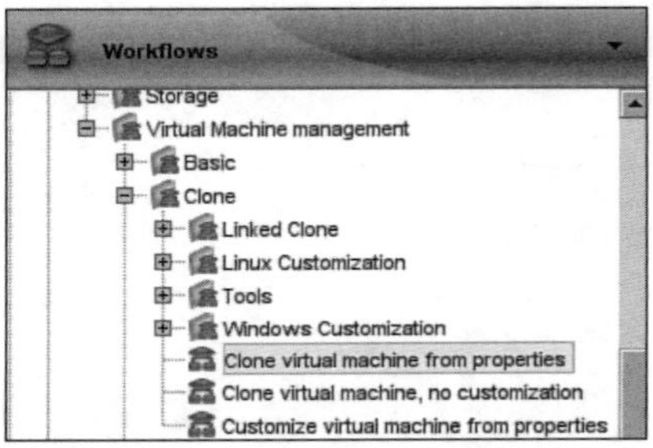

Figure 9.6 Workflows related to clone management

The workflow we specifically dig into is "Clone Virtual Machine, No Customization." First, let's take a look at the schema for this workflow, as shown in Figure 9.7.

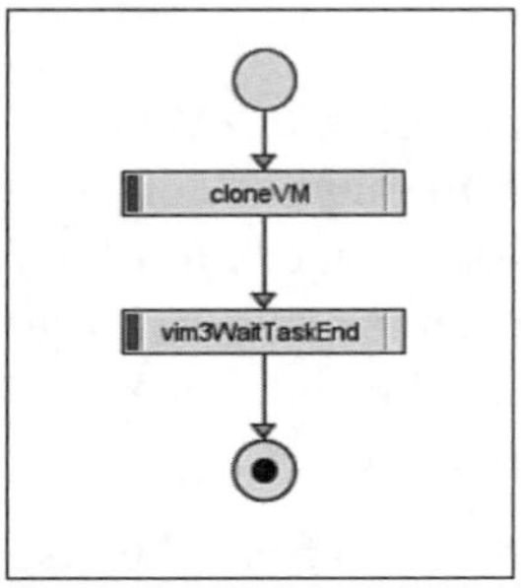

Figure 9.7 "Clone Virtual Machine, No Customization" schema

"Only two scripting blocks?" I see you mouth in disbelief. Although there are only two, we need to dig a bit deeper to begin to see the complexity. Figure 9.8 shows the required inputs for this workflow.

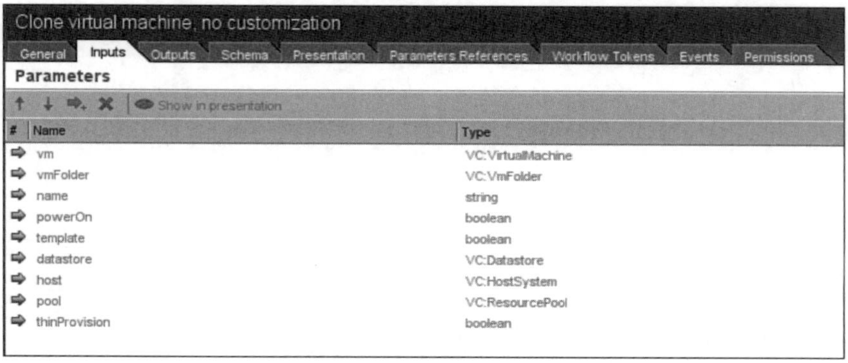

Figure 9.8 Inputs for "Clone Virtual Machine, No Customization"

You can see that a number of inputs cover everything from the basic "name this VM" to the datastore location and whether to thin provision the VM's disks. Now let's look at the code for the first script block:

```
actionResult = System.getModule("com.vmware.library.vc.basic").
cloneVM(vm,vmFolder,name,powerOn,template,datastore,host,pool) ;
```

NOTE

That's all one line, really. The spacing in the book doesn't allow for it to work out that way. If you've got vCO installed as covered earlier in this book, you should be able to see it correctly.

This line takes all the inputs from the start of the workflow and launches a "cloneVM" task against the vCenter. The second scripting block, `vim3WaitTaskEnd`, is the same task as we examined before. So, what can we do with this to make it more valuable for Amazing Smoothies? Glad you asked. Let's take a look.

Customization for Amazing Smoothies

It's a pretty simple workflow we're looking at, but that does not mean there is not room to hard set some values to make it so that each execution provides consistent, predictable results. As we did with the "logistics" set of workflows, we first produce two copies of the workflow, one for our Linux VMs and a second for our Windows VMs, as shown in Figure 9.9.

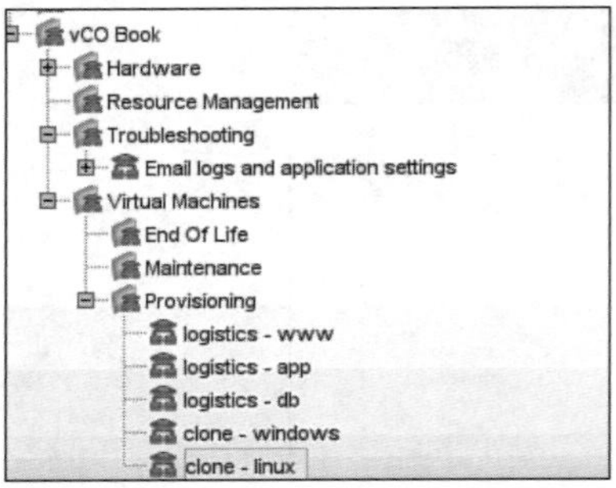

Figure 9.9 Copied workflows

Also, we do as we did with the "logistics" workflows and show you the customization of one workflow, allowing you to download the others. With this one, there is only one value we need to move around, and that is the `vm` value of type `VC:VirtualMachine`. Figure 9.10 shows the value moved from inputs to attributes.

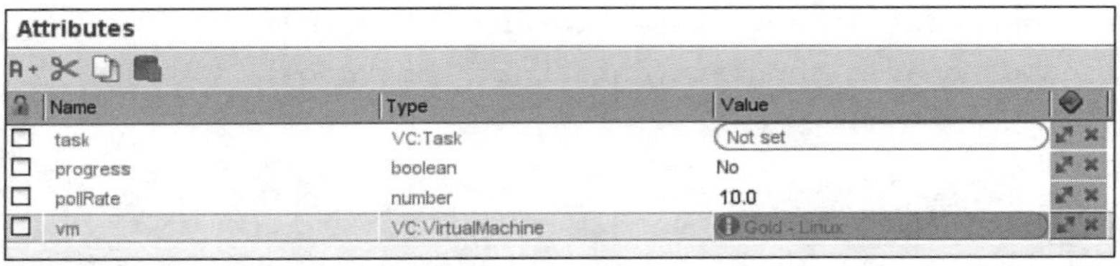

Figure 9.10 `vm` of `VC:VirtualMachine` moved from inputs to attributes

Now that it has been modified to clone a specific VM, the result when each user executes it will be identical, providing you with an exact replica on which to begin customization.

Customization with VMware VIX

Now that we can produce standardized images and produce them from a small handset of base images, we still need to address customization. That is, we still need to take our base images and manipulate them so that they have the packages and settings needed to take on their specific role. To do that, we examine a downloadable plug-in that makes use of VMware's VIX API set.

> **NOTE**
>
> Check the VMware website for more information about VMware VIX, its installation, and what it can be used for. There is quite an amazing amount of power here that could fill a book of its own; we just scratch the surface. It is also important to note that the VMware VIX plug-in does not ship with vCO, nor does the vCO team supply it.

VMware VIX Built-In Workflows

The VIX plug-in contains quite a few workflows that are helpful for post processing a VM clone. Take a look at Figure 9.11 and notice the following few workflows:

- "Check for File"
- "Copy File from vCO to Guest"
- "Run Program in Guest"
- "Run Script in Guest"

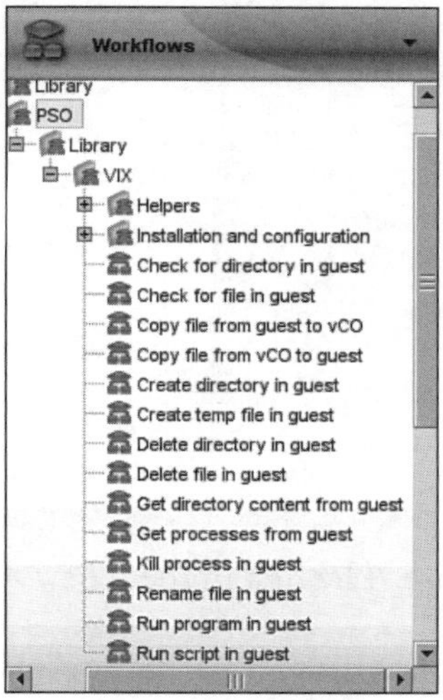

Figure 9.11 VMware VIX plug-in workflows

Each of the these workflows can serve a purpose when customizing a cloned VM. Take, for example, "Copy File from vCO to Guest." When used in conjunction with "Run Program in Guest," you can use it to copy over an installation package and then execute the installation. For our customization exercise, we focus on the "Run Program in Guest" workflow. We begin by looking over the schema and then dissecting the interesting bits of the script. Figure 9.12 shows the schema for "Run Program in Guest."

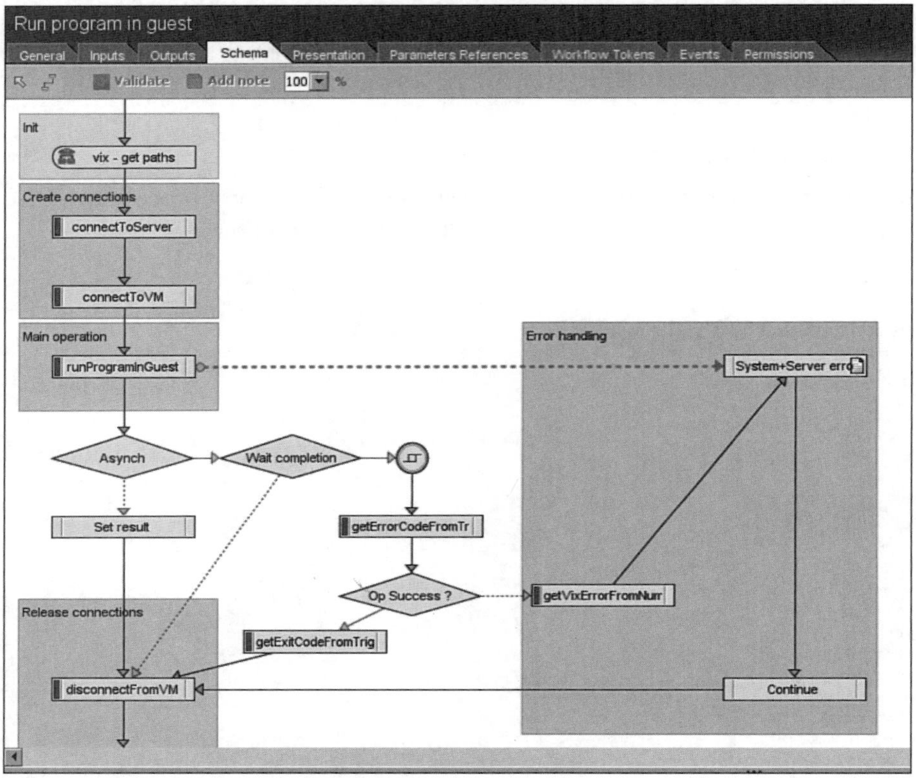

Figure 9.12 "Run Program in Guest" workflow

There are a few bits to this workflow that you haven't seen before. The first of these new areas is the workflow *notes*, or the shaded areas of the workflow.

> **NOTE**
>
> In the vCO Client, the gray boxes in Figure 9.12 are in color and are used much like comments in the JavaScript code to let you know what a particular block is doing.

Duplicate the Workflow

Right-click the existing workflow and select Duplicate. As in other workflows, for this example I duplicated the workflow to vCO Book, Virtual Machines, Provisioning, with a name of "SetIPWindows," as shown in Figure 9.13.

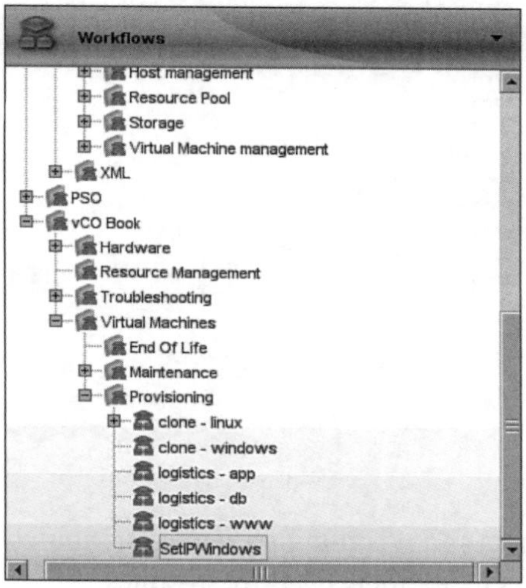

Figure 9.13 Duplicated workflow

Add Inputs

Table 9.3 shows the inputs that need to be added and the type.

Table 9.3 Inputs to Add

Variable	Type	Description
`ipAddress`	`String`	IP address for the VM
`Netmask`	`String`	Netmask for the VM
`gatewayIP`	`String`	Gateway address for the VM

Take a look at Figure 9.14 to see these completed.

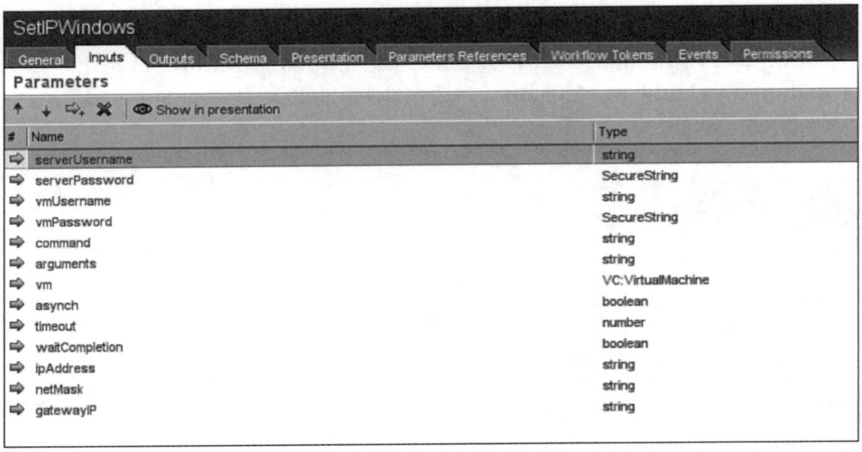

Figure 9.14 New inputs added to the workflow

Move Inputs to Attributes

We also need to take care of moving some of the inputs and positioning them as attributes. Table 9.4 shows the two values we moved from inputs to attributes and their values.

Table 9.4 Values Moved from Inputs to Attributes

Variable	Type	Value
`command`	`String`	`C:\windows\system32\netsh.exe`
`arguments`	`String`	`interface ip set address name="Local Area Connection" static`

Windows administrators will recognize a few things missing from the arguments in the table. That's because we are handling that in the next section.

Modify Scripting

For this we need to get our metaphorical Exacto knives out as the `RunProgramInGuest` block cannot be modified directly and needs to be removed for something more functional. You need to select the `RunProgramInGuest` block and press the Delete key. The results will look much like Figure 9.15.

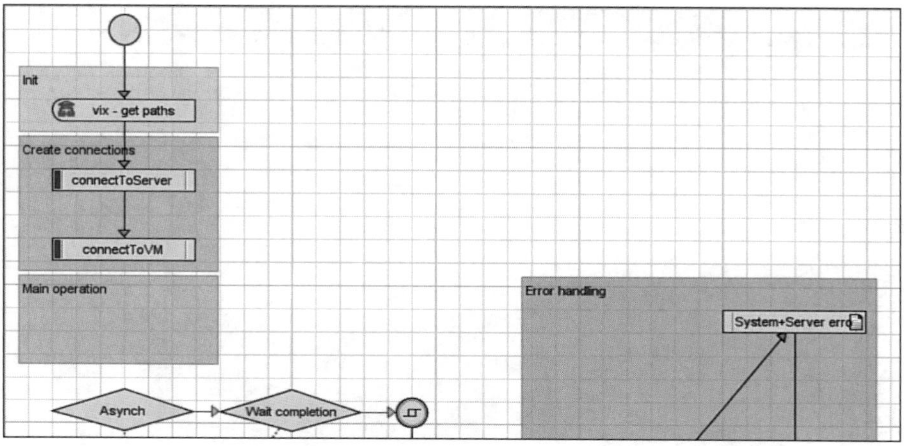

Figure 9.15 Schema with `RunProgramInGuest` removed

Next, you want to drag in a new scripting task. The lists that follow describe the inputs and outputs that need to get assigned, respectively. After those have been assigned, take a look at Figure 9.16 to see how the new scripting task should be linked to the other elements in the workflow.

- In
  - `vixVM`
  - `vmUsername`
  - `vmPassword`
  - `command`
  - `arguments`
  - `async`
  - `timeout`
  - `ipAddress`
  - `netMask`
  - `gatewayIP`
- Out
  - `actionResult`

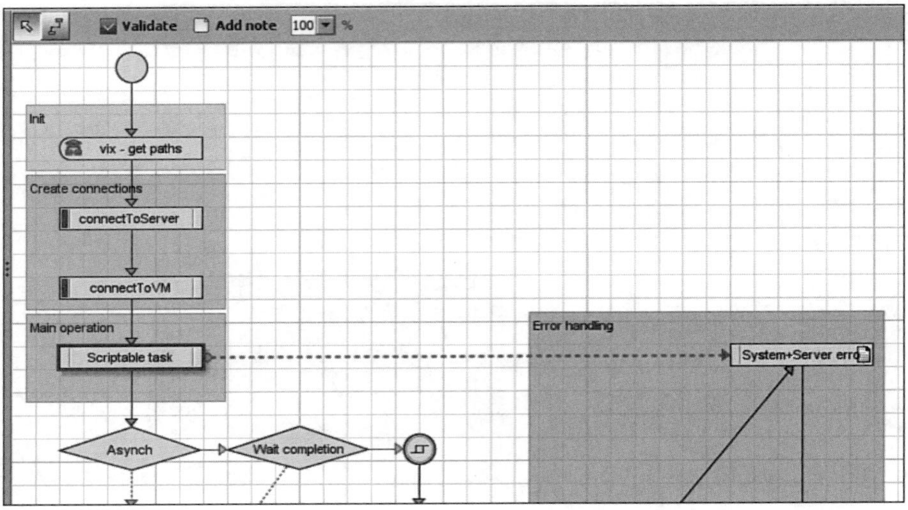

Figure 9.16 Schema with scriptable task linked in

With the output parameter, you won't find this on the list, at least not directly. You must select Trigger [Attribute] and change the name accordingly.

Finally, the code is presented in the following listing:

```
01 // Compute the arguments with IP and NetMask
02 var allArguments = arguments + " " + ipAddress + " " + netMask + " " +
gatewayIP + " 1";
03
04 // Apply the changes
05 actionResult = System.getModule("com.vmware.pso.vix").runProgramInGuest
(vixVM,vmUsername,vmPassword,command,allArguments,asynch,timeout) ;
```

Note the following about this code:

- Line 2 takes all our input parameters and forms them into a legitimate set of arguments for `netsh`.
- Line 5 is mostly borrowed from the prior workflow. Note the addition of `allArguments` in place of the old `arguments` attribute.

Approval Process

As a last step to help further reduce VM sprawl, you work with senior IT staff on an approval process that requires signoff for any new VM provisioned at Amazing Smoothies. To do this, the vCO library has some workflows that will provide this functionality.

> **NOTE**
>
> You might have noticed that earlier releases of vCO supported an Authorizations feature. The documentation for vCO 4.2 indicates, however, that this functionality is deprecated going forward. That said, the method we use here is a workaround. If you have a more robust system in place already, there is likely a way or two to integrate it with vCO.

Built-In Approval Processes

Because we do not cover the "deprecated" authorizations functionality, we need to look for some functional alternatives in vCO. Thankfully for us, some workflows in the email plug-in enable us to accomplish this.

In the vCO Client, drill down to Library, Mail, Example Interaction with Email and take a look at Figure 9.17.

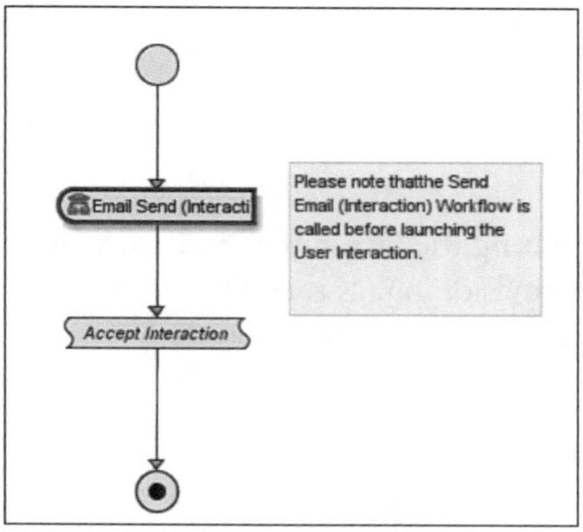

Figure 9.17 "Example Interaction with Email" schema

> **NOTE**
>
> Email likely isn't the optimal medium for this, for a few reasons. One of the big ones, tracking, comes to mind. There are other third-party systems that enable REST, SOAP, or other integration that you can use to kick off an approval process. However, these are many and beyond the scope of the book. Amazing Smoothies uses Request Tracker, which supports email integration, so we can keep the requests for later review.

What this workflow does at runtime is present you with a prompt to input the address to send email to and a selector box for AD user groups who will be authorized to click the link to continue the workflow. This looks like it's just what we need to get started, but instead of jumping right into customizing this for Amazing Smoothies, what we do at this stage is duplicate this workflow and use it as the base for the next section on putting the entire provisioning process together.

All Together Now

Now that you have built all of the prerequisite pieces, the time comes to stitch them all together into a workflow-containing workflow. No, I didn't go all *Inception* on you; in fact, as you get further along in working with workflows, using a workflow to string together other workflows opens up all manner of interesting possibilities. For our specific case, let's take a look at the requirements:

- New VM request comes in.
- Fire off approval for new VM.
- Clone VM from "gold."
- Assign an IP address.

As stated in the preceding section, let's begin by duplicating the "Example Interaction with Email" workflow into vCO Book, Virtual Machines, Provisioning, as the "Provisioning" workflow. After you've duplicated it, open the editor and let's begin to work on the schema. Figure 9.18 shows our clean slate.

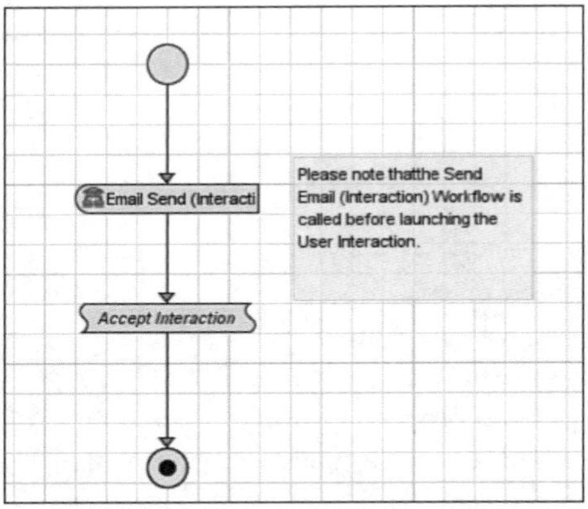

Figure 9.18 "Provisioning" workflow

NOTE

The difference between Figure 9.17 and Figure 9.18 is that we are using the same workflow as a starting point. Figure 9.18 is editable, and we will be expanding from there.

Next, we add the workflows that we've created so far:

- "Clone – Windows"
- "SetIPWindows"

The resulting schema looks like Figure 9.19.

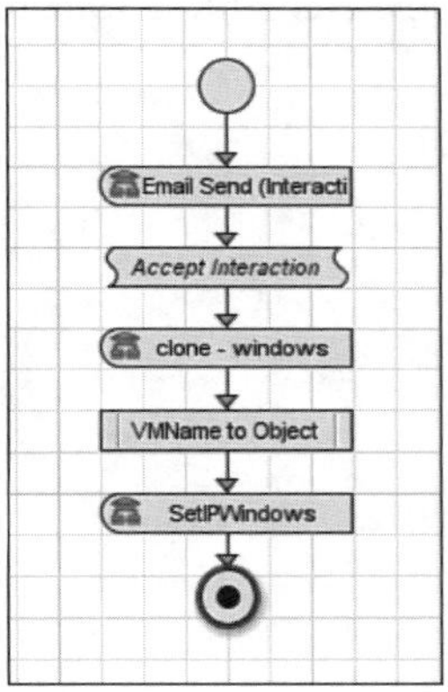

Figure 9.19 Our workflow-containing workflow

It looks pretty straightforward. However, we need to sort out a few things, as you can see by the yellow and red indicators on the "Clone – Windows" and "SetIPWindows" elements. We cover each of the sub-workflows and scripting blocks in order.

First, at the master workflow level (the workflow we are working on, not one of the sub-workflows), we need to move the `toAddress` and group inputs to attributes. To do this, first delete them as inputs, and then add the attributes in Table 9.5.

Table 9.5 Inputs to Be Made Attributes

Name	Type	Description	Value
`toAddress`	`String`	Who gets the email	`talkingheads@amazing.corp`
`Group`	`LdapGroup`	LDAP group for users who can approve new VMs	`vmApprovers`

Next, we need to confirm that the "Email Send" step has inputs that are mapped, as shown in Figure 9.20.

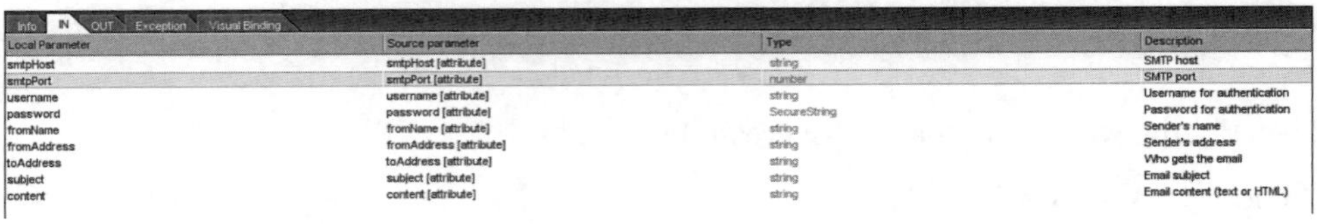
Info
IN
OUT
Exception
Visual Binding
Local Parameter
Source parameter
Type
Description
smtpHost
smtpHost [attribute]
string
SMTP host
smtpPort
smtpPort [attribute]
number
SMTP port
username
username [attribute]
string
Username for authentication
password
password [attribute]
SecureString
Password for authentication
fromName
fromName [attribute]
string
Sender's name
fromAddress
fromAddress [attribute]
string
Sender's address
toAddress
toAddress [attribute]
string
Who gets the email
subject
subject [attribute]
string
Email subject
content
content [attribute]
string
Email content (text or HTML)

Figure 9.20 Input mapping for "Email Send" workflow

We can skip the "Accept Interaction" element because our mappings were updated automagically. This brings us to "Clone – Windows." For this workflow element, we again start by taking a look at the inputs it requires:

- `vmFolder`
- `name`
- `powerOn`
- `template`
- `datastore`
- `host`
- `pool`
- `thinProvision`

From this list, we take the following and add them as inputs to the master workflow with the attributes listed in Table 9.6.

Table 9.6 Add the Following as Inputs to the Master Workflow

Name	Type	Description
`name`	`String`	Name of the new VM
`datastore`	`VC:Datastore`	Datastore for the new VM
`host`	`VC:HostSystem`	Host for the new VM
`thinProvision`	`Boolean`	Thin disks?
//## auto_generated <<cit>>		

The inputs for the master "Provisioning" workflow should now look as shown in Figure 9.21.

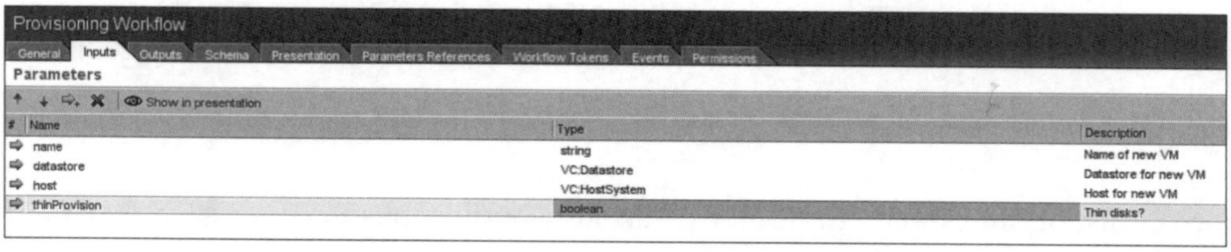

Figure 9.21 Inputs for "Provisioning" workflow

In addition, we now need to create a few attributes for the master workflow to tie the remainder of the values back to the "Clone – Windows" workflow. To do that, add the attributes shown in Table 9.7 to the workflow.

Table 9.7 Add the Following Attributes

Name	Type	Value	Description
`vmFolder`	`VC:VmFolder`	Select your folder for new VMs.	Folder for new VMs.
`powerOn`	`Boolean`	`False`	Do not power on new VMs.
`template`	`Boolean`	`False`	Also to mark them as templates.
`pool`	`VC:ResourcePool`	Set as appropriate for your environment.	Resource pool for the VMs.

NOTE

Depending on the complexity of your specific environment, you might want to take `vmFolder` and `pool` and make them inputs or configuration elements.

Next, you need to link all these modifications back to "Clone – Windows," as shown in Figure 9.22.

Finally, to finish up with "Clone – Windows," we need to create another attribute on the workflow called `newVM` of type `VC:VirtualMachine`. This does not need to be set because this will be linked to the output of the "Clone – Windows" element.

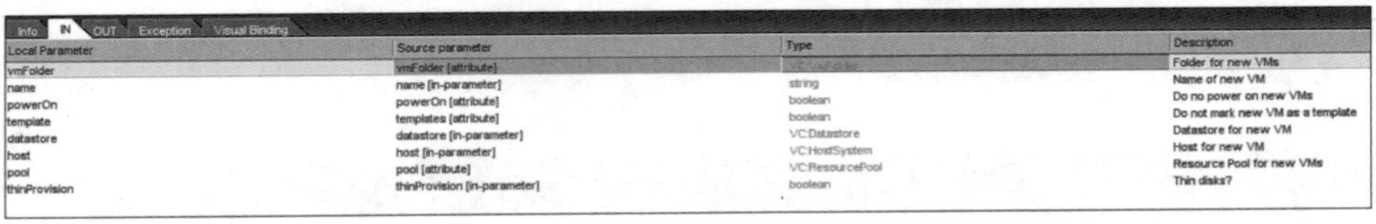

Figure 9.22 Inputs mapped for "Clone – Windows"

Next on our list of things to do to tie all the various workflow bits together is do the same input linkings on the "SetIPWindows" workflow. First, our list of required inputs follows:

- `Async`
- `Timeout`
- `waitCompletion`
- `ipAddress`
- `netMask`
- `gatewayIP`

Of these, we make the attributes presented in Table 9.8.

Table 9.8 Workflow Attributes

Name	Type	Value	Description
`Async`	`Boolean`	`False`	Force the workflow to wait for the IP to be set
`timeoutIP`	`Number`	`300`	Time in seconds to wait for failure
`waitCompletion`	`Boolean`	`True`	Wait for IP to be set

The remainder is created as workflow inputs as presented in Table 9.9.

Table 9.9 Workflow Inputs

Name	Type	Description
`ipAddress`	`String`	IP address for the VM
`netMask`	`String`	Netmask for VM
`gatewayIP`	`String`	Default gateway for VM

> **NOTE**
>
> These inputs are just that: strings. The workflow will likely fail if you input them incorrectly. That said, if you want to build error handling into your script, that's cool, too. All these workflows are provided on ProfessionalVMware.com for your modification.

The completed input map for "SetIPWindows" is shown in Figure 9.23.

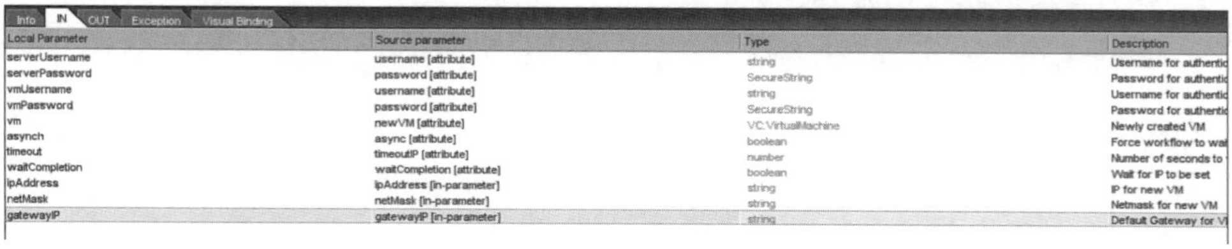
Info
IN
OUT
Exception
Visual Binding
Local Parameter
Source parameter
Type
Description
serverUsername
serverPassword
vmUsername
vmPassword
vm
asynch
timeout
waitCompletion
ipAddress
netMask
gatewayIP
username [attribute]
password [attribute]
username [attribute]
password [attribute]
newVM [attribute]
async [attribute]
timeoutIP [attribute]
waitCompletion [attribute]
ipAddress [in-parameter]
netMask [in-parameter]
gatewayIP [in-parameter]
string
SecureString
string
SecureString
VC:VirtualMachine
boolean
number
boolean
string
string
string
Newly created VM
Wait for IP to be set
IP for new VM
Netmask for new VM

Figure 9.23 Completed input mappings for "SetIPWindows"

Now that you have the completed workflow, save and close it, and start it up (see Figure 9.24).

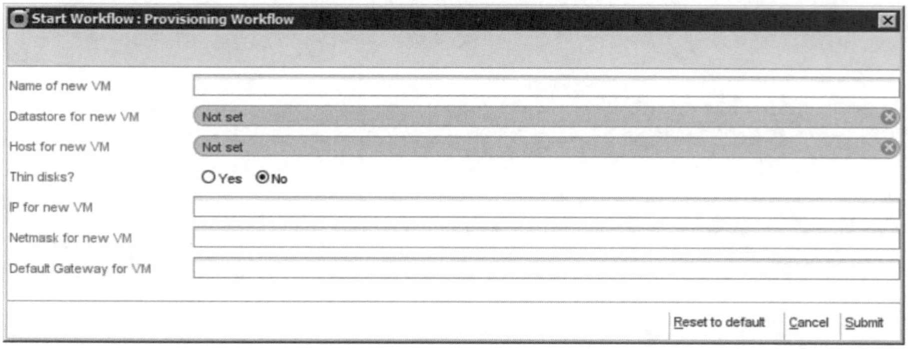

Figure 9.24 "Provisioning" workflow in all its glory

Summary

Phew! Today was a long but fruitful day at the Amazing Smoothies headquarters. However, as you sit back with your strawberry-mango infusion, you take a moment to reflect on what you have knocked out. That is, in this chapter we covered how to build VMs with vCO in a number of ways, created golden templates form which to build VMs, performed post-clone customization with the VMware VIX plug-in, and finally tied it all together in a single VM provisioning workflow.

Chapter 10

Amazing Smoothies Day 4: VM Decommissioning

Decommissioning, an often-forgotten task in the world of virtualization, what with it being so simple to throw new virtual machines (VMs) online with a few clicks, is the subject of this chapter. The proliferation of VMs can lead to a condition called *VM sprawl*. Sprawl, in turn, leads to increased management overhead because administrators must maintain each new VM. There are also some security implications to sprawl.

You can defeat sprawl with a good VM lifecycle process. Although this book does not detail the entire process for you, Chapter 9, "Amazing Smoothies Day 3: VM Provisioning," covered the beginning of this lifecycle. Now, in this chapter, you learn about the end of the VM lifecycle. Specifically, this chapter covers the following:

- The current Amazing Smoothies VM decommissioning process
- Optimizing the process
- vCenter Orchestrator workflows for the various stages
- Tying it all together for Amazing Smoothies

Amazing Smoothies VM Decommissioning Process

As you have undoubtedly discovered in earlier chapters, the deeper we look at Amazing Smoothies, the more we see an organization that hasn't had much time to mature their processes (because of the period of hyper-growth they have experienced). With that in mind, it is no surprise that the process to decommission a VM is in much the same state, that is to say, it is ad hoc.

An ad hoc VM decommissioning process risks a few problems, including the following:

- Inconsistency
- VM sprawl
- Security
- Management

The following sections examine each of these so that you gain a better understanding of the problem as it exists at Amazing Smoothies.

Inconsistency

Hyper-growth, or any growth in your virtual environment, can lead to a number of interesting inconsistencies. In the case of Amazing Smoothies, hyper-growth led to the current state of the environment. That is, based on the open policy for VM provisioning before you came onsite, most business units would spin up a number of VMs for a project. At the end of the project, if the VMs were no longer in use, they were sometimes powered off, sometimes not. The converse to this is that sometimes VMs were taken offline without a final copy/backup, leading to expensive data-loss issues. Thankfully, the proprietary Amazing Formulas were stored as hard copy.

VM Sprawl

Because VMs were not always removed at the end of their service life, the Amazing Smoothies IT team has witnessed exponential growth of VMs under management. Each VM online past its usable life costs just a bit of cash to run when you consider the storage, memory, and computing resources that could be allocated to production VMs.

Management

With the now huge number of VMs under management, in addition to physical resources, Amazing Smoothies now also has expensive IT resources dedicated to keeping these VMs patched and running smoothly. There is also the side effect of licensing costs to keep all of these VMs operational. Consider that each VM has at a minimum an OS license, antivirus license, and a license for the management software in use. You can see where running more VMs than required can end up costing the company more than is necessary.

Security

VM sprawl has led to some interesting security issues for Amazing Smoothies, as well. First, information-leak potential increases with each VM that is online past its service life. Second, keeping the antivirus software and operating system updates applied has become a losing battle. Finally, firewall rules must be maintained for each VM. If the VM is not in service or does not need to be Internet accessible any longer, it should be taken offline.

So, how do we address these concerns for Amazing Smoothies? We need to optimize the way old VMs are brought offline.

Optimizing the Decommissioning Process

Now that you understand the problem facing the staff at Amazing Smoothies a bit better, let's deconstruct it and figure out what an optimal VM decommissioning process should look like. This will allow us to make the process both consistent and to address VM sprawl. The steps in such a process are as follows:

1. Identify VMs to decommission.
2. Power them off.
3. Remove snapshots.
4. Perform a final copy/backup.
5. Check the VM's classification.
    a. If the classification is below sensitive, delete the VM.
    b. If classification is above sensitive and below secret, migrate to archive storage and remove from inventory.
    c. If the classification is above secret, notify business owners.
6. Clean up third-party systems.
7. Send notification.

Figure 10.1 shows a flow chart of this optimized workflow.

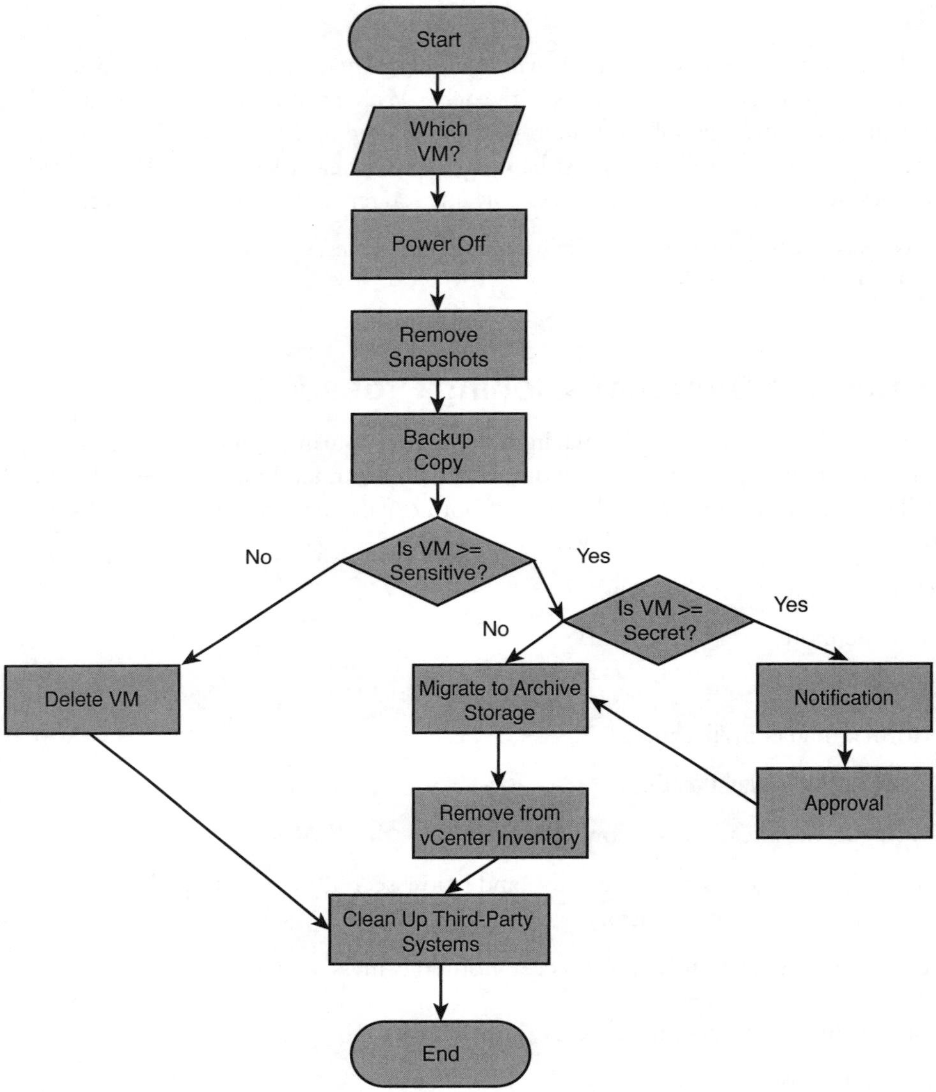

Figure 10.1 Optimized VM decommissioning workflow

Keep in mind it just looks complicated on the surface. When you consider the individual steps, however, you see that we have addressed the management concerns by performing a cleanup of third-party systems and have created a final backup of the VM. We have also addressed security concerns by basing decisions on the classification of the data the VM contains and acting accordingly. Now, how do we make this happen in vCenter Orchestrator (vCO)?

vCenter Orchestrator Workflows

First, let's look at the areas in which vCO has built-in workflows to address our process. Where it does not have a workflow, we must build our own. We need to look for workflows for the following:

- Power management
- Snapshot management
- Clone/copy VM
- Move VM
- Delete VM
- Notification and approval (via email)
- Third-party cleanup

We're lucky: vCO has most of these covered. Let's start with power management and see where we end up.

Power Management

The vCO workflows for power management, like most of the others we have worked with so far, come form the vCenter Server Library. Specifically, we're looking at the following workflows:

- "Power Off Virtual Machine and Wait"
- "Shut Down Guest OS and Wait"
- "Shut Down and Delete Virtual Machine"

Of these, "Shut Down and Delete" is more or less out of the question for this particular use case. We get to delete VMs later. That leaves us with "Shut Down Guest OS and Wait" and "Power Off Virtual Machine and Wait." Of these two, "Shut Down Guest OS" is generally the safer of the two options if we want to bring the VM back to life later, so let's take a look at the schema for this workflow, shown in Figure 10.2.

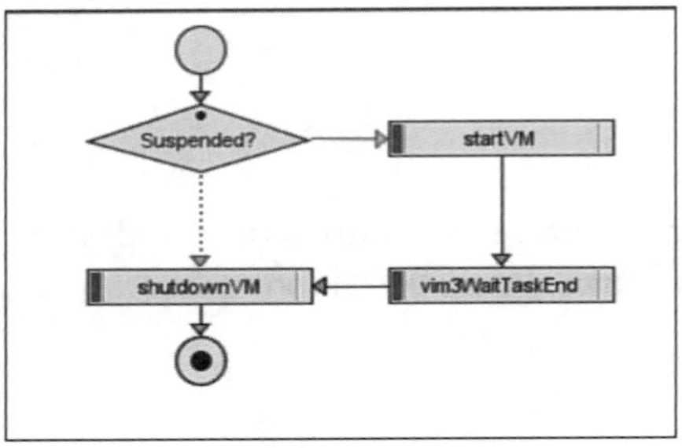

Figure 10.2 "Shut Down Guest OS and Wait" schema

Also, take a look at the code in the `shutdownVM` block:

```
System.getModule("com.vmware.library.vc.vm.power").shutdownVM
  (vm,timeout,polling);
```

As you can see, it's a relatively straightforward workflow and set of commands. It first checks to see whether the VM specified is suspended. Based on this, the workflow will either resume the VM and then perform a guest OS shutdown or just send the guest OS shutdown command to the VMware tools, making it a good choice for our use again later when we make the master workflow.

Snapshot Management

Next up is snapshot management, which we covered in detail in Chapter 8, "Amazing Smoothies Day 2: Dealing with Snapshots." This time, however, we want to remove all snapshots rather than just those over a specific age. You can find these in the vCenter Server Library of workflows (Library, vCenter, Virtual Machines, Snapshot); the workflow we are going to use is called "Remove All Snapshots." Yeah, I was surprised it was that easy, too. Figure 10.3 shows the schema for this workflow.

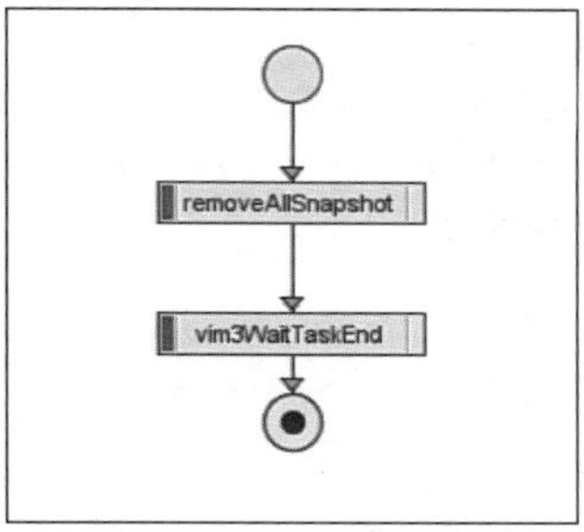

Figure 10.3 "Remove All Snapshots" schema

Like the power management workflow we chose, this workflow is also straightforward and executes just one bit of code, as well:

```
actionResult = System.getModule("com.vmware.library.vc.vm.snapshot")
  .removeAllSnapshot(vm) ;
```

Having seen a few JavaScript examples in other chapters, you should be able to guess what this is doing. If not, well, it is setting a variable `actionResult` to the outcome of the `removeAllSnapshot` action contained within the `com.vmware.library.vc.vm.snapshot` library of actions. Again, this one will be useful as we work through the following sections of this chapter.

Clone/Copy VM

Now that we have a workflow to use for powering the VM down and a workflow to use to remove all the snapshots on the VM, we can take care of handing the final copy to "archive" storage.

> **NOTE**
>
> Archive storage may mean any number of things, and I fully expect that your organization will have a different interpretation of it than what is described here. For our use case, this is an iSCSI export from my home filer for just such uses. My "retention" policy is more or less as long as it takes to write this chapter. That said, make sure that if you will be archiving a copy of the VM you have enough storage (de-duped, thin provisioned, and so on) to store the VM for as long as you are required to keep it.

As with our other workflow areas, we start in the vCenter Server Library section but drill down into the Virtual Machine Management, Clone section. Because we don't need to customize anything, we use "Clone Virtual Machine, No Customization" as a starting point. Why? Well, we want to reduce the amount of information that the end user is prompted for, so we will specify a few attributes instead of taking them as input. To begin, duplicate this workflow and give it a handy name: **Decommission VM – Clone**. From there, we move the variables in Table 10.1 from inputs to attributes.

Table 10.1 Values to Move from Inputs to Attributes

Name	Type	Value
`Name`	`String`	`n/a`
`Datastore`	`VC:Datastore`	*`Ix4-200d-iscsi`*
`thinProvision`	`Boolean`	`True`

Changing the values from Table 10.1 enables us to do a few things:

- Ensure the VM takes up as little space as possible on the backup medium
- Specify the backup location
- Calculate the name to use for the copied VM

Figure 10.4 shows the completed modifications.

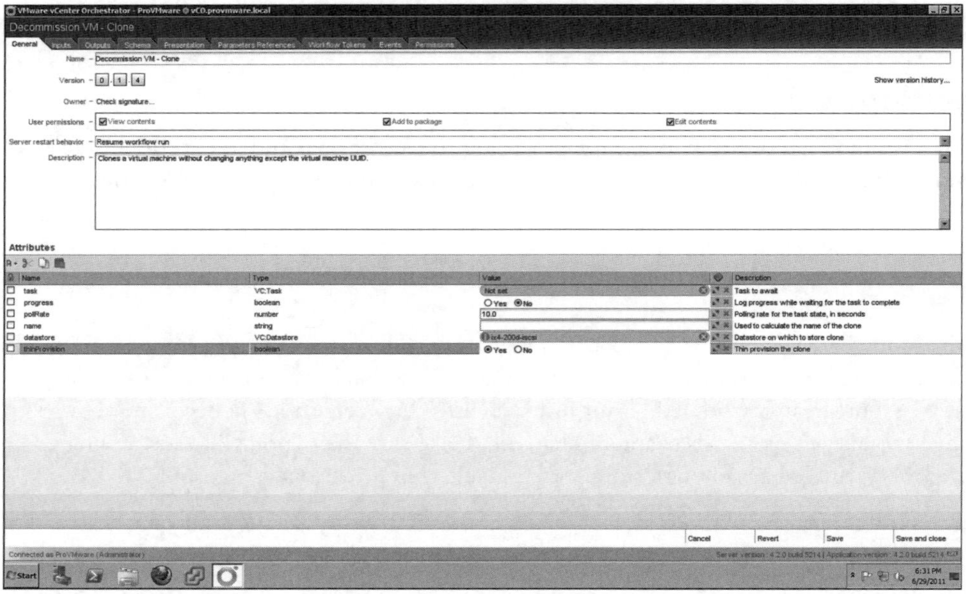

Figure 10.4 "Decommission VM - Clone" with inputs moved to attributes

The scripting contained in the `cloneVM` scripting block is as follows:

```
actionResult = System.getModule("com.vmware.library.vc.basic").cloneVM
  (vm,vmFolder,name,powerOn,template,datastore,host,pool) ;
```

This is followed by a wait task until the clone has finished. Our next stop is to move or delete the VM.

Move VM

As you saw in Figure 10.1, if the VM has some "secret" or above classified information we need to shelter the VM from deletion by the "low-orbit ion cannon." To do that, we are still working in the vCenter Server Library, but we now move our sights to Virtual Machine Management, Move and Migrate. There are a few workflows here, and you will want to spend a few minutes reviewing them. However, the one for our use is "Relocate Virtual Machine Disks."

We're using this task because the VM itself is already powered off and only needs to be moved to the metaphorical cryogenic storage facility until it needs to be powered up later or can be disposed of safely. With that in mind, take a look at the schema for this task in Figure 10.5.

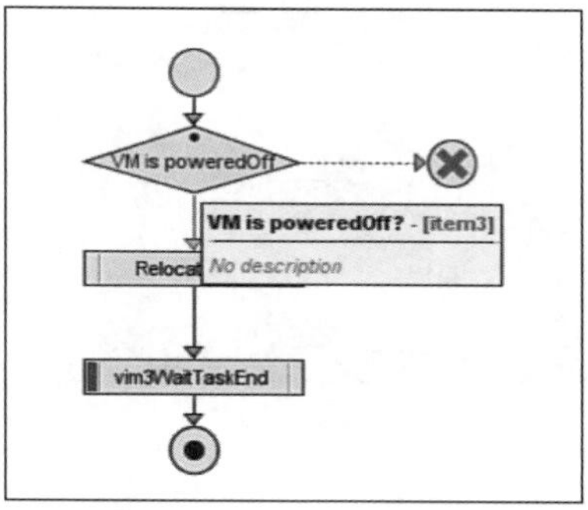

Figure 10.5 "Relocate Virtual Machine Disks" workflow

As we did for the clone task that performed our final backup, we will duplicate the workflow to "Decommission VM – Move" and move a few inputs to attributes. Table 10.2 shows the input, type, and value of the input we will be migrating.

Table 10.2 Add This Input

Name	Type	Value
`Datastore`	`VC:Datastore`	`Ix4-200d-nfs`

> **NOTE**
>
> If you've been paying attention to my lab setup thus far, you'll notice that most of the VMs live on the ix4-200d-nfs export. Although that might be my live storage and my cold storage, you want to either imagine it as being a different device or replace the value with one appropriate for your environment.

Figure 10.6 shows "Decommission VM – Move" in its new home with the inputs moved to attributes.

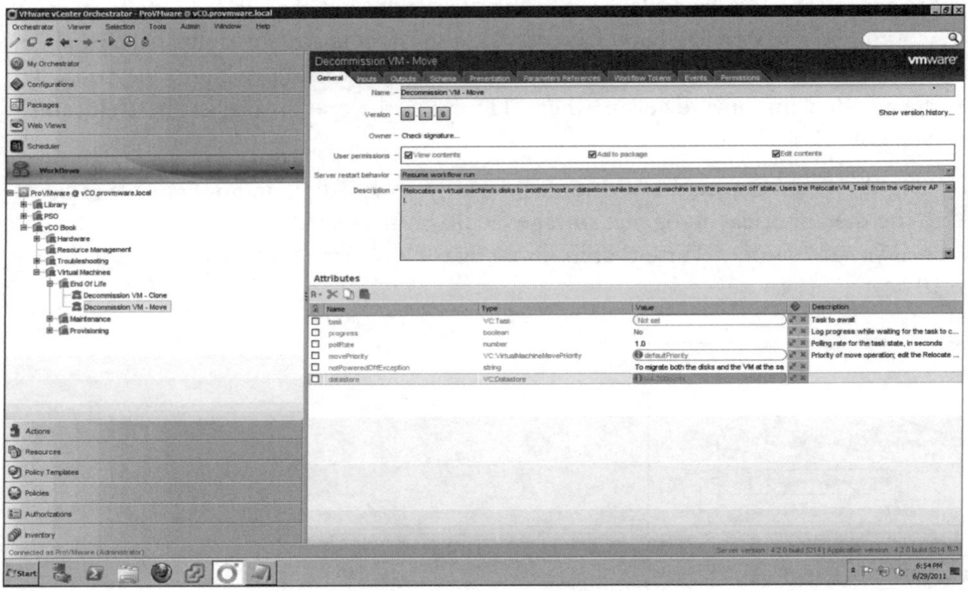

Figure 10.6 "Decommission VM - Move" workflow and attributes

Now that you know you can save a VM for later, let's take a look at the workflow we use to remove one.

Delete VM

How do you delete a VM? I sometimes envision it as if I were nuking them from orbit. Let's take a look around the vCenter Server Library of workflows and see whether something a bit more practical exists. Specifically, look here: vCenter, Virtual Machine Management, Basic, and then take a look at Figure 10.7 for the schema of our workflow of choice.

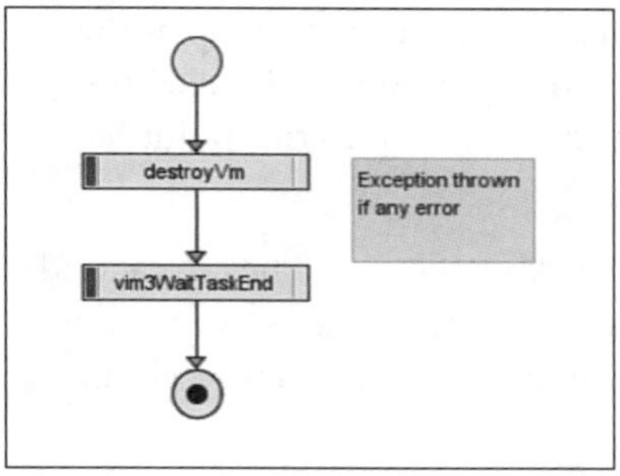

Figure 10.7 Schema for the "Delete Virtual Machine" workflow

This one is pretty straightforward and uses the `destroyVM()` method that is part of the com.vmware.library.vc.vm section of the APIs provided by vCO:

```
actionResult = System.getModule("com.vmware.library.vc.vm").destroyVm(vm) ;
```

That's really all there is to this one: Fire it up, and destroy away!

Notification and Approval (via Email)

We now need to incorporate the feedback and approval mechanism. To do this, we use the vCO-provided "Example Interaction with Email" workflow. The only modification we need to make when including it is to link the input parameter of `toAddress` to an attribute of the same name on the master workflow.

Third-Party Cleanup

In our grand master workflow in the next section, this is left as an exercise for the end user. Keep in mind that most of your systems will have either an API or scripting interface that vCO can latch on to. This, in turn, will allow you to get quite creative when removing the VM from Active Directory, antivirus, and your configuration management database (CMDB).

NOTE

I had intended to include examples here for a common CMDB system or something similar. However, because of the timelines associated with getting this book to press and the complexity in getting something going, I settled for removing a computer object from AD. Look for a future blog post on my website, ProfessionalVMware.com, on how to use the SOAP/REST plug-in to knock this out.

The example shown here comes from the Active Directory plug-in, using a copy of the "Destroy a Computer" workflow. Why a copy? Well, the AD workflow itself takes as input an object of `AD:ComputerAD`, and what we have been working with up to this point has been a VM of type `VC:VirtualMachine`.

In nonprogrammer speak, this means that we have been working with a domestic car and now need to change out our tool set to work on a foreign helicopter. That is, we need to figure out how to tell vCO we're looking for an AD computer when all we know about is a VM, and it's not as straightforward as you would think.

First, take a look at the schema of our duplicated workflow, as shown in Figure 10.8.

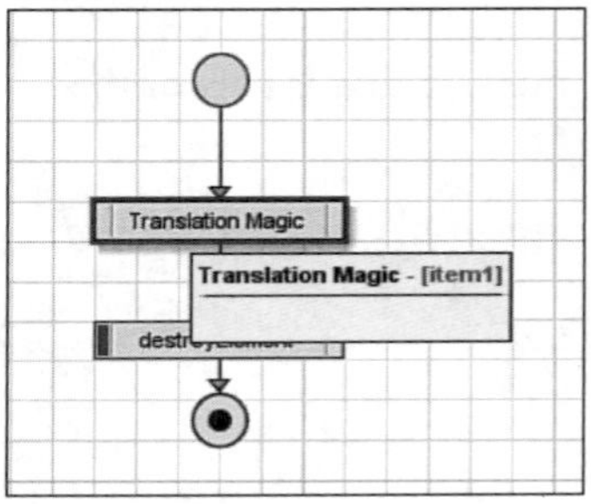

Figure 10.8 Modified schema to translate `VC:VirtualMachine` to `AD:ADComputer`

Notice the Translation Magic block; that's where our metaphorical mechanic retools so that he can work on new objects. More specifically, we use the following code:

```
computer = ActiveDriectory.getComputer(VM.name);
System.log (computer);
```

The first line takes the `ActiveDirectory` object and calls the `getComputer()` method on it. The `getComputer` method takes a string or computer name as input, searches the AD for a computer object with the same name, and returns it. The second line prints this value out to the system log.

When our translation is successful, the next scripting block picks up and deletes the AD computer object:

```
System.getModule("com.vmware.library.microsoft.activeDirectory")
  .destroyElement(element) ;
```

With that, we've completed our tour of all the prerequisite parts for building the "master" workflow. The next section covers putting it all together.

Tying It All Together

Cool! You've made it this far. This section first shows you a completed schema that will look like the flow chart from Figure 10.1. From there, we talk about the custom script/decisions at each point, top to bottom, along the way. Our new workflow, "Nuke Virtual Machine from Orbit," has the schema shown in Figure 10.9.

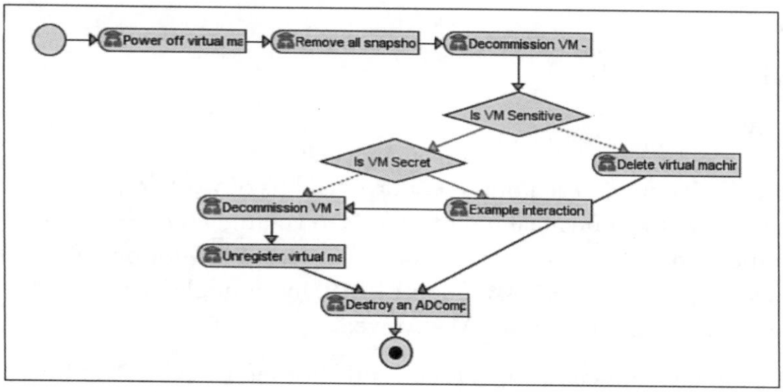

Figure 10.9 "Nuke Virtual Machine from Orbit" schema

As you can see, this looks very much like Figure 10.1, with some minor adjustments to fit the screen. Now let's open our workflow for editing and get down to the dirty work. Follow these general steps:

1. Open the workflow for editing.
2. Add input.
3. Adjust the input/output parameters for workflows.

Opening for editing like we've done so many times before is as simple as right-clicking the workflow in the Inventory list and selecting Edit. Next, we need to add an input with the values shown in Table 10.3.

Table 10.3 Move This Value

Name	Type	Description
`Vm`	`VC:VirtualMachine`	Name of the VM to be deleted

That takes care of items one and two from our list of tasks. Now for item three, let's move over to the Schema tab and work our way from left to right editing the input and output parameters of the various workflows:

Power Off Virtual Machine/Remove All Snapshots and Others

You must modify the input parameter bindings of several subworkflows, including the following:

- "Power Off Virtual Machine"
- "Remove All Snapshots"
- "Delete Virtual Machine"
- "Unregister Virtual Machine"
- "Destroy AD Computer"

Rather than cover moving the inputs for each of these individual bits of workflows, we cover how to part once and leave the individual modifications to you the user. To perform the input parameter modification, do this: Select the block in the workflow for one of the bindings just listed and display its Input tab. Take Figure 10.10, for example; here we are editing the input parameters of "Decommission VM – Move."

Under Source Parameters for VM, notice that this is currently not set. Clicking Not Set will present you with the dialog box in Figure 10.11, in which you can select a parameter to bind it to. In our case, they have an identical name: vm.

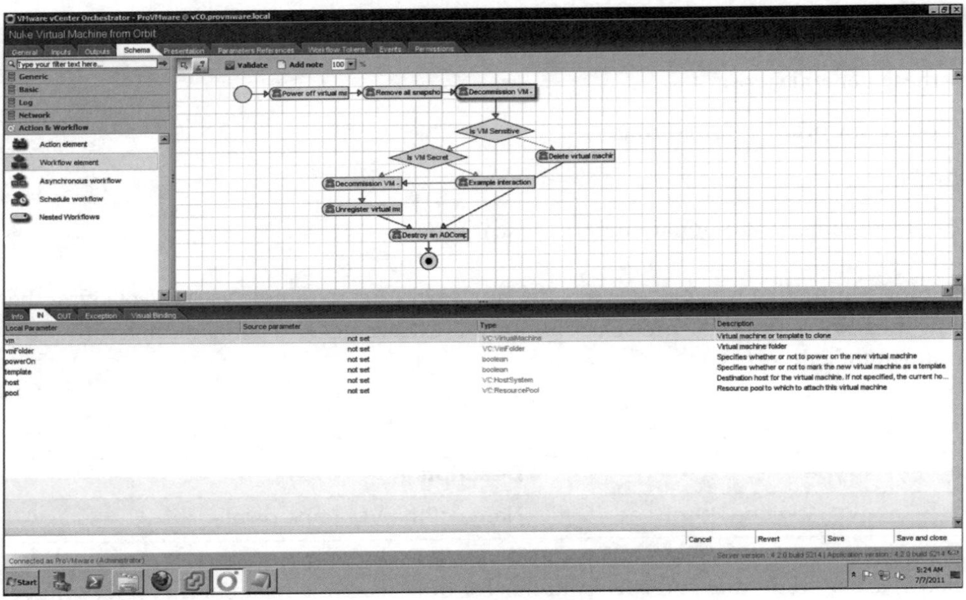

Figure 10.10 Input parameters of "Decommission VM – Move"

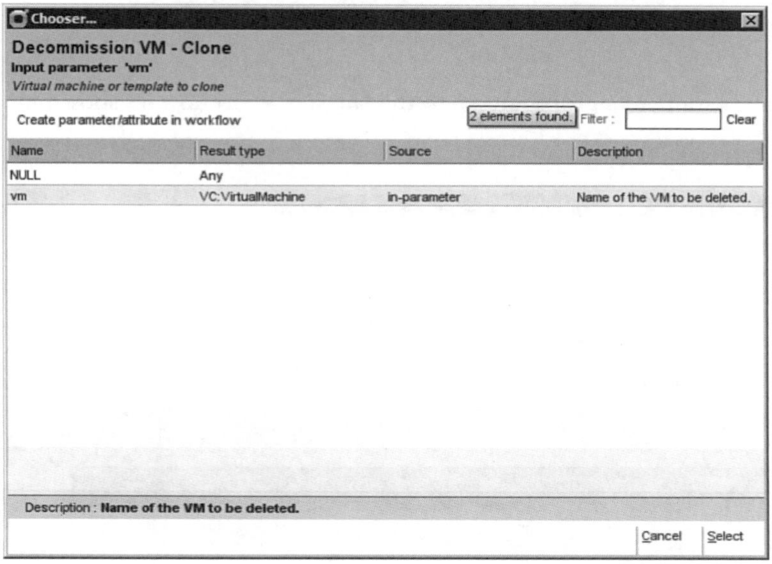

Figure 10.11 Input parameter binding dialog box

Decommission VM – Clone and Decommission VM – Move

The "Decommission VM – Clone" and "Decommission VM – Move" workflows are a bit different, in that in addition to adding the `vm` input parameter as listed in the preceding section, we need to provide a facility to take its other input values as part of the master workflow. To do this, we right-click the workflow and select Synchronize, Synchronize Presentation.

> **NOTE**
>
> This might seem a bit obtuse at first, and frankly I didn't understand it either until I got the following information from the folks on the vCO team at VMware:
>
> **Synchronize Parameters:** This option updates changes in the input/output parameters of an embedded workflow only; it does not carry up to the workflow being edited. (This is important when you have an embedded workflow that you have either added or removed input parameters from. Synchronizing the parameters only updates the bindings of that embedded workflow in the workflow you are editing.)
>
> **Synchronize Presentation:** This option adds input parameters of embedded workflow-to-workflow being edited.

If you select Synchronize Presentation, you are prompted with the dialog box shown in Figure 10.12 asking you to confirm your intention.

If you click OK, the input parameters propagate up to the "master" workflow, as shown in Figure 10.13.

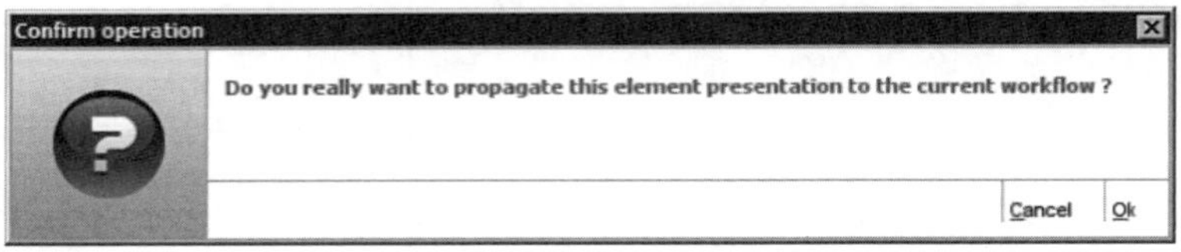

Figure 10.12 Synchronize presentation confirmation dialog box

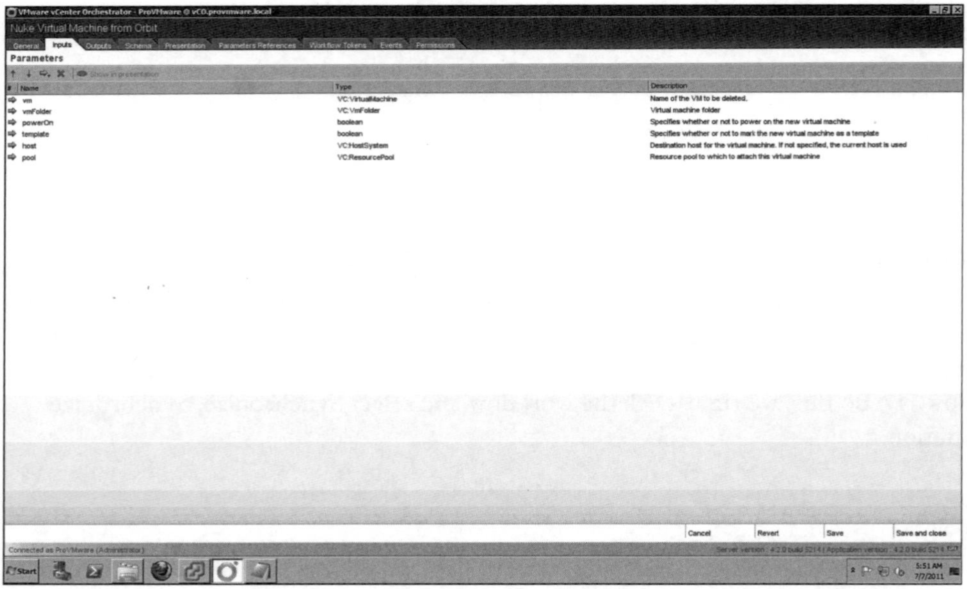

Figure 10.13 Additional input parameters after synchronization with "Decommission VM – Clone"

Is the VM Secret? How About Sensitive?

Before getting too deep into the scripting behind the decision blocks here, I want to point out that, like many shops, you might not have these values assigned to either your data or the VMs that contain the data. It is also a bit beyond the scope of this book to tell you the *how* and the *why* behind classifications. That said, the workflow is easily modifiable to make this work for you if you do not classify VMs.

Decisions, decisions... Our custom decision blocks will both take an input of the same `vm` parameter that we have been working with so far and use it to grab the custom attributes of the VM. The decision tree will work as follows:

If classification is

- Not defined, delete the VM
- Defined, assume classification is at least Sensitive
- Defined as Secret, proceed with notifications

To implement this in code, let's look at the first decision block's (Is VM Sensitive) custom scripting:

```
var classification = ConfigurationElement.getAttributeWithKey(secret);
if (classification != null){
        return true;
} else {
        return false;
}
```

Our first line grabs the "secret" or `classification` attribute set on our VMs; the next five lines are the logic that decides what to do with the VM. If it's undefined, proceed down the true branch of the workflow (green line in the figure); otherwise, proceed down the false or red branch of the workflow.

The next decision block is implemented with the following code:

```
var classification = ConfigurationElement.getAttributeWithKey();
if (classification == "secret"){
        return true;
} else {
        return false;
}
```

Like the code before it, the first line grabs the `classification` custom attribute from the VM to do our comparison. Next, the code proceeds down the secret path (acknowledgments and so on) if true; otherwise, it proceeds to finish the decommissioning process.

The final step is to modify the notification script. To do this, we need to hard set the `toAddress` field. So, we add a `toAddress` attribute to the main workflow, and then change the input binding of the "Email Notification" workflow.

What did I just say? On our "Nuke Virtual Machine from Orbit" workflow, once open for editing, display the General tab and add an attribute with the values in Table 10.4.

Table 10.4 Input Value Needed for Nuke Virtual Machine from Orbit

Name	Type	Value
toAddress	string	theboss@smoothie.corp

This is also shown in Figure 10.14.

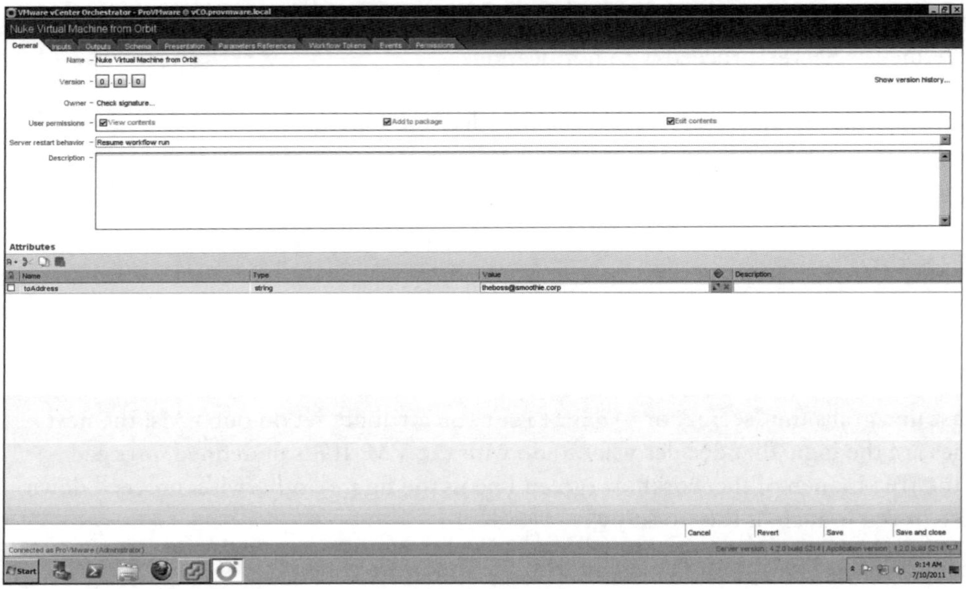

Figure 10.14 Custom attribute on "Nuke Virtual Machine from Orbit" workflow

We now need to bind this attribute to the inputs of the "Email Interaction" workflow that we called. Under the Schema tab, select the "Example Interaction" workflow and its associated Input tab, as shown in Figure 10.15.

After you have done this, the last step is to synchronize the presentation to catch the last parameter.

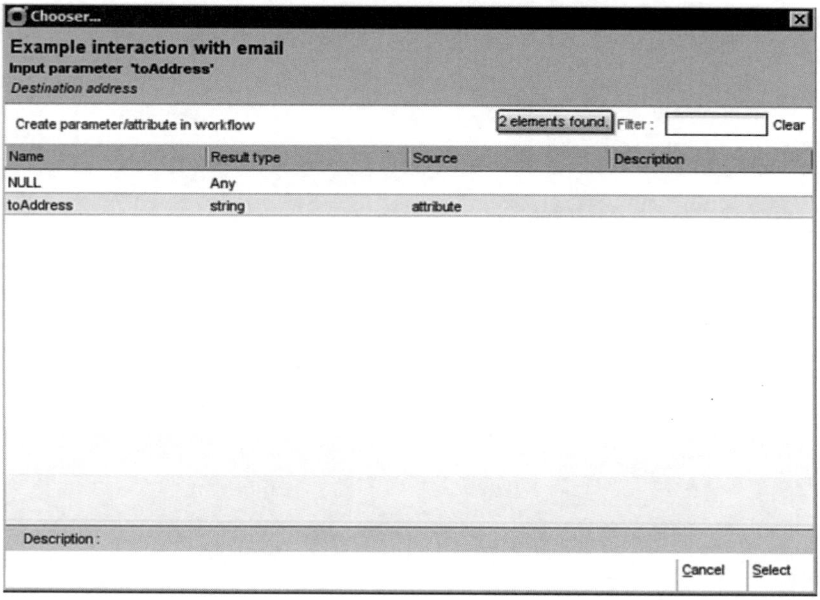

Figure 10.15 Binding workflow attributes to inputs

Summary

This chapter took you on quite a journey. First we discussed the need for a decommission process for VMs. Then we discussed the various parts that go into a good decommission process and reviewed what that process looks like. We then looked at the various workflows included with vCenter Orchestrator that could be tied together or modified slightly to fit our new process. Toward the end of the chapter, we began to tie it all together.

Chapter 11

Amazing Smoothies Day 5: Other VM Management

Now that you have thoroughly impressed the leadership staff at Amazing Smoothies, they're chomping at the bit to see what it is you will do next. After all, in the past 4 days you have resolved some of their most painful issues and helped put in place processes and their associated workflows that both help save time and ensure consistent results.

As you roll into the office and grab your Amazing orange, kiwi, banana smoothie for the morning, it hits you that today you need to take care of some of the other bits of virtual machine (VM) management. This includes spring cleaning and other various bits of ensuring that the Amazing Smoothies vSphere environment is humming along, as it should.

Specifically, this chapter covers the following:

- Exporting vCO logs
- Checking for orphaned VM files
- Maintaining VMware tools
- Deleting unused files
- Conducting a mass VM migration

Although this seems like a pretty tall order, implementing these is mostly straightforward.

Exporting vCO Logs

vCenter Orchestrator (vCO) keeps an extensive set of logs for just about everything that happens within its world. Things such as who ran what workflow and when and information on the various internal workings of the vCO service itself are among what you will find kept in the vCO logs. Getting at them, however, is not always the most straightforward of affairs. Thankfully, vCO includes a workflow for exporting the logs to a more manageable location.

To run the workflow, browse to Library, Troubleshooting, as shown in Figure 11.1.

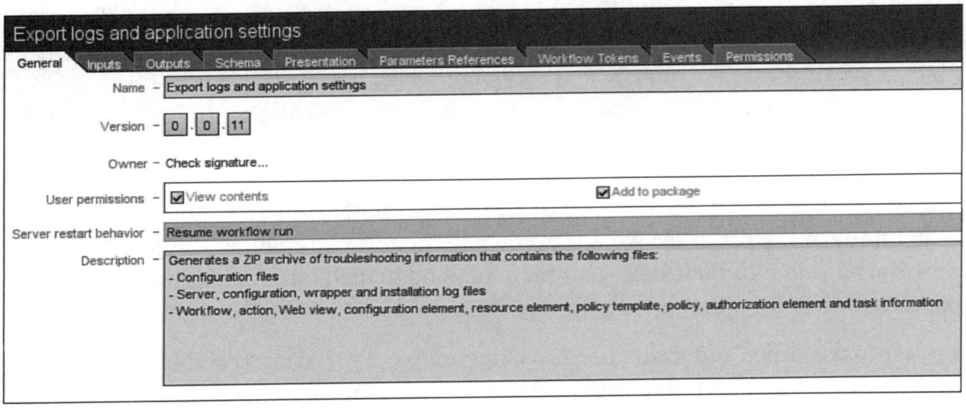

Figure 11.1 "Export Logs vCenter Orchestrator" workflow

When you start the workflow, it prompts you for the location to which to export the logs. If not specified, the logs are exported to C:\Orchestrator; however, you need to create this folder. Figure 11.2 shows the input dialog, and Figure 11.3 shows the actual exported ZIP file containing the logs.

> **NOTE**
>
> These logs are exported to the directory specified on the vCO server. This is key for recovering them.

> **NOTE**
>
> Like any system logs, the vCO server logs can contain sensitive information about your system and the systems vCO interfaces with. Therefore, you want to exercise caution when moving the log files between systems or exporting them for external consumption.

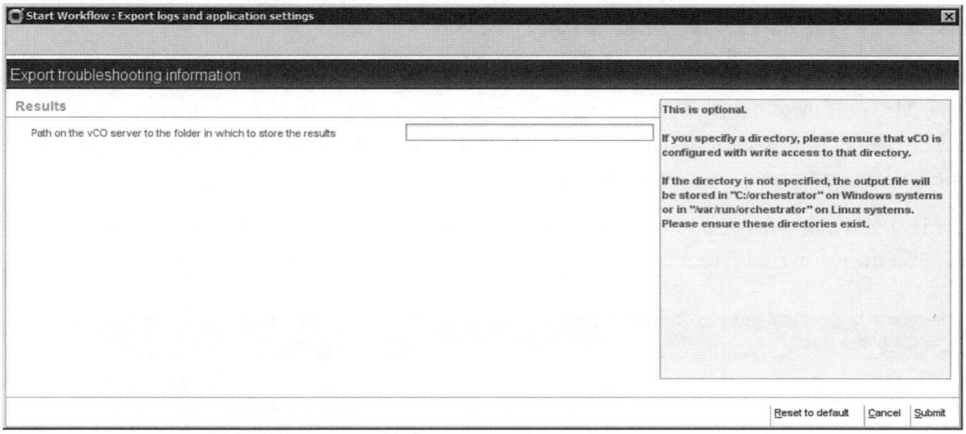

Figure 11.2 vCO Export Logs input dialog

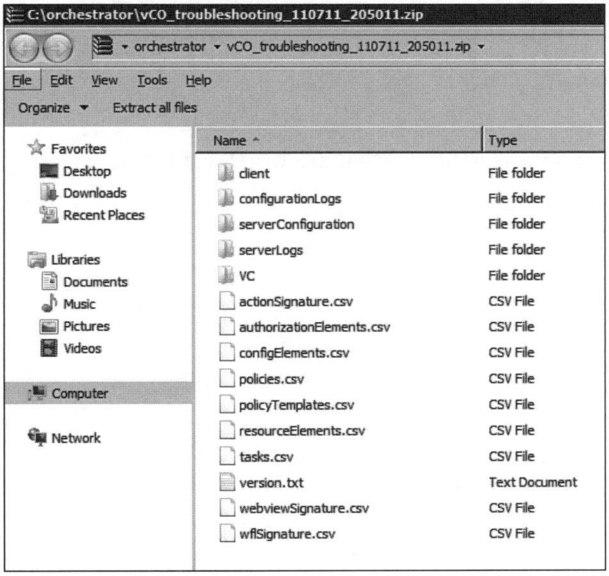

Figure 11.3 Exported vCO logs

These log files are useful when figuring out why a workflow is not operating in the way you expect or why a plug-in does not seem to be behaving in the expected way.

Checking for Orphaned VM Files

Now that you've taken care of cleaning up snapshots and provided a process to create and remove VMs, you now need to perform some spring cleaning. As part of this, you need to find and clean up various ancillary files of VMs that might have been improperly decommissioned before the new process was put in place.

To do this, we work with the "Find Orphaned Virtual Machines" workflow found in Library, vCenter, Virtual Machine Management, Others, also shown in Figure 11.4.

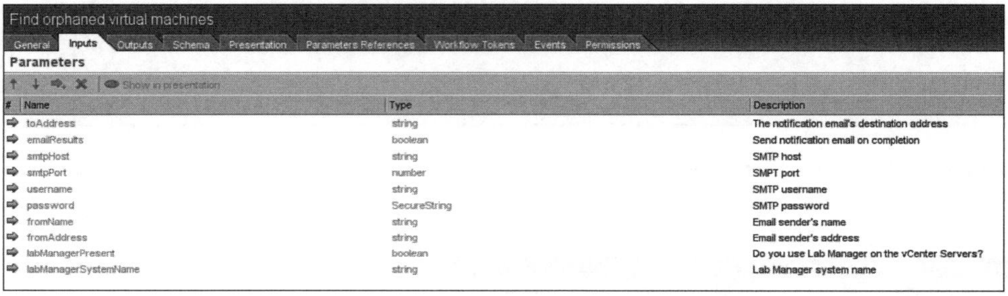

Figure 11.4 "Find Orphaned Virtual Machines" workflow

The workflow itself has some interesting scripting blocks that are worth exploring. Let's first take a look at the schema, shown in Figure 11.5.

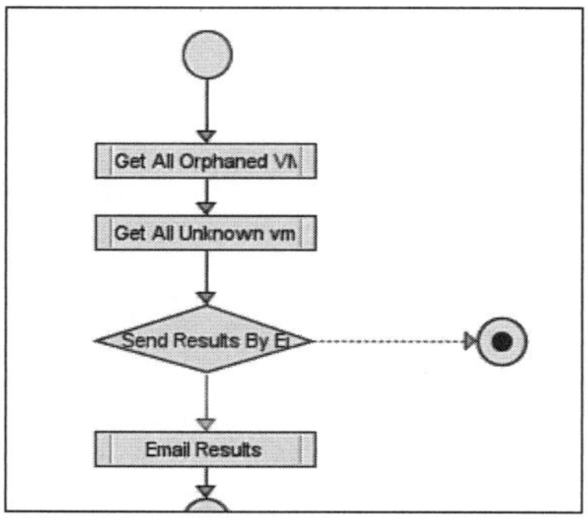

Figure 11.5 Schema for the "Find Orphaned Virtual Machines" workflow

The first block we look at is Get All Orphaned VMs, which contains the following lines of code:

```
01 // Get all Virtual Machines for all vCenter connections defined for this
plugin
02 var allVms = VcPlugin.getAllVirtualMachines(new Array());
03 emailContent = new Array();
04 // Check to see if each Virtual Machine is orphaned
05 var orphans = new Array();
06 for (var i in allVms) {
07         if (allVms[i].summary.runtime.connectionState ==
VcVirtualMachineConnectionState.orphaned) {
08                 emailContent.push("VM: " + allVms[i].name + " is an
orphaned VM");
09                 orphans.push(allVms[i]);
10                 System.log( "VM: " + allVms[i].name + " is an orphaned
VM");
11                 Server.log( "VM: " + allVms[i].name + " is an orphaned
VM");
12         }
13 }
14 orphanList = orphans;
15 if (emailContent.length == 0) {
16         emailContent.push("No VMs were found in orphaned state");
17         System.log("No VMs were found in orphaned state");
18         Server.log("No VMs were found in orphaned state");
19 }
```

Note the following about this code:

- Line 2 gathers a list of all VMs known to all vCenter Server instances that are known to vCO.
- Lines 6 through 13 parse the list from line 2 and check for VMs in the "orphaned" state.
- Line 7 does the actual checking.

The next scripting block that is of some interest is the Get All Unknown VMs block. The Get All Unknown VMs block checks all datastores known to vCenter Server for VM files that are not otherwise linked to any VMs. The following code is how it accomplishes this task:

```
for (var i in allDatastores) {
        ds = allDatastores[i];
        System.log( "Checking datastore: " + ds.name + " for unknown vmdk
files");
```

```
    Server.log( "Checking datastore: " + ds.name + " for unknown vmdk files");
    try {
        // Get all vmdk files for a datastore
        files = System.getModule("com.vmware.library.vc.datastore.files").getAllVmdkFile(ds);
        var fileFodund = false;
        for (var x in files) {
            //ignore esx console
            var filename = System.getModule("com.vmware.basic").getFileName(files[x]);
            if (filename == "esxconsole.vmdk") {
                continue;
            }
            var vmFound = false;
            for (var y in allVmFiles) {
                if (files[x] == allVmFiles[y].name) {
                    vmFound = true;
                    break;
                }
            }
            if (vmFound == false) {
                if (isLabManagerFould(files[x]) == false) {
                    fileFound = true;
                    emailContent.push("The file " + files[x] + " is not associated with any vm known to vCO.");
                    fileList.push(files[x]);
                    System.log("The file " + files[x] + " is not associated with any vm known to vCO."  );
                    Server.log("The file " + files[x] + " is not associated with any vm known to vCO."  );
                }
            }
        }
        if (fileFound == false) {
            System.log("No File found on datastore " + ds.name);
            Server.log("No File found on datastore " + ds.name);
        }
    }
```

Note the following about this code:

- Line 1 starts a loop for each individual datastore.
- Line 7 gets a list of all Virtual Machine Disk (VMDK) files on the datastore.
- Lines 9 through 31 contain nested loops to check each individual file to determine whether there is an associated VM.
- Lines 12 through 14 ignores the ESX service console if using ESX Classic.
- Lines 16 through 21 check the VMDK file on the datastore against a list of known VMDK files; if true, skip to the next VMDK file in the search.
- Lines 22 through 30: If the VMDK is not associated with a VM, put it in the list to be logged and mailed.

As we have noted previously when talking about sections of code, this code will not run by itself; this is only a relevant selection of the code included with the workflow.

Once run, this workflow reports all VMDK files on disk not associated with a VM and any VMs that are in the orphaned state. This proves quite useful when it's spring-cleaning time or to run periodically to see whether folks have fallen outside using your newly defined VM decommissioning process.

Maintaining VMware Tools

Next on our list of things to automate is to check the status of VMware tools and keep them up to date. Why are the VMware tools important? Well, a full answer to this is somewhat beyond the scope of this discussion, but suffice it to say the VMware tools offer any number of features and performance enhancements that make them worth your while. In the realm of vCO, when used in conjunction with the VMware VIX plug-in, the VMware tools are critical to making this work.

To help in maintaining the VMware tools, vCO offers several workflows under Library, vCenter, VMware Tools. Specifically, we look at the following workflows:

- "Mount Tools Installer"
- "Unmount Tools Installer"
- "Upgrade Tools"
- "Upgrade Tools at Next Reboot"

Mount Tools Installer

The "Mount Tools Installer" workflow is pretty straightforward; in fact, check out Figure 11.6. You cannot find a simpler workflow schema.

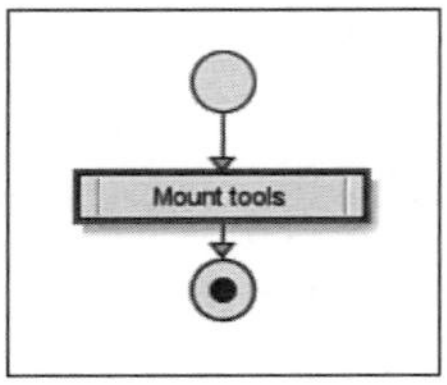

Figure 11.6 "Mount Tools Installer" schema

As input, the workflow takes a `VC:VirtualMachine`, a.k.a. a VM, and runs a single line of code:

```
vm.mountToolsInstaller();
```

Although interesting for mounting the Tools Installer on a single VM, imagine if you had 300 or 3,000 that needed a tools installation. It starts to get much more interesting. To do that, you'd need to make it a part of a larger workflow with a schema similar to the one shown in Figure 11.7.

Unmount Tools Installer

The schema for "Unmount Tools Installer" is identical to the one for "Mount Tools Installer" in that it has a start, stop, and scripting block. The amazing thing is that the scripting block is nearly identical to the "Mount Tools Installer" script. Also, it contains the following code:

```
vm.unmountToolsInstaller();
```

Indeed, it is quite simple, but that enables us to use it over and over again in workflows of our own, as in the example in Figure 11.7.

> **NOTE**
>
> vCO includes plenty of these one-liner scripting block/workflows. It includes them for two reasons: 1) to show a reference implementation of a common use case in workflow form as a building block for more complex scripts, and 2) as an example of how to properly form workflows.

Yes, you can include all the various steps in a single scripting block; however, breaking it out into several single-use blocks can make troubleshooting and reuse easier.

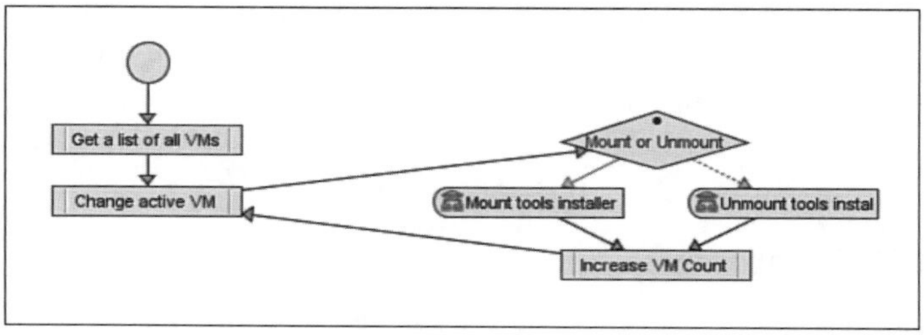

Figure 11.7 Workflow for using "Mount/Unmount Tools Installer"

Upgrade Tools

Next on the list is the "Upgrade Tools" workflow. This workflow and its brother "Upgrade Tools at Next Reboot" are invaluable as components of larger workflows to upgrade the VMware tools on multiple VMs within your infrastructure. Figure 11.8 shows the schema for the "Upgrade Tools" workflow.

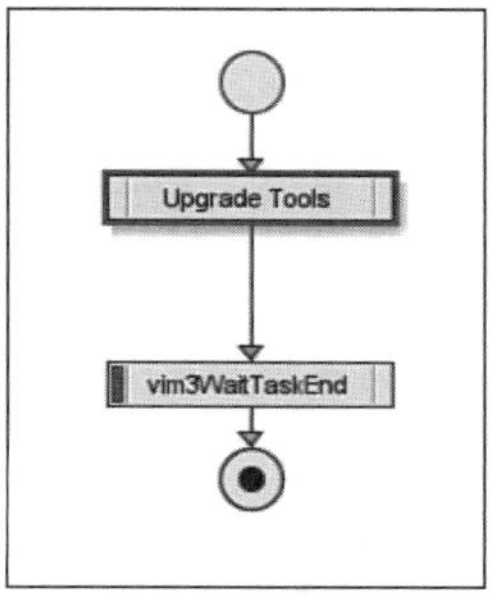

Figure 11.8 "Upgrade Tools" schema

The actual JavaScript magic that makes this work is as follows:

```
task = vm.upgradeTools_Task(installerOptions);
```

This runs the VMware tools upgrade task API function against the VM specified when the workflow was launched while storing a reference to the resulting task in vCenter Server in the `task` variable. Basically, it kicks off the tools upgrade task and stores the task so that we can check on it again later.

Specifically, you use this workflow to initiate an unattended VMware tools upgrade, which may in turn result in an unscheduled reboot of a VM. Now mind you, if you are within a maintenance window and reboots are otherwise expected, then by all means, use this workflow and allow the reboots to happen. If you want to stage the upgrades until there is a scheduled reboot, however, take a look at the sibling workflow, "Upgrade Tools at Next Reboot," in the next section.

Upgrade Tools at Next Reboot

This workflow is the "more cautious" sibling of the "Upgrade Tools" workflow. That is to say that when you run this workflow, it first checks to see whether the VM specified needs its tools upgraded. If so, it schedules them for the next reboot. To see how it does this, take a look at the schema in Figure 11.9.

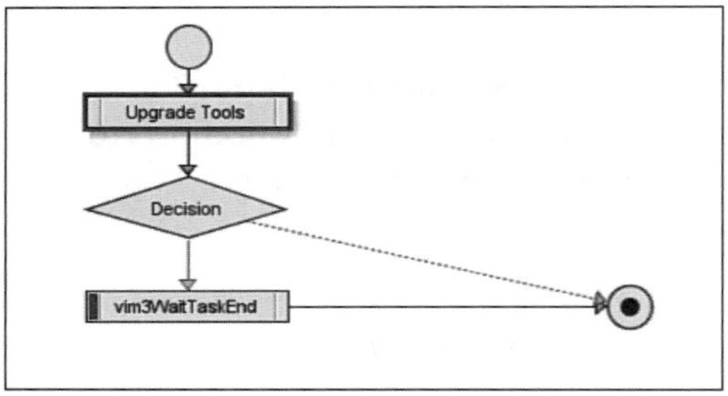

Figure 11.9 "Upgrade Tools at Next Reboot" schema

The first scripting block is where all the magic for this workflow happens. To take a peek behind the proverbial curtain, let's review the JavaScript contained within:

```
if (vm.summary.guest.toolsVersionStatus != "guestToolsNeedUpgrade") {
        System.log("Tools do not require upgrade for vm: " + vm.name);
}
else {
        System.log("Upgrading tools for vm: " + vm.name);
        task = System.getModule("com.vmware.library.vc.vm.tools")
  .upgradeToolsAtNextReboot(vm);
}
```

The first three lines check whether the VMware tools indeed need an upgrade. If not, they write a note to the vCO log and move on. If the VMware tools do need an upgrade, lines 4 through 7 take care of this. More specifically

- Line 5 writes a note in the vCO log that the tools are being upgraded for the VM.
- Line 6 calls the "Upgrade Tools at Next Reboot" vCenter Server API call for the specified VM. It records the resulting action in the variable `task`.

The decision block that follows this code determines whether the workflow needs to pause while the task executes or, if no task was created, ends the workflow.

Delete Unused Files

Delete unused files! Like checking for orphaned VMs, deleting unused files should be used as part of a periodic cleanup or "spring cleaning" on your datastores. Deleting the various files that may once have been associated with a living VM but are no longer can help you reclaim valuable storage space. In addition, it helps keep your datastores organized, in turn lowering the likelihood of errors.

You can find the workflow that we are working with under Library, vCenter, Datastore and Files, Delete All Unused Datastore Files (see Figure 11.10). Figure 11.11 shows the schema for "Delete All Unused Datastore Files."

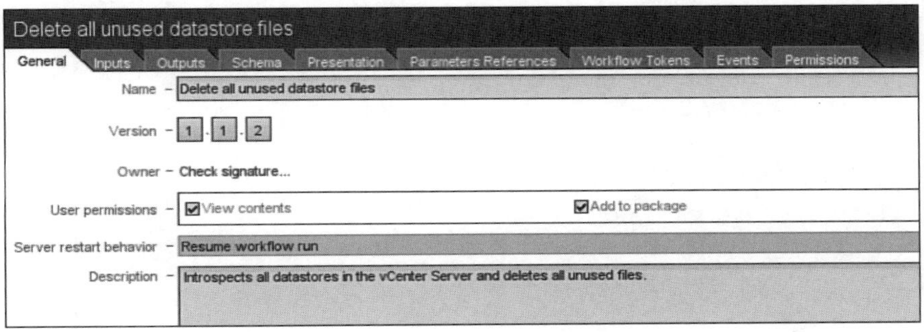

Figure 11.10 Location of the "Delete All Unused Datastore Files" workflow

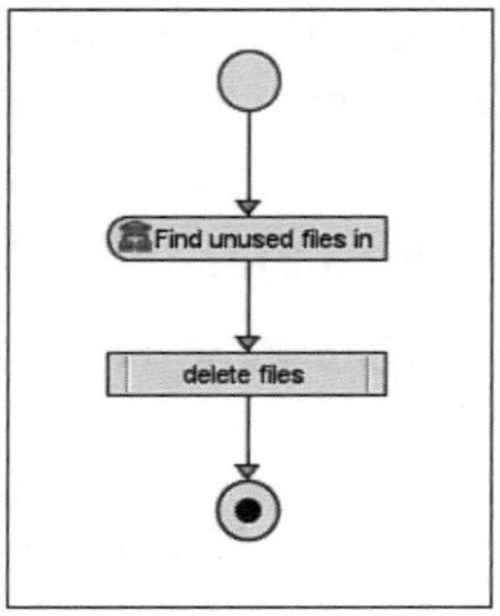

Figure 11.11 "Delete All Unused Datastore Files" schema

As you can see from the schema, this is another workflow containing workflows, and as always, there is more than meets the eye going on. The workflow that our "Delete All Unused Datastore Files" workflow calls is "Find Unused Files in Datastores," which in turn calls "Get All Configuration, Template, and Disk files from Virtual Machines," the schema for which is shown in Figure 11.12.

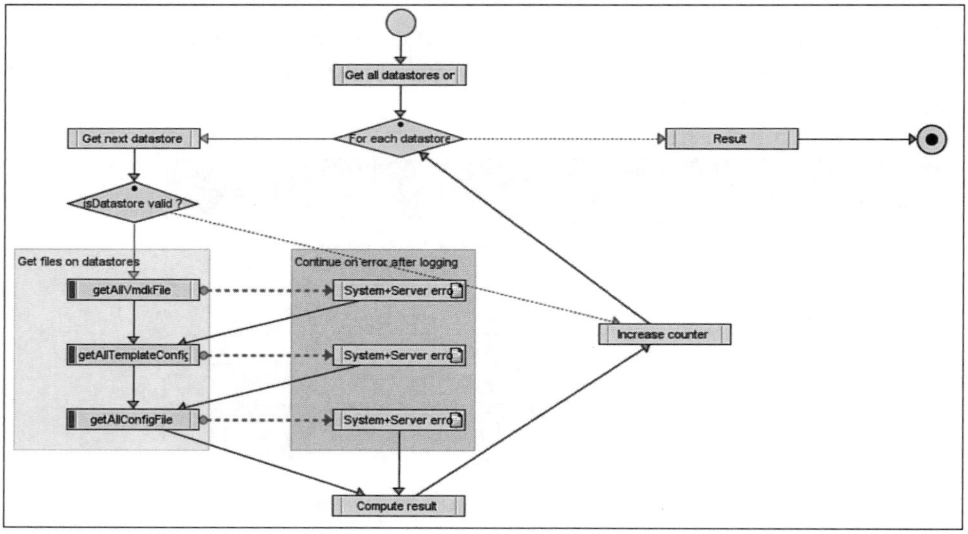

Figure 11.12 "Get All Configuration, Template, and Disk Files from Virtual Machines" schema

In addition, the "Delete All Unused Datastore Files" workflow has a second step, a scripting block. The delete files scripting block, shown in Figure 11.11, takes a list of the files found by the prior step in the workflow and actually deletes them with the following script:

```
01 var files = new Array();
02
03 for (var i in diskFiles.keys) {
04      files.push(diskFiles.keys[i]);
05 }
06
07 for (var i in vmFiles.keys) {
08      files.push(vmFiles.keys[i]);
09 }
10
11 var datastores = System.getModule("com.vmware.library.vc.datastore")
   .getAllDatastores();
12
13 for (var i in files) {
14     var a = /\[(.+)] (.+)/(files[i]);
15     var dsName = a[1];
16     var fPath = a[2];
17     for (var j in datastores) {
18            if (datastores[j].name == dsName) {
19                   System.getModule("com.vmware.library.vc.
                     datastore.files").deleteFile(datastores[j],fPath)
20            }
21     }
22
23
24 deletedFiles = files;
```

Note the following about this code:

- Lines 1 through 10 set up an array of files to be deleted from the values passed into the scripting block.
- Line 11 creates another list, this one containing all datastores known to the vCenter Server instances registered with vCO.
- Lines 13 through 22 do the actual deleting by looping through both the file and datastore lists. The actual delete is executed on line 19.

Mass VM Migration

Our final topic of VM workflow goodness, also in the name of spring cleaning or purchasing/migrating to new storage, is mass VM migration. Of the mass VM migration workflows, I believe that one is specifically quite handy: "Mass Migrate Virtual Machines with vMotion." You can find this workflow under Library, vCenter, Virtual Machines, Move and Migrate.

The "Mass Migrate Virtual Machines with vMotion" workflow is somewhat misnamed, in that it uses vMotion, svMotion, or a combination of the two to relocate the VMs you select to the desired location. The workflow is quite clever in that it stacks the two tasks in order because vCenter Server cannot simultaneously execute both a vMotion and an svMotion on a powered-on VM. Figure 11.13 shows the schema for this workflow.

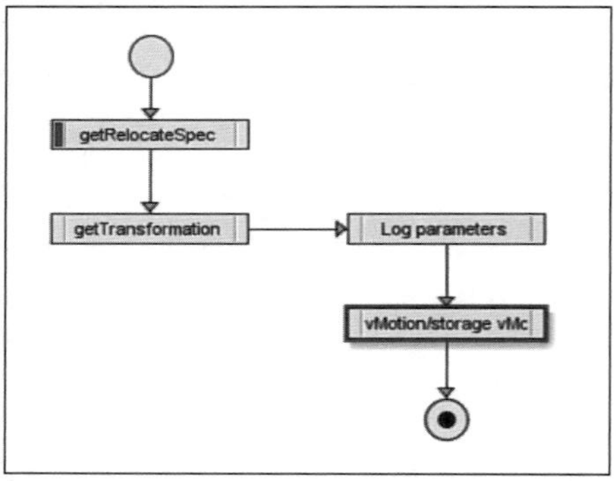

Figure 11.13 "Mass Migrate Virtual Machines with vMotion" schema

Summary

On our fifth day at Amazing Smoothies, we took a look at the various places where we can clean up and make our future day-to-day lives more efficient. We did this first with workflows that helped us export the vCO logs. Next, we ensured all VMs were performing optimally and had the latest VMware tools installed across the board. From there, we looked at cleaning up orphaned VMs and deleting unused files. Finally, we mass migrated some VMs from storage that were going "end of life" by our storage vendor onto our newly purchased storage. All in all, a busy day.

Chapter 12

Amazing Smoothies Day 6: New Hardware

There is no better day in a vSphere admin's life than when there is new hardware on hand to expand the vSphere cluster! After all, a bigger cluster means that business is expanding and that the resources required, as well as redundancy requirements, have gotten greater. Or perhaps you are much like the author of this book and you just like the feel of newer, faster, and more awesome hardware (read: shiny toys).

In this chapter, Amazing Smoothies needs to grow one of their branch offices from a single host into a clustered solution with shared storage and vMotion. As the Amazing Smoothies administrator, you are going to knock this out with vCenter Orchestrator (vCO). Specifically, we will be doing the following with Orchestrator:

- Add a new host to vCenter Server
- Add a cluster to vCenter Server
- Configure shared storage on hosts
- Add the hosts to the new cluster

As in earlier chapters, we first take a look at the individual workflows and snippets of code that are used to make these tasks happen. We then tie everything together at the end in a master workflow to accomplish our goal.

Add a New Host to vCenter Server

So, the hardware has been unloaded from the truck and rolled into the datacenter. You've racked, stacked, and cabled it up and confirmed it can ping vCenter Server. That was the easy part. Now you need to add the host into vCenter Server. Rather than fire up the vSphere Client, you browse to Library, vCenter, Host Management, Registration in the vCO Client and take a look at the "Add Standalone Host" workflow, the schema of which is shown in Figure 12.1.

> **NOTE**
>
> There is also an "Add Host to Cluster" workflow that has a nearly identical schema to that of "Add Standalone Host" and nearly identical scripting. Both can be used nearly interchangeably. Choose the one that fits your environment.

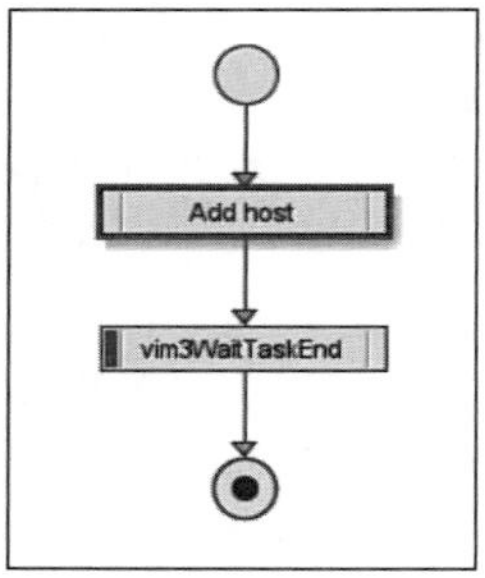

Figure 12.1 "Add Standalone Host" workflow

It looks more or less like a number of the basic workflows we have looked at in earlier chapters, containing both a scripting block to do the work and a wait block to pause the workflow until the task completes. Before looking over the scripting in that block, I've started the workflow itself to show you the input dialog, shown in Figure 12.2, to help you understand what the scripting block is doing with these values.

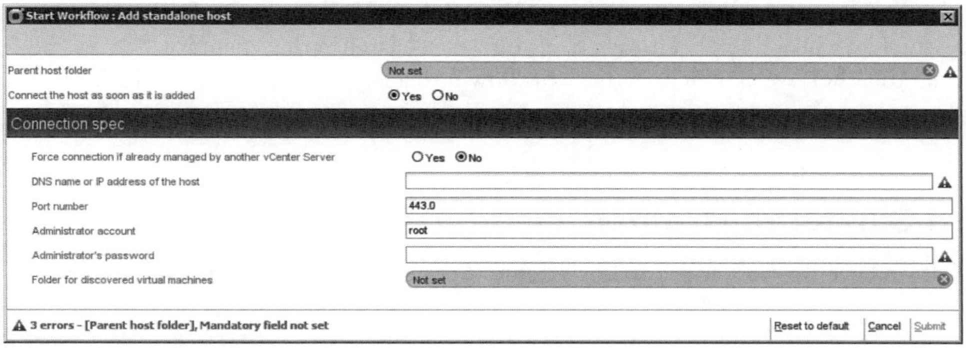

Figure 12.2 Input dialog for "Add Standalone Host"

These inputs correlate with the various values in the following script. What is in that scripting block, however? Let's take a look:

```
01 // define default if params is null
02 if (asConnected == null) asConnected = true;
03 if (force == null) force = false;
04 if (port == null) port = 443;
05
06 var hostConnectSpec = new VcHostConnectSpec();
07 hostConnectSpec.force = force;
08 hostConnectSpec.hostName = hostName;
09 hostConnectSpec.port = port;
10 hostConnectSpec.userName = userName;
11 hostConnectSpec.password = password;
12 if (vmFolder != null) hostConnectSpec.vmFolder = vmFolder.reference;
13
14 task = cluster.addHost_Task(hostConnectSpec, asConnected, resourcePool);
```

Note the following about this script:

- Lines 1 through 4 define values to use when connecting the host.
- Line 6 sets up an object to contain the values needed to connect the host.
- Lines 7 through 12 take values from the input dialog (refer to Figure 12.2) and assign them to properties of the `hostConnectSpec` object created on line 6.
- Line 14 takes all the values and executes the connection.

Now, although excellent in its own right, the workflow only adds a single host to vCenter Server, which can be a limiter. However, as you will see later in this chapter when we bring it all together, we can include this workflow into a larger workflow to add a force multiplier to it.

Add a Cluster to vCenter

Now that we have the host added to our vCenter Server, we need to build out the cluster.

NOTE

Honestly, this step and the add host to vCenter Server step can be done in reverse order. The beauty of vCO is that it is flexible enough to enable you to create the most elegant solution for your environment.

To build out the cluster, we head to a slightly different area of the vCenter Server Plug-In Workflow Library: Library, vCenter, Cluster and Compute Resources (and we're looking specifically for Create Cluster).

Like the "Add Standalone Host" workflow we just looked at, the "Create Cluster" schema also only consists of a scripting block, as shown in Figure 12.3.

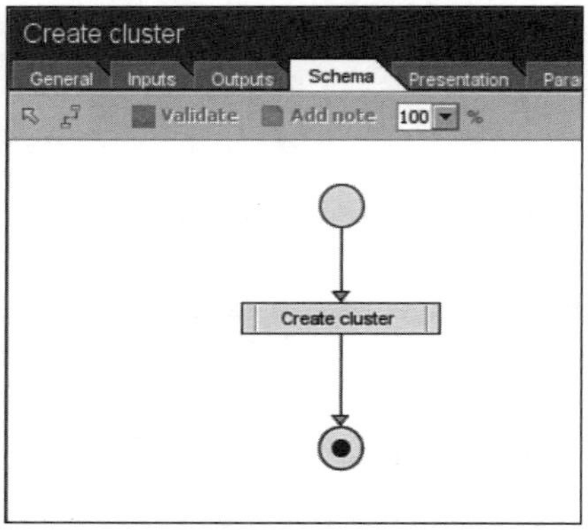

Figure 12.3 "Create Cluster" schema

The important parts in this workflow, however, just like before, are under the cover of the scripting block. The code contained within is as follows:

```
01 var clusterConfigSpec = new VcClusterConfigSpecEx();
02 clusterConfigSpec.dasConfig = new VcClusterDasConfigInfo();
03 clusterConfigSpec.dasConfig.enabled = haEnabled;
04 clusterConfigSpec.dasConfig.admissionControlPolicy = new VcCluster
   FailoverLevelAdmissionControlPolicy();
05 clusterConfigSpec.dasConfig.admissionControlPolicy.failoverLevel = 2;
06 clusterConfigSpec.drsConfig = new VcClusterDrsConfigInfo();
07 clusterConfigSpec.drsConfig.enabled = drsEnabled;
08 clusterConfigSpec.dpmConfig = new VcClusterDpmConfigInfo();
09 clusterConfigSpec.dpmConfig.defaultDpmBehavior =
   VcDpmBehavior.automated;
10
11 cluster = folder.createClusterEx(name, clusterConfigSpec);
12 if (cluster == null) {
13       throw "ReferenceError: Unable to create cluster for unknown
reason";
```

Note the following about this code:

- Lines 1 through 9 set up a `ConfigSpec` using the input values for the new cluster.
- Line 11 creates the cluster.
- Lines 12 through 13 perform error checking.

Now let's take a quick look at the input box that is generated when you run this workflow, shown in Figure 12.4.

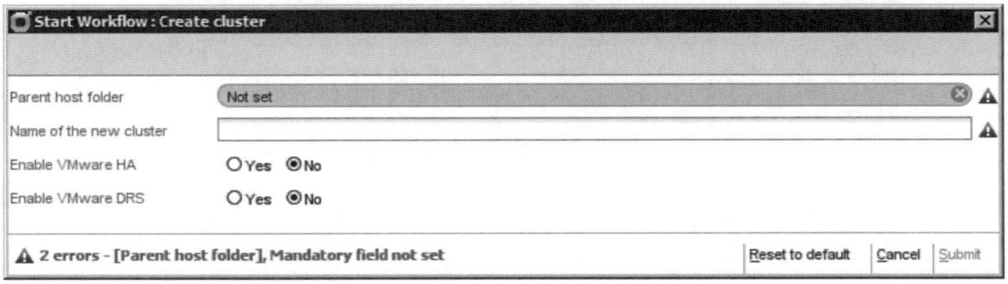

Figure 12.4 Input dialog for "Create Cluster"

In addition to the prompt for parent folder and the input box for the name of the cluster, note that there are two additional questions. These will allow you to enable HA and DRS on the cluster if needed.

Configure Shared Storage on Hosts

Next in the list of tasks to be completed is to configure a shared storage datastore on the hosts in your cluster. At this time, there is no built-in workflow within the plug-ins that ship with vCO to handle this. However, all is not lost, and we have a perfect opportunity to put the scripting APIs that are part of the vCenter Server plug-in to use for us and create our own workflow: "Add NFS Datastore." The steps we take to create this workflow are much the same as for the other workflows we have created so far in the book:

1. Add inputs.
2. Create the schema.
3. Link the inputs.
4. Add the scripting.

Add Inputs

First things first: We need to determine the values we need inputs for and the types of data that go along with the values. To do this, we look to the vSphere Client when adding an NFS datastore, as shown in Figure 12.5.

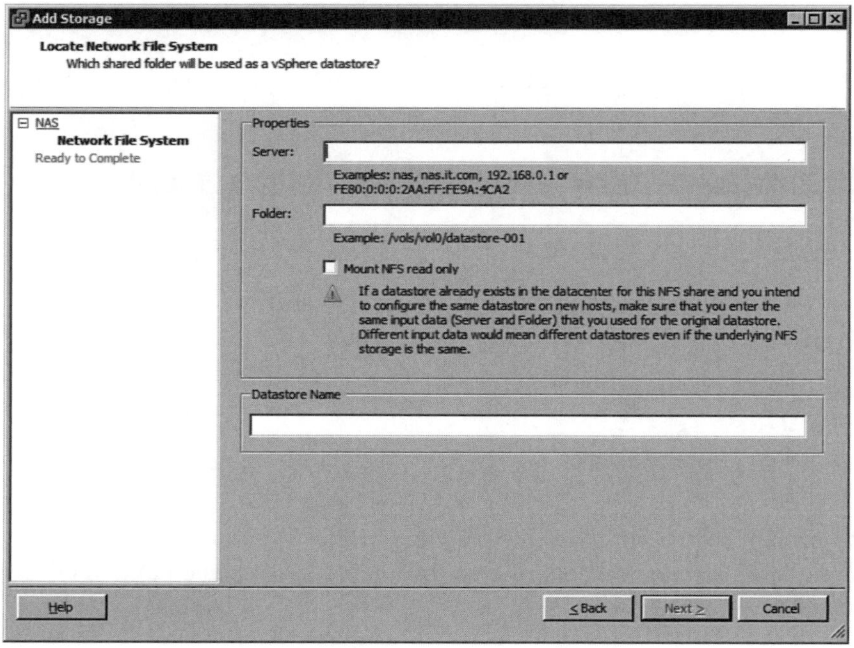

Figure 12.5 Adding an NFS datastore in the vSphere Client

> **NOTE**
>
> The assumption here is that you know your way around the vSphere Client. Explaining the features and specific actions are beyond the scope of what we're trying to achieve in this book.

As you'll note in the wizard, adding an NFS datastore requires three things: the NFS server, a path to the NFS export, and the datastore name. In addition, when firing up the wizard, you open it on a specific host, so we also need to add that to the inputs.

After you have created the workflow, open it for editing and select Inputs. The inputs we will be adding are the specific ones presented in Table 12.1.

Table 12.1 Inputs for "Add NFS Datastore"

Name	Type	Description
`Host`	`VC:HostSystem`	Host to add datastore to
`DatastoreName`	`String`	Name for the datastore
`remoteHost`	`String`	Host with the NFS export
`remotePath`	`String`	Path to the NFS export

Figure 12.6 shows these inputs added to our workflow.

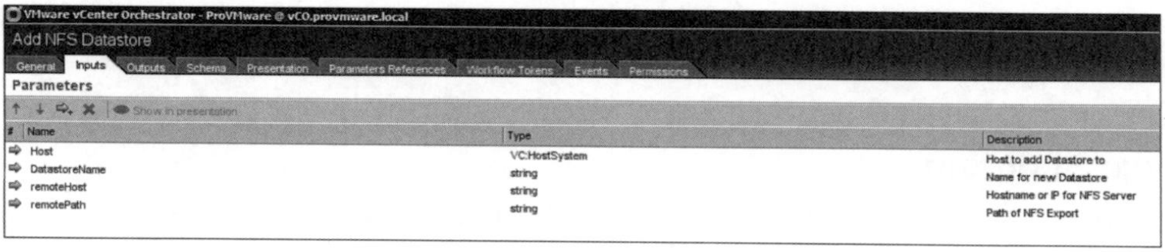

Figure 12.6 Inputs to the "Add NFS Datastore" workflow

Create the Schema

Our next step is to create the schema for this workflow. In that vein, because it is a single, specific task, we use a start, stop, and scripting block, as shown in Figure 12.7.

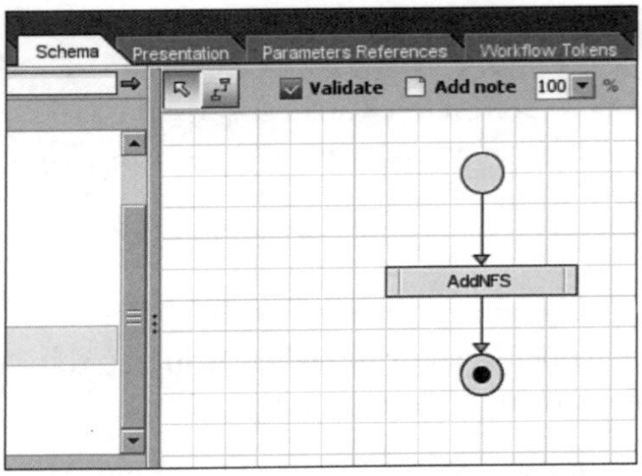

Figure 12.7 "Add NFS Datastore" schema

Link Inputs

Next, we link the inputs we take for the workflow directly to the scripting block, as shown in Figure 12.8.

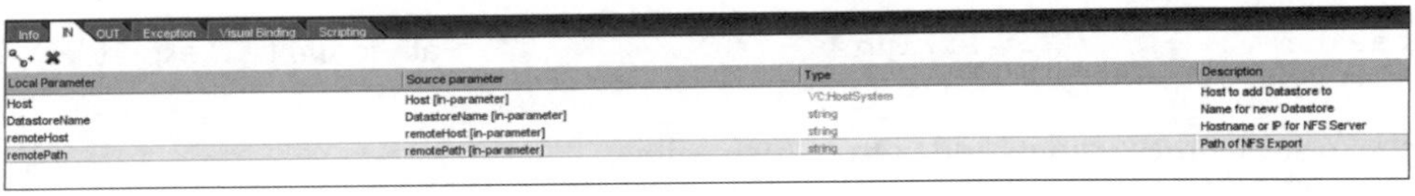

Figure 12.8 Workflow inputs linked to the scripting block

Add the Scripting

Here comes the fun part, actually adding the scripting to the scripting block. In way of explanation, I first give you all the code in the scripting block and then break down by line number what's going on:

```
01 var datastore_mgr = Host.configManager.datastoreSystem;
02
03 var new_spec = new VcHostNasVolumeSpec();
04 new_spec.accessMode=VcHostMountMode._readWrite;
05 new_spec.localPath=DatastoreName;
06 new_spec.remoteHost=remoteHost;
07 new_spec.remotePath=remotePath;
08 new_spec.type="nfs";
09
10 try {
```

```
11        var newDatastore=datastore_mgr.createNasDatastore(new_spec);
12 }
13
14 catch (ex) {
15        System.log ( ex + " creating datastore " + remoteHost + ":" +
remotePath + " on " + Host.name + " as datastore " + DatastoreName );
16 }
```

Here is a breakdown of what's going on in the script:

- Line 1 creates an instance of the datastore system object that we'll use to perform the actual work.
- Line 3 creates an object to store the parameters of our new datastore.
- Lines 4 through 8 assign our input values to specific values of the object created in line 3.
- Lines 10 through 12 attempt to create the datastore using the specifics built in lines 4 through 8.
- Lines 14 through 16: If we could not successfully add the datastore, write the *why* of it to the log.

Looking at this JavaScript, I would be remiss as an author if I did not point out that Appendix A, "Working with VMware Onyx," shows off VMware Onyx, which provides an easy method for using your vSphere Client to produce JavaScript vCO can use. Now that you've created the workflow, you should save it and run a quick validation. Failing that, you can download it from my website, ProfessionalVMware.com.

Add the Hosts to the New Cluster

Okay, so now we have hosts added to vCenter Server, a cluster built, and have added storage to these hosts. Next, we move the hosts into the cluster. To do this, we use the "Move Host into Cluster" workflow that is found under Library, vCenter, Host Management, Basic, also shown in Figure 12.9.

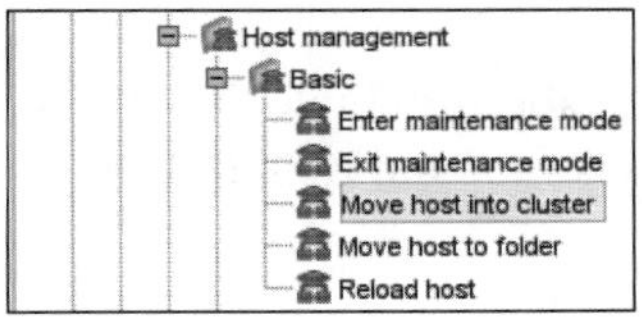

Figure 12.9 "Move Host into Cluster" workflow

This workflow, like many of the others discussed in this chapter, has a main component that consists of a scripting block; this is then followed by a wait task block, as shown in Figure 12.10.

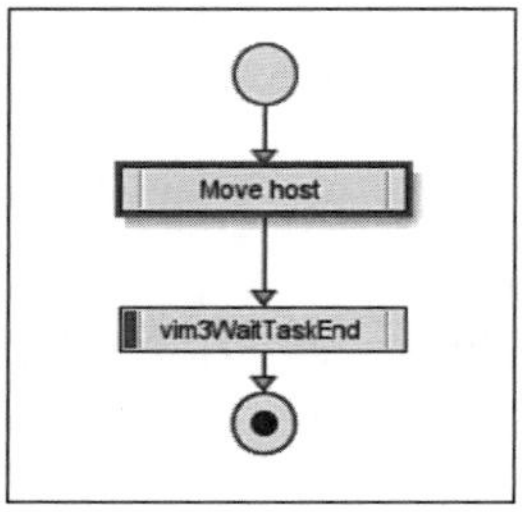

Figure 12.10 "Move Host into Cluster" schema

The scripting in the "Move Host Block" is just as straightforward:

```
01 var array = new Array();
02 array.push(host);
03 task = folder.moveIntoFolder_Task(array);
```

The first line creates an array to contain the host object we will be working with. Line 2 then pushes the host into the array, followed by line 3, which makes the magic happen.

Tying It All Together

Now that we have taken a tour of the various pieces needed to add a host at Amazing Smoothies, we need to do something about it. That is to say, following the theme of making things easier for ourselves and other Amazing Smoothies administrators down the road, we shouldn't just document the various workflows used to add a host to a cluster. No, we instead need to give them a master workflow to further simplify the task. To do that, we look first at what we want the workflow to look like, and then assemble or modify the pieces we discussed earlier into this workflow.

The Workflow

In Figure 12.11, I've created a flow chart for the workflow we are about to build. This will give you an idea as to what we need schema-wise. Let's take a look first and then discuss.

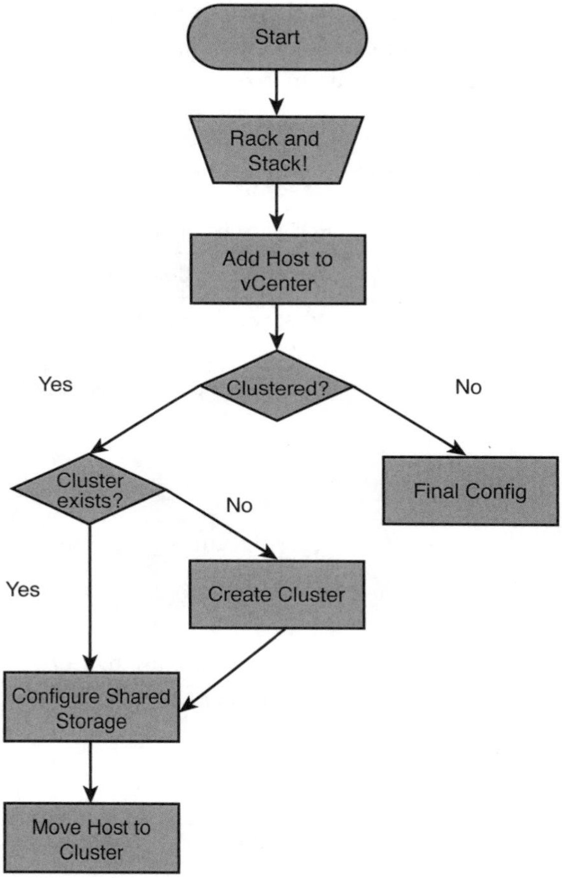

Figure 12.11 Flow chart for master "Add Host to Amazing Smoothies" workflow

NOTE

The flow chart, and indeed the chapter, makes some assumptions as to how you will get the host online in the first place. Depending on your licensing level with vSphere, you might have available to you Host Profiles and Autodeploy (a new feature in vSphere 5.x). However, configuring these is beyond the scope of this book.

From this, you can start to see we need a number of inputs at the beginning of our master workflow: Hostname/IP address; will the host be clustered, and if so, what's the name of the cluster, also the shared storage does it need? Table 12.2 summarizes the inputs needed.

Table 12.2 Inputs

Name	Type	Description
`Hostname`	`String`	FQDN or IP of host.
`isClustered`	`Boolean`	Will the host be clustered?
`clusterName`	`String`	What will the cluster be called?
`datastoreName`	`VC:Datastore`	Which datastore do we add?

NOTE

There will be many more inputs when we are done. However, they will be inherited from some of the additional workflows, as you'll see as we go.

In addition to inputs, we need to add some specific attributes or variables we use to store values and objects as we move between steps in the workflows. Table 12.3 shows the attributes.

Table 12.3 Attributes for New Host Workflow

Name	Type	Value
`RootFolder`	`VC:HostFolder`	`host`
`True`	`Boolean`	`Yes`
`False`	`Boolean`	`No`
`nfsHost`	`String`	`10.0.1.10`
`nfsPath`	`String`	`/iso/`
`vmHost`	`VC:HostSystem`	N/A
`clusterObject`	`VC:ClusterComputeResource`	N/A

Next, we build out the schema, link the blocks together, and set up the inputs/outputs per block. Figure 12.12 shows the schema and its linkages.

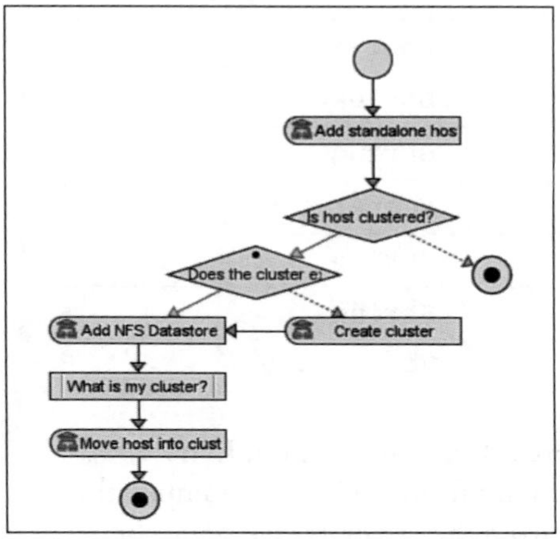

Figure 12.12 "New Host – Amazing Smoothie" schema

Next up is to show the various input/output links between the nested workflows, which we do from top to bottom:

- "Add Standalone Host"
- Is Host Clustered?
- Does the Cluster Exist?
- "Create Cluster"
- "Add NFS Datastore"
- "Move Host into Cluster"

Add Standalone Host

For the "Add Standalone Host" workflow, Table 12.4 provides the input and value linkages.

Table 12.4 Input and Value Linkages

Local Parameter	**Source Parameter**	**Type**
`hostFolder`	`RootFolder`	`VC:HostFolder`
`addConnected`	`True`	`Boolean`
`Force`	`True`	`Boolean`
`hostname`	`Hostname`	`String`
`Port`	`NULL`	`Number`
`userName`	`userName`	`String`
`Password`	`Password`	`String`
`vmFolder`	`NULL`	`VC:VmFolder`

The important part to pay attention to is in the Source Parameter section. In here, we choose not just the variable to link to, but where it comes from. Take, for example, the input `hostFolder` where we link it to `RootFolder` from the attributes we set at the beginning of the workflow. Figure 12.13 shows this more clearly.

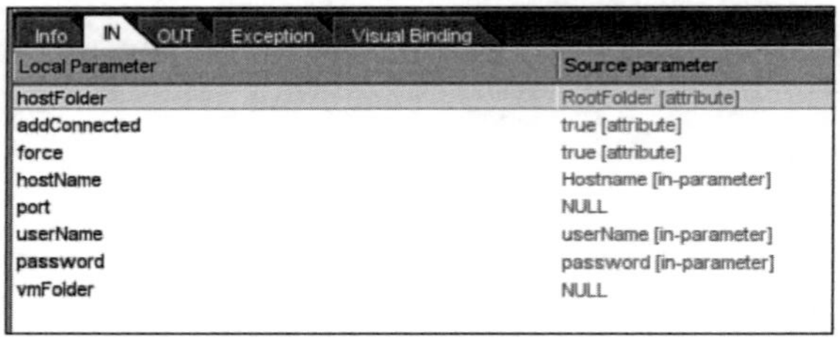

Figure 12.13 Source parameters for "Add Standalone Host"

Is Host Clustered?

Next up is the "is host clustered?" decision, which only has one parameter on which we are making a decision. Instead of hidden under inputs like a scripting block, for this decision block it's actually held under the Decision tab, as shown in Figure 12.14. The input we're basing our decision on was provided at the start of the workflow and is stored in the `IsClustered` value.

Figure 12.14 Decision whether the host is clustered

If the host isn't to be clustered, we end the workflow because there is nothing left for us to do.

NOTE

There likely is more work to do depending on your specific environment. However, for the sake of this example, we would be finished.

If we are to be in a cluster, however, our next step is to decide whether the actual cluster exists.

Does the Cluster Exist?

To make this decision, we need to get a little bit more creative than a basic decision block. To do this, we turn to a custom decision block and provide it the `clusterName` variable as input. From there, we use some scripting to correlate the string to search for a cluster with the same name. If it's not found, we move down the path to create it; otherwise, we use the cluster and roll with it into adding the datastore. The scripting used in this block is as follows:

```
01 // Get a list of all clusters
02 var clusters = VcPlugin.getAllClusterComputeResources();
03
04 // Parse that list looking for our cluster. If it's there, we're done.
If not, make it so!
05 for (var i=0; i<clusters.length; i++) {
06         if(cluster[i].name == clusterName){
07                 return true;
08                 break;
09         }
10 }
return false;
```

NOTE

Appendix A covers using the vSphere Client and PowerCLI to help with figuring out the bits of JavaScript needed in instances such as this.

Like the comment says, line 2 gets a list of all the clusters in the vCenter Server and stores them in the `clusters` variable. Lines 5 through 10 iterate through each cluster stored in `clusters`, comparing the `name` property to our variable `clusterName`. This search returns `true` if found and `false` if not found.

NOTE

This search is case sensitive, as is the vCenter Server when considering such things.

Create Cluster

Okay, so the cluster wasn't found, either that or you spelled it wrong. In either case, we need to now build the cluster. For this nested workflow, we provide the variables presented in Table 12.5 as the inputs to the "Create Cluster" workflow.

Table 12.5 Variables

Name	Source Parameter	Type
`Folder`	`RootFolder`	`VC:HostFolder`
`Name`	`clusterName`	`String`
`haEnabled`	`haEnabled`	`Boolean`
`drsEnabled`	`drsEnabled`	`Boolean`

Add NFS Datastore

Next we add the NFS datastore. To do this, we link the workflow we created earlier in this chapter. Table 12.6 shows the inputs we are passing to this workflow.

Table 12.6 Inputs to "Add NFS Datastore"

Name	Source Parameter	Type
`Host`	`vmHost`	`VC:HostSystem`
`DatastoreName`	`datastoreName`	`String`
`remoteHost`	`remoteHost`	`String`
`remotePath`	`remotePath`	`String`

If you supply a valid host and path, the workflow will then mount up the datastore against your new host.

What Is My Cluster?

This particular scripting block is here to make sure we have the `VC:ClusterComputeResource` required by the next workflow, "Move Host into Cluster," because all we have worked with up to this stage is the `clusterName`. To do this, we use some scripting magic to make it all happen.

Table 12.7 shows the inputs we provide to "What Is My Cluster?"

Table 12.7 Inputs to "What Is My Cluster?"

Name	Source Parameter	Type
`clusterName`	`clusterName`	`String`
`clusterObject`	`clusterObject`	`VC:ClusterComputeResource`

Next, we use some scripting magic to determine whether we already have the object we need. Failing that, we move along:

```
01 // Get a list of all clusters
02 var clusters = VcPlugin.getAllClusterComputeResources();
03
04 // Parse that list looking for our cluster. If it's there, we're done.
05 for (var i=0; i<clusters.length; i++) {
06         if(cluster[i].name == clusterName){
07                 clusterObject = cluster[i];
08                 break;
09         }
10 }
```

You'll notice looking at this script that it is nearly identical to the one we used before. The important change to note is line 7. Instead of returning `true` or `false`, it takes the match found on `clusterName` and sets `clusterObject` to the correct object.

Now that we've got the variable we need, we can move our host into the correct cluster.

Move Host into Cluster

Now we've reached the last part of the workflow, the area where we finally move the host into the cluster. To do this, we call the VC plug-in's "Move Host into Cluster" workflow with the inputs presented in Table 12.8.

Table 12.8 Inputs for "Move Host into Cluster"

Name	Source	Type
`cluster`	`clusterObject`	`VC:ClusterComputeResource`
`host`	`vmHost`	`VC:HostSystem`
`resourcePool`	`NULL`	`VC:ResourcePool`

With that, we're done setting up and configuring the schema and inputs for this workflow. Now we need to run it and make sure everything is happy.

Running the Workflow

After clicking Save and closing for the final time on the editor, you take a deep breath and with the anticipation of an inventor testing his first invention, you click Start Workflow, to be presented with the dialog box in Figure 12.15.

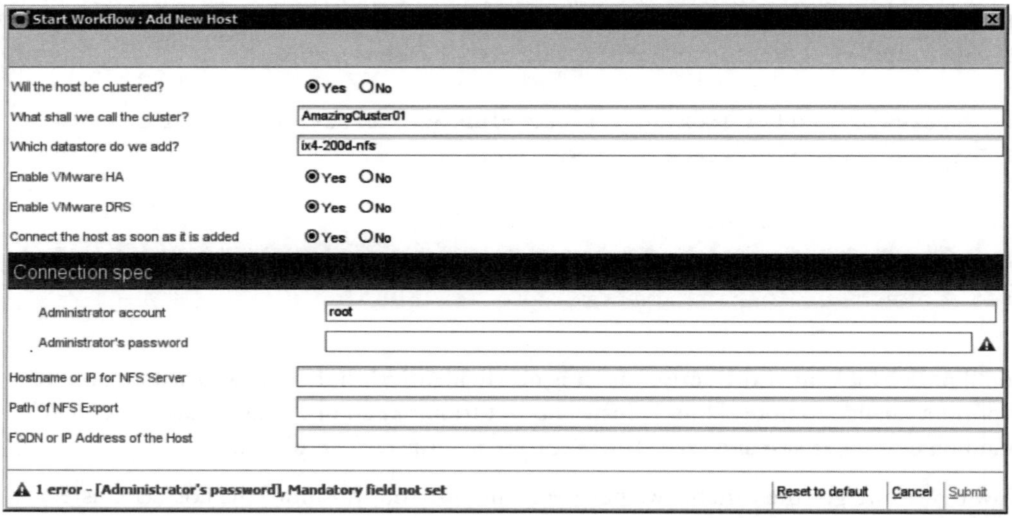

Figure 12.15 Starting workflow for "Add New Host"

Summary

At the beginning of Day 6, management asked you to rack, stack, and expand the computing power at a branch office. Again, you have amazed the higher-ups at Amazing Smoothies by not only building a new cluster and adding the host and shared storage to it in record time, but also doing it with a workflow that is easily repeatable at the next branch office.

Part IV

Appendices

Appendix A

Working with VMware Onyx

There will come a time when building out workflows that you find yourself in a position where you are not sure what bits of vCO code you need to write. Or, if JavaScript is not your native scripting language and you'd rather work in PowerCLI, you will need to figure out how to translate from one language to the other, which, itself, can be quite interesting. Thankfully, VMware has a tool that you can add to your workflow-building tool belt to make this simple, and that is Onyx.

In this appendix, we cover the following:

- What is Onyx?
- Installing Onyx
- Configuring Onyx output
- Using Onyx with the VI Client
- Using Onyx with VMware PowerCLI

What Is Onyx?

As touched on in the introduction, Onyx is a wonderful little tool from VMware to help you translate actions you take in the VI Client into some manner of script, code, or raw API call. Here is the product description from the VMware page:

Project Onyx is a new tool that generates code based on the mouse clicks you make in the vSphere Client. Project Onyx makes it easy to see what is happening behind the covers and can help with development of scripts and automation solutions.

It does this by sitting on your local Windows and acting as a proxy for all requests to vCenter. When it receives these requests, it translates them into code for the selected language. Take a look at Figure A.1.

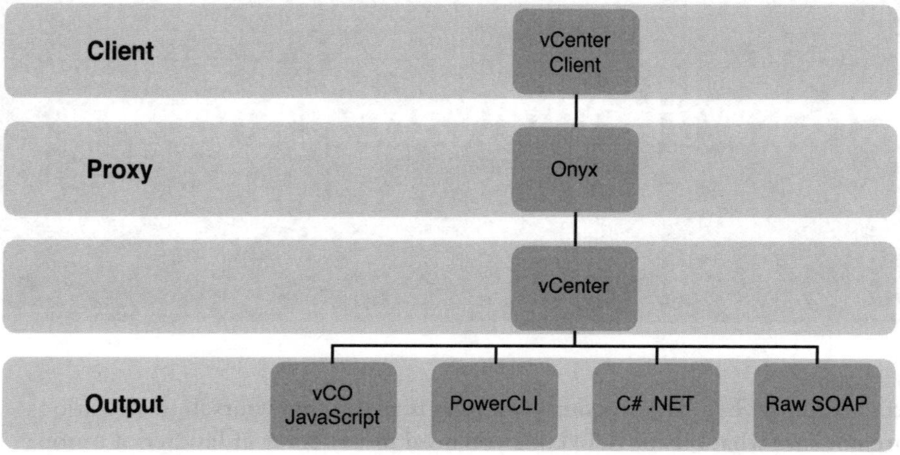

Figure A.1 Where Onyx fits

Installing Onyx

Installing Onyx is a straightforward process because it is basically a standalone executable file. Therefore, the steps to get Onyx up and running are as follows:

1. Download Onyx (vmware.com/go/onyx).
2. Unzip Onyx.
3. Launch Onyx.exe.

Figure A.2 shows the files in the Onyx bundle.

From here, double-click Onyx and you'll be up and running, as shown in Figure A.3.

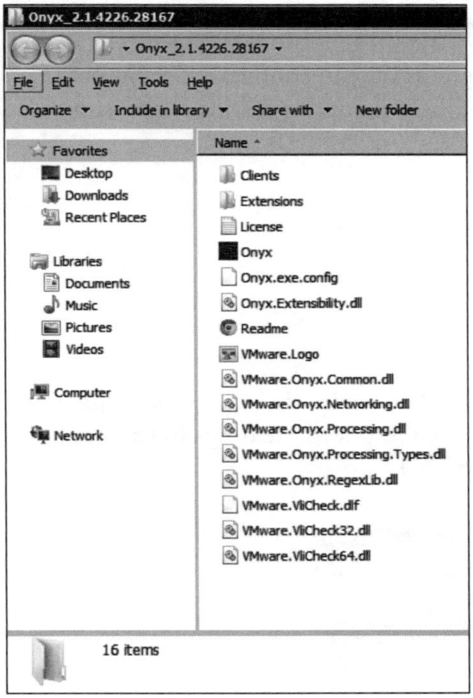

Figure A.2 Onyx bundle

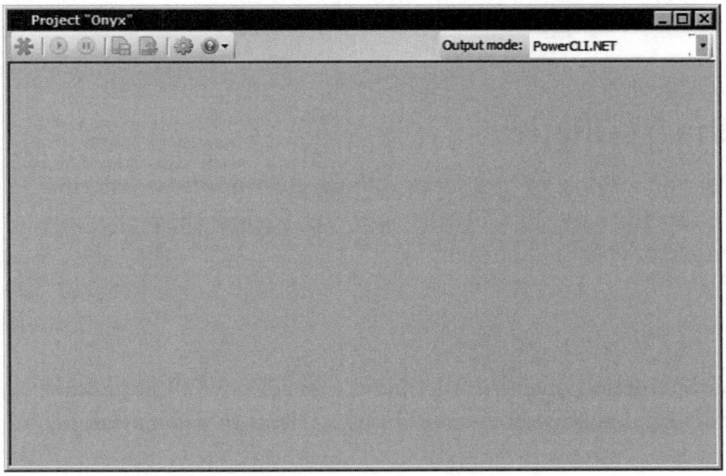

Figure A.3 Onyx running

Configuring Onyx Output for vCO

Now that you have Onyx downloaded and running, it is time to configure it to output in a way that we can use with vCenter Orchestrator. At the time of this writing, Onyx supports four different kinds of output:

- vCO JavaScript
- PowerCLI.NET
- C#.NET
- Raw SOAP

Of the four options, for this exercise we are concerned only with the vCO JavaScript. To configure Onyx to output vCO JavaScript, change the Output Mode drop-down in the upper right of the Onyx window, as shown in Figure A.4.

Figure A.4 Onyx with vCO JavaScript selected

Pretty simple stuff so far, and that is more or less how Onyx works. You will see where this simplicity becomes beautiful in the examples in one of the following sections.

Using Onyx with the VI Client

Now that you've selected that you want vCO JavaScript output, you must be wondering how to actually capture the clicks from the VI Client. To do this, we first show you how to connect, followed by an example of collected output.

Connecting

To connect Onyx to vCenter Server and open the VI Client, first select vCO JavaScript. Next, click the yellow asterisk in the upper-left corner of Onyx Client to get started, as shown in Figure A.5.

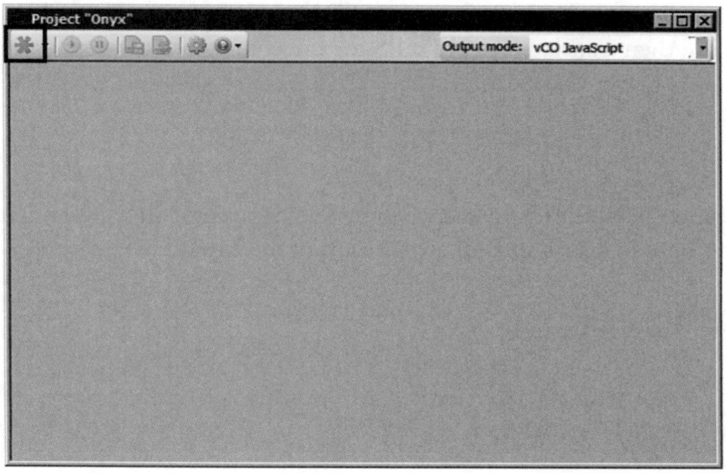

Figure A.5 The yellow asterisk

By so doing, you open the connection window shown in Figure A.6.

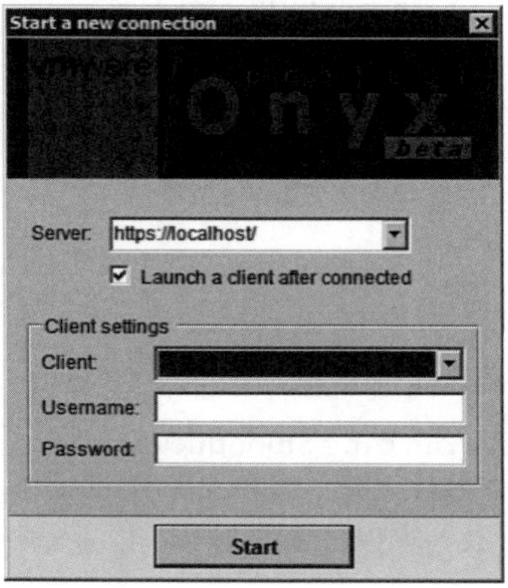

Figure A.6 Onyx connection window

Note that I've also checked the Launch a Client box. What this does is have Onyx automatically fire up either the vSphere Client or PowerCLI, which we cover in the next section. When selecting the VI Client, after providing credentials and clicking start you are prompted with a dialog prompting you about connecting over a nonsecure connection. This is due to Onyx being a proxy between your VI Client and the vCenter Server. All the commands you send from the VI Client to Onyx are plain HTTP web service calls; the calls from Onyx to vSphere are then translated to HTTPS for the connection between Onyx and vCenter.

Example

Now that we've got a connection between Onyx and vCenter Server running, let's walk through adding a custom attribute to a VM and collect the output in Onyx. This process works as follows:

1. Connect Onyx to vCenter Server (done).
2. Start recording in Onyx.
3. Perform actions.
4. Stop recording in Onyx.

Start Recording in Onyx

Being that we're already connected to vCenter Server with Onyx, our next step is to start recording. To do this, click the Play icon in the Onyx window, shown in Figure A.7.

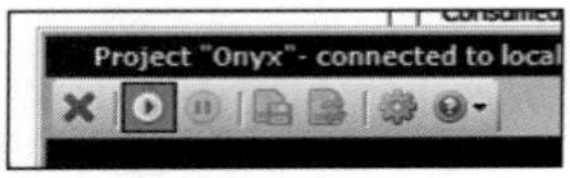

Figure A.7 Start Onyx recording

Perform Actions

In this example, we take an example we used in Chapter 12, "Amazing Smoothies Day 6: New Hardware," specifically in the section on "Add NFS Datastore." To do this, you normally use the following sequence of events in the vSphere Client:

1. Select a host.
2. Select the Configuration tab.
3. Select Add Storage.
4. Select Network File System. Click Next.
5. Provide the server, the NFS mount, and a name for the datastore. Click Next.
6. Click Finish.

This generates the following vCO code in the Onyx window:

```
// ------- CreateNasDatastore -------
var spec = new VcHostNasVolumeSpec();
spec.remoteHost = "10.0.1.10";
spec.remotePath = "/nfs/ISO";
spec.localPath = "ISO";
spec.accessMode = "readOnly";
spec.type = "nfs";
managedObject.createNasDatastore(spec);  // HostDatastoreSystem
```

The following is a rather short and sweet bit of vCO code that can be built in to a scripting block or custom action and called in any of your workflows:

```
Stop Recording [Same heading as start]
```

You can use two methods to stop recording. The first is to use the large red X in the upper left of the Onyx client. The other is to use the pause button, also at the top of the Onyx client near the X. The difference between the two is the red X completely stops and disconnects your Onyx session, in turn closing out Onyx.

Using Onyx with VMware PowerCLI

Most administrators generally interface with vCenter in one of two ways: via the Windows vSphere Client or via VMware PowerCLI. This section works much like the preceding one in that it shows you where you need to modify the connection and then follows up with an example of this in action.

> **NOTE**
>
> Yes, there are others. In fact, Onyx, being a proxy to vCenter Server, will work with them, as well, with little additional work. However, instead of covering each and every one of these, it's best to show you the two common ones and let you build from there.

Note one more thing before we move on, and it's something I consider important enough to not use a note block. That is, translating PowerCLI to vCO JavaScript with Onyx will not carry over any of the logic or looping constructs that PowerCLI performs. This is also because of how Onyx interacts with vCenter Server. That is, Onyx is only catching the calls made to vCenter Server and not the logic of what is running *in* the PowerCLI script.

Connecting

Connecting Onyx to vCenter and having it launch PowerCLI is as simple as changing it in the drop-down, as shown in Figure A.8.

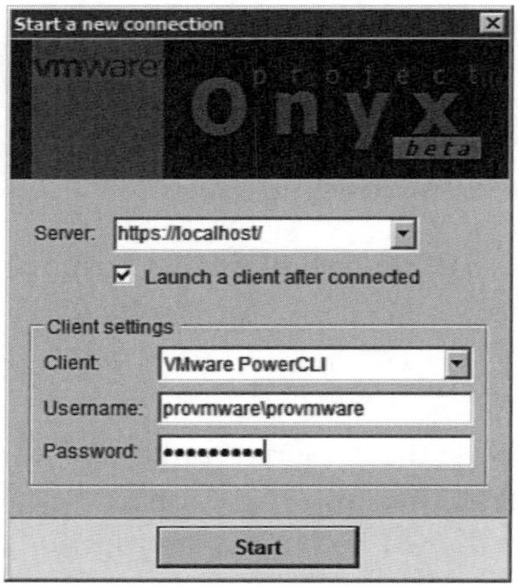

Figure A.8 Onyx connection screen with PowerCLI selected

> **NOTE**
>
> To see this option, you must have PowerCLI installed on the machine you are running Onyx from. When you have it installed, click Start and the connection will be made and PowerCLI launched.

Example

For this example, we're going to get a powered-off VM and power it on. As in the preceding section, make sure you start recording first.

Here is the PowerCLI we use:

```
Get-VM | Where {$_.PowerState -eq "PoweredOff"} | Select -First 1 |
Start-VM
```

Here is the resulting vCO JavaScript:

```
// ------- PowerOnVM_Task -------
managedObject.powerOnVM_Task(null);  // VirtualMachine
```

Although not as interesting as the earlier example, this example highlights how, if you are uncertain or unable to find the commands you need in vCO JavaScript but are familiar with the PowerCLI calls, you can use Onyx to easily proxy the PowerCLI to get the commands you need.

Summary

This appendix showed you where to find VMware's Onyx and explained what Onyx is and how it can help you. You also saw how to connect Onyx to vCenter Server and produce vCO JavaScript that you can use in your workflows.

Appendix B

Troubleshooting vCO Workflows

This appendix covers what to do when vCenter Orchestrator (vCO) or a workflow breaks. Despite my best efforts to teach you how to build out a vCO environment and construct sound workflows, technology would not be nearly as much fun if it didn't break. Specifically, this appendix covers the following:

- Basic troubleshooting
- Finding information
- Debugging workflows

For each of these, when we need to show something broken, we use the "Add New Host" workflow that we built in Chapter 12, "Amazing Smoothies Day 6: New Hardware." For reference, Figure B.1 presents the schema again.

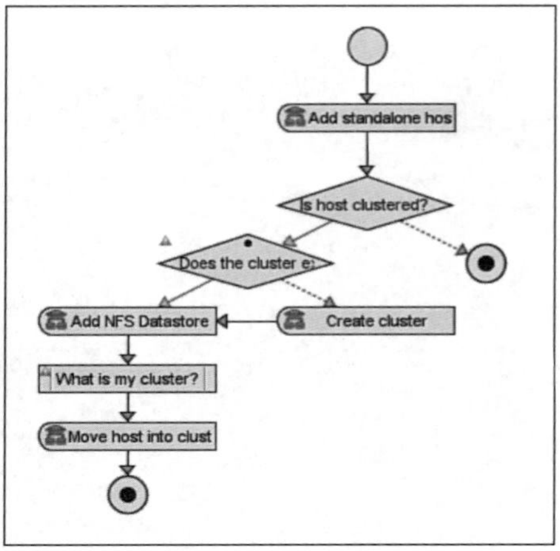

Figure B.1 "Add New Host" schema

Basic Troubleshooting

Basic troubleshooting! We all do it, but we cover it again in this section to ensure that we are all starting from the same baseline. This section also shows you an example of where the vCO engine has dependencies on external systems that can cause some headache.

Basic Troubleshooting

First things first: To troubleshoot, you need to have an idea as to how to get to a resolution from the problem you have. To do this, there are a number of troubleshooting methodologies about. For the sake of being brief, I'll save you the lecture on following one and just mention the elements common to most of them:

- Problem statement
- Find what changed
- Identify and test likely fixes
- Implement the fix

Just to make sure we're on the same page as to what each of these means, I touch on each briefly.

Problem Statement

The problem statement, otherwise known as the *description*, is just that: a description of what is broken. How you will state problems in your environment will vary depending on the type and magnitude of a problem. Another important thing to note during this step is to identify not only what is broken, but also what the definition of *fixed* is.

For example: "My computer is slow" is not a good problem statement. However, it is a good jumping-off point for open-ended questions to help narrow down "what" about the computer is slow and what the expected speed is.

Find What Changed

Ideally, the system was in a working state beforehand. Otherwise, how would we know it's broken? Once you know what the problem is, the next step is identifying the change in the system that either caused or is causing it. Sometimes it is as simple as a network flap or service account with an expired password. Other times, it is a bit more complex, like identifying the line in a scripting block that changed.

Identify and Test Likely Fixes

After you have identified the source of the problem, you must then identify and test a few different fixes.

NOTE

In a vCO environment, it is important that you test your fix somewhere that is not production. You do not want to test a fix over and over again, for example, if that fix is for a workflow that deletes a virtual machine (VM) or some such thing.

Implement the Fix

Last but not least, after you have all prior steps done and documented, it is time to schedule a maintenance window and get the fix put into place.

Knowing Where vCO Fits

When working with any system of a decent amount of complexity, and vCO is one of them, it is important to know not only what dependencies there are to make the system work, but also where and how that system is dependent on them. Figure B.2 shows where these connections occur with the basic vCO engine and the default packages that it ships with.

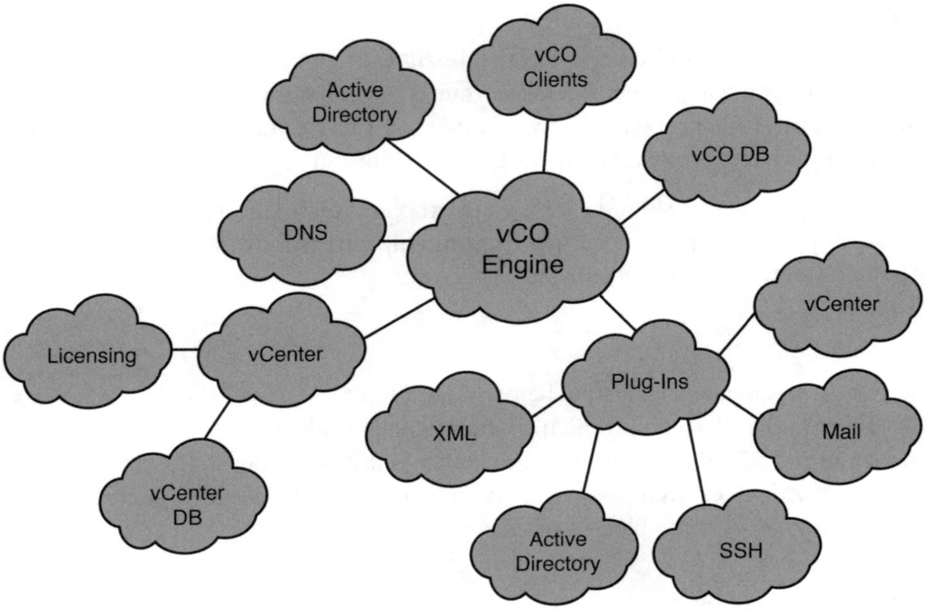

Figure B.2 vCO system interconnections

You can see in Figure B.2 that the vCO engine has any number of interdependencies on both internal and external systems to operate correctly. In the case of our "Add New Host" workflow, if the DNS link is broken, vCO cannot have vCenter add the host by name, thus causing the workflow to fail. The troubleshooting methodology mentioned earlier and the interconnections map in Figure B.2 will form the basis for a good deal of the troubleshooting you do around vCO.

Finding Information

In addition to having a workable troubleshooting methodology and a good understanding of how vCO interconnects with your other systems, you need to know where to find information about what went wrong. Like most software, vCO keeps information about its various actions in a log of some sort. Obtaining these logs and finding other information about basic workflow execution can be a challenge if you've not had to look for it before. This section covers a number of ways to obtain information about how the vCO engine is operating. In addition, you learn about finding out information about the state of workflow execution.

Where vCO Hides Log Files

So, there are actually two places to find log files for vCO. The first of these is the helpful built-in workflow to collect a log bundle. To use this workflow, fire up the vCO Client and do the following:

1. Open the vCO Client.
2. Log in as an administrator user.
3. Click Workflows.
4. Drill down to Library, Troubleshooting.
5. Click Export Logs and Settings.

Figure B.3 shows the description for the workflow.

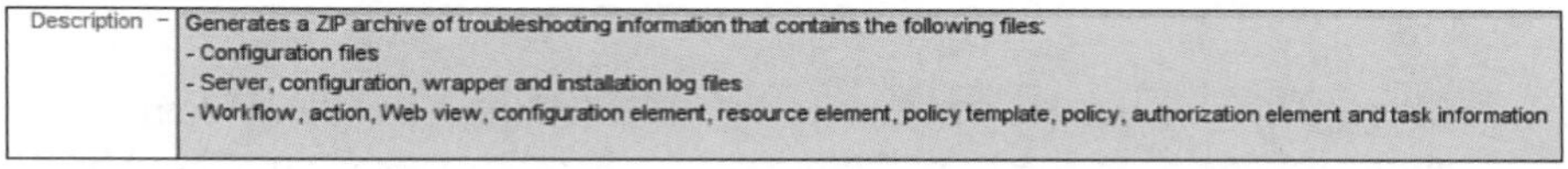
Description
Generates a ZIP archive of troubleshooting information that contains the following files:
- Configuration files
- Server, configuration, wrapper and installation log files
- Workflow, action, Web view, configuration element, resource element, policy template, policy, authorization element and task information

Figure B.3 Description for the "Export Logs and Settings" workflow

Running this workflow is as simple as right-clicking and providing a path on the vCO server to store the resulting ZIP file. The default path on Windows is C:\orchestrator; however, this path needs to exist on the vCO server before exporting the files.

> **NOTE**
>
> That does indeed say path on the vCO server. Meaning, if you are running the vCO Client from your workstation, you need to either view the log files on the server or copy them somewhere else for analysis.

If you're following along, or currently do have a legitimate vCO issue, now is a good time to right-click and run the workflow. Figure B.4 shows the resulting files on a Windows installation.

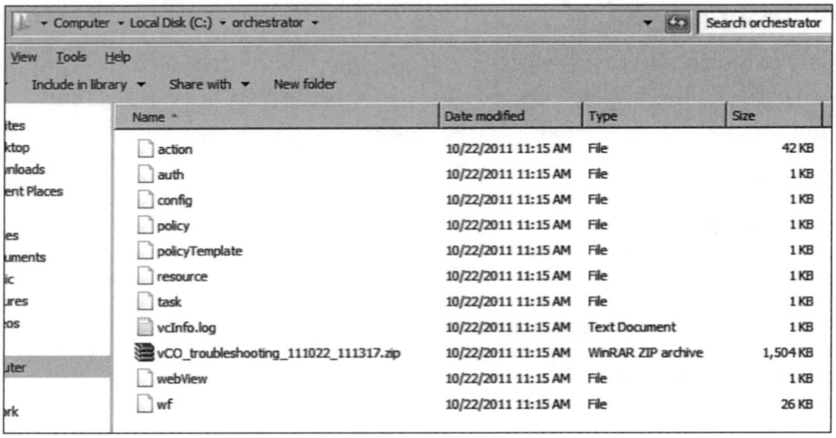

Figure B.4 Files generated by the "Export Logs and Settings" workflow

What you see in Figure B.4 are the files that make up a vCO support bundle. When the going gets tough and you need to raise a support case, these files are what should be uploaded. In addition, when troubleshooting your own issues, it is helpful to know what each file contains. Table B.1 lists the filename and what that file contains.

Table B.1 Filenames and Contents

Name	Contents
Action	A CSV listing of all actions available in the system
Auth	A CSV of pending authorizations
Config	A CSV containing custom configurations
Policy	A CSV containing information about configured policies
policyTemplate	Same as Policy, but for policy templates
Resource	A CSV containing information about configured resources
Task	A CSV containing information about running or pending tasks
vcInfo.log	The URLs and version of the vCenter Server vCO is configured to interface with
webView	A CSV containing information about the web views configured on vCO

The second place to get vCO logs from lies within the logs portion of the vCO configuration interface. To get to this page, do the following:

1. Open a web browser and go to: http://<vCO server address>:8282.
2. Log in as an admin user. The default is vmware/vmware.
3. Click Log.

Configuring Logging Levels

Depending on the size of the disk in your vCO server and the type of incident you are trying to troubleshoot, the information you need might not be in the default logging level, and you may need to change the logging to contain either more or less information.

The logging levels available are familiar to anyone who has worked with a syslog server before. For those who haven't, Table B.2 describes these levels.

Table B.2 Logging Levels and What They Mean

Level	What It Does
Off	Turns off logging.
Fatal	Only logs fatal events, very minimal.
Error	One step up from fatal. Includes fatal and additional error messages.
Warn	One step up from error. Contains all prior levels + warnings.
Info	This level includes everything up to the Warn level, with the addition of informational and status messages during the normal operation of vCO.
Debug	Logging doesn't get much more verbose than this. You'll likely only need this level if prompted by VMware support.
All	Remember how I said it couldn't get much more verbose? It did. Again, this level gets you all prior levels and then some. You generally end up here only when prompted by VMware support.

To change the logging level, do the following:

1. Open a web browser and go to: http://<vCO server address>:8282.
2. Log in as an admin user. The default is vmware/vmware.
3. Click Log.
4. Change the logging level (see Figure B.5).
5. Click Apply Changes.

Figure B.5 shows the logging page on the vCO configuration site.

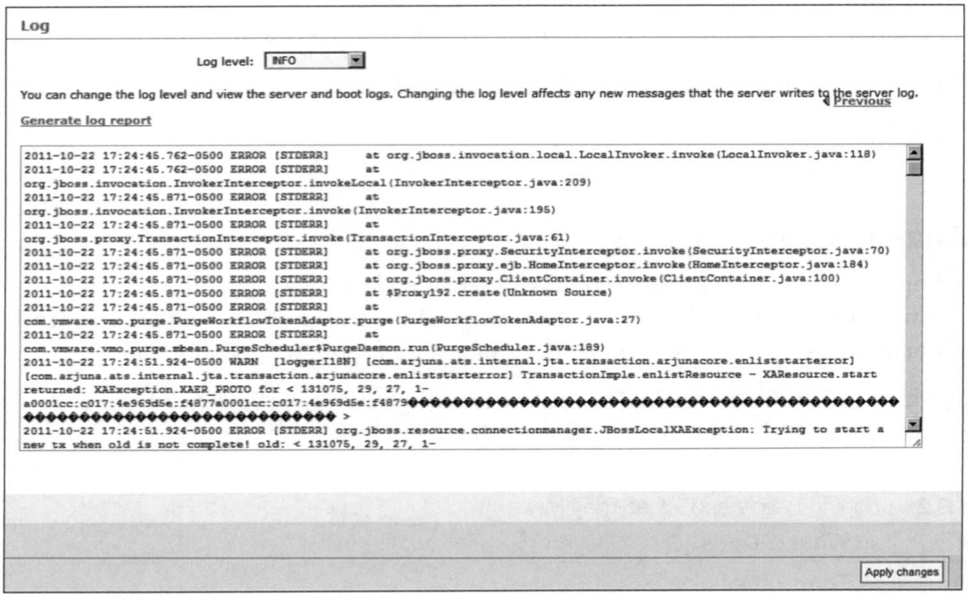

Figure B.5 The logging page under the vCO configuration service

Finding the Last Time a Workflow Ran

Another useful bit of information when troubleshooting the result of a workflow, or to find out whether a workflow actually ran, is to be able to find the last time the workflow itself ran. Thankfully, vCO makes this incredibly easy. In fact, if you have tested any of the workflows thus far in the book, you will likely have seen where vCO presents this already. In case you haven't, the most straightforward way to find the last time a workflow ran is to do the following:

1. Open the vCO Client.
2. Log in as a user with permissions to view workflows.
3. Select Workflows from the menu on the left.
4. Drill down to the workflow you want to know about.
5. Expand the workflow.

This can be found in Figure B.6.

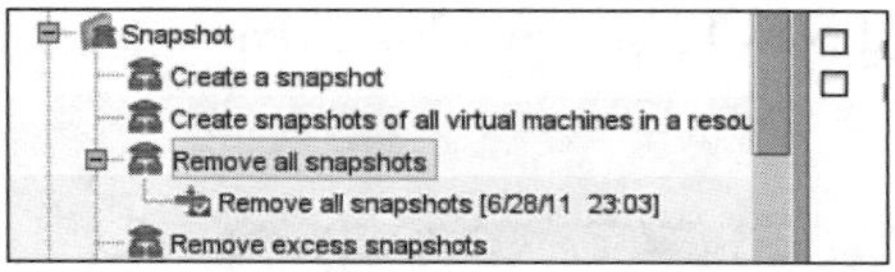

Figure B.6 Screenshot showing the last time a workflow ran

In addition, when selecting a previous run, you can view the success or failure and any relevant logging information that occurred during the workflow run. This additional information can prove quite handy when coming back from a 3-day weekend and finding that a workflow did not behave as expected.

Debugging Workflows

Another useful skill to have when trying to find out what went sideways in your operations is the ability to debug workflows. This will help when developing your own workflows and when working with those downloaded from third parties. The steps to debugging a workflow that we cover are as follows:

1. Workflow validation
2. `System.Log()` and `Server.Log()`
3. Locking

Workflow Validation

Built in to vCO is the ability to validate the flow of a workflow. That is to say, workflow validation makes sure all the different actions, decisions, scripting blocks, and nested workflows all link together properly. Validation also tells you when you have attributes and inputs that are not used or that conflict.

To validate a workflow that you have developed, follow these steps:

1. Open the vCO Client.
2. Log in with a user ID that has at least Inspect permissions.
3. Select Workflows from the menu on the left.
4. Drill down to your workflow (for example, “Add New Host”) and right-click.
5. Select Validate.

Figure B.7 shows the validation run against the "Add New Host" workflow from Chapter 12.

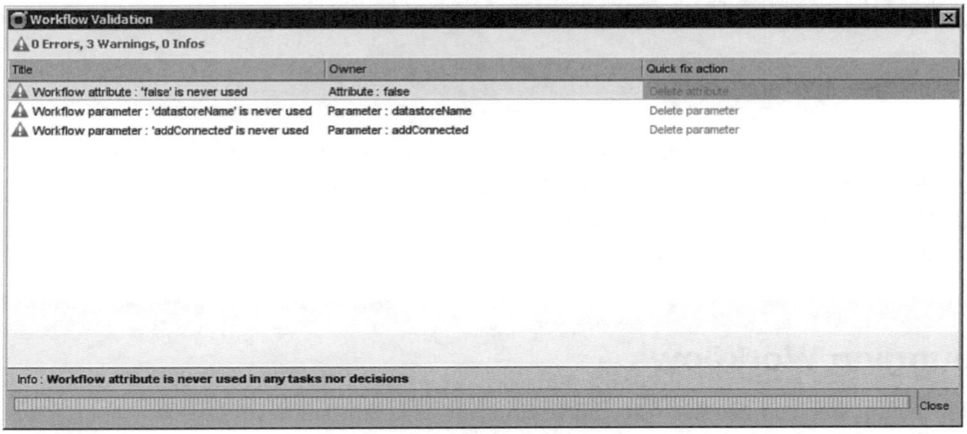

Figure B.7 Validation report for "Add New Host" workflow from Chapter 12

As you can see, we have a number of noncritical failures for attributes and parameters that never get used within the workflow. The validation report also provides a number of recommended fixes for this. Figure B.8 shows the workflow again after I went back and changed something that would break other elements.

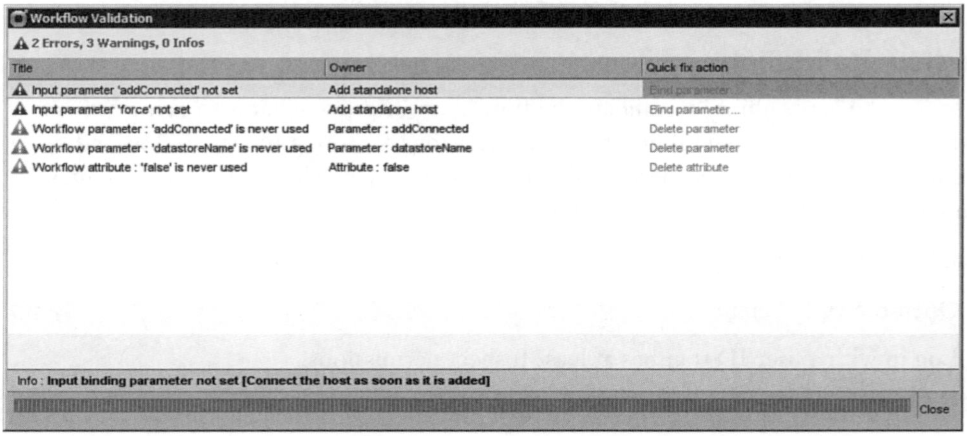

Figure B.8 Validation report for "Add New Host" with critical errors

You can see from the figure that the errors marked in red prevent the workflow from executing. As you are developing your workflows, it is a best practice to validate early and validate often. Doing so will save you quite a bit of rework in the long run.

`System.Log(), Server.Log()`

Workflow validation provides some help at a workflow level to help figure out why a particular workflow won't run. But what do you do when the workflow itself runs, but does not do, as you would expect? Well, that's where `System.Log` and `Server.Log` come in handy. You can use these two functions within a scripting block to return a string of text, status, or the value of a variable from within the scripting block.

Both of these functions accept the same parameters; the difference is in where the output goes. `System.Log("Hello World")` places its output into the log files, whereas the output from `Server.Log("Hello World")` shows up under the Events tab after a workflow has run.

To use these within your own scripting block, the syntax is as follows:

```
System.Log("Hi Mom!");

Server.Log("Hi Dad!");
```

You can use and manipulate the bits between the parentheses as you would any string within JavaScript. For most of us that will involve some text and perhaps a variable that would look something like this:

```
Server.Log("Deleting Snapshot: " + serverSnapshot);
```

> **TIP**
>
> To get really advanced, you can use `Server.Debug()` to trace variable content.

Locking

Locking isn't as much of a debugging mechanism as it is an operational mechanism to use while moving from debugging to production. vCO allows for the editing of a workflow while it's in flight, which can indeed be quite handy when developing or debugging a workflow. However, when said workflow is going to become production ready, you want to lock it to prevent accidental editing.

To lock a workflow, follow these steps:

1. Open the vCO Client.
2. Log in with a user who has at least Inspect permissions.
3. Select Workflows from the menu on the left.
4. Drill down to your workflow (for example, "Add New Host") and right-click.
5. Select Locking.
6. Choose either Lock or Lock with Dependencies.

The choice between Lock and Lock with Dependencies allows you to lock only the current workflow at runtime or to lock any additional workflows the first workflow is dependent on. In the case of our "Add New Host" workflow from Chapter 12, the third step in the workflow is to call the "Add NFS Datastore" workflow. If we are placing the "Add New Host" workflow into production, we want to Lock with Dependencies to prevent the "Add NFS Datastore" workflow from becoming the source of future troubleshooting.

Other Resources and Techniques

What follows here is a collection of other techniques and resources for finding and fixing that last bug or unexpected behavior in your workflows.

vSphere Client

One of the most useful methods to finding out why a workflow is not operating as expected is to manually run through the actions with the vSphere Client to determine whether you can reproduce the same results. For our workflow example "Add New Host," let's pretend it is failing on "Add NFS Datastore." In this case, you first review the relevant logs and then attempt to manually walk through the steps for "Add NFS Datastore":

1. Open the vSphere Client.
2. Drill down to your host.
3. Select the Configuration tab.
4. Select Storage.
5. Select Add Storage.

6. Choose Network File System and click Next.
7. Put in the IP address and NFS export of the NFS server.
8. Provide a datastore name.
9. Click Next, and then click Finish.

If you are able to successfully walk through these steps, you should in turn be able to successfully execute the "Add NFS Datastore" section of the "Add New Host" workflow.

Onyx

One of the best things to do along with walking through an action in the vSphere Client is to perform that action in conjunction with VMware Onyx. VMware Onyx is essentially a proxy that sits between the vSphere Client and the vSphere Server that translates the API requests made into a variety of languages. To demonstrate Onyx, we follow the steps from the "vSphere Client" section, earlier in this appendix.

Before you can get started with Onyx, you need to download it onto the same workstation you are running the vSphere client from. You can download Onyx from http://vmware.com/go/onyx. After you have the files downloaded, extract them and follow along to get Onyx up and running.

1. Open the folder where you extracted Onyx.
2. Double-click Onyx.exe.
3. For output mode, select vCO JavaScript.
4. Click the orange star Connect.
5. Provide the address of your vCenter Server.
6. Check the Launch a Client After Connected box and select the VMware VI Client.
7. Provide login credentials.
8. Click Start.

Now that Onyx is running, the last thing to do is to click what looks like the VCR play button to start recording the API interactions. After you have started recording, you can run through any sequence of events in the vSphere Client and get the resulting vCO JavaScript.

Figure B.9 shows steps 5 through 7. Figure B.10 shows the resulting Onyx screen.

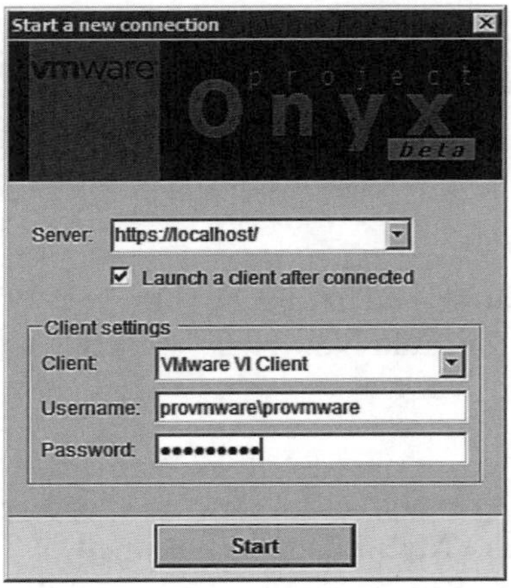

Figure B.9 Onyx Connection window (steps 5 through 7)

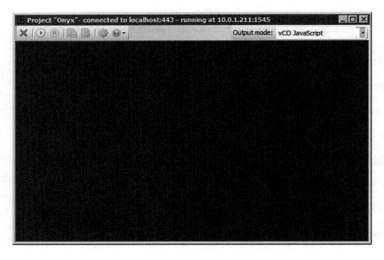

Figure B.10 Onyx connected to vCenter Server

Troubleshooting Examples

Now that you have a basic troubleshooting methodology as well as some vCO-specific tools in your troubleshooting tool belt, let's delve into some real-world vCO troubleshooting examples.

Unable to Add vCenter to vCO

In this example we troubleshoot the process of adding a vCenter to vCO for management.

Problem Statement

Your organization just added a second vCenter Server. Upon configuring vCO to work with this vCenter Server, you could not establish communication. Specifically, you received the error shown in Figure B.11.

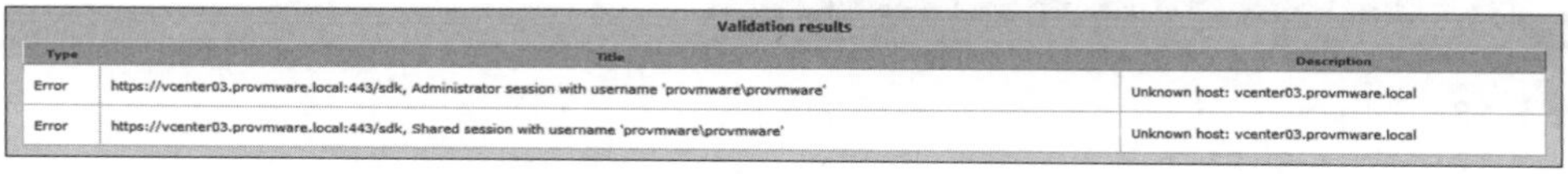

Validation results		
Type	Title	Description
Error	https://vcenter03.provmware.local:443/sdk, Administrator session with username 'provmware\provmware'	Unknown host: vcenter03.provmware.local
Error	https://vcenter03.provmware.local:443/sdk, Shared session with username 'provmware\provmware'	Unknown host: vcenter03.provmware.local

Figure B.11 Unable to add vCenter02

What Changed

In this instance, the change is obvious: a new vCenter Server. What is less obvious is what is different about this vCenter Server compared to the first vCenter Server. When attempting to add the vCenter Server, you used the DNS name provided by the engineer who built the vCenter Server; this DNS name was vcenter03.provmware.local. As you see in Figure B.11, however, this doesn't appear to be working, so it's likely we've identified the change.

Identify and Test Fixes

With the DNS name not working, you call the engineer who built the new vCenter Server and confirm that vCenter03.provmware.local is indeed the address. Because the error indicated "Unknown host," you then ask the engineer to confirm the IP address assigned to the host: 10.0.1.212.

With the proper information in hand, you log in to the console of the vCO server, open a command prompt, and perform the following tests:

1. Ping the vCenter Server by name (see Figure B.12).

Administrator: Windows PowerShell
PS C:\> ping vcenter03.provmware.local
Ping request could not find host vcenter03.provmware.local. Please check the name and try again.
PS C:\> _

Figure B.12 Ping by name

2. Ping the vCenter Server by IP address (see Figure B.13).

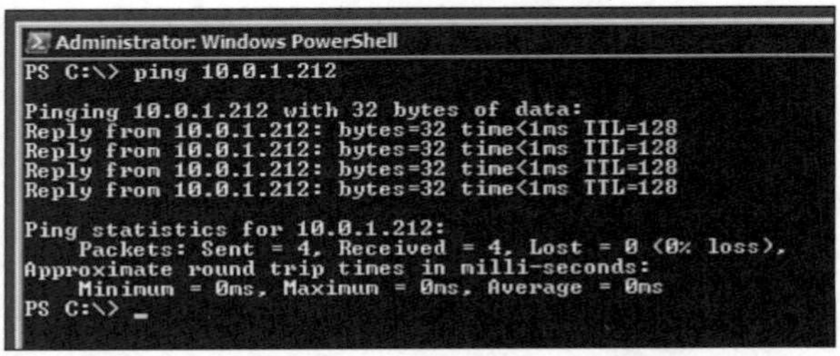

Figure B.13 Ping by IP

As you see in Figure B.12, the problem is very much with the DNS name provided. To be doubly sure, let's add it to the hosts file on the local system to test our fix before replying to the owner of vcenter03 and asking him to correct it:

1. Add an entry to C:\Windows\system32\drivers\etc\hosts for the name/IP (see Figure B.14).
2. Ping the vCenter Server by name (see Figure B.15).

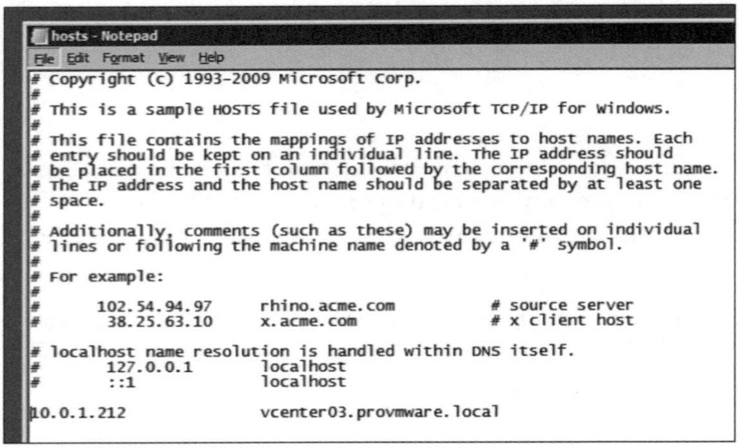

Figure B.14 Editing the hosts file

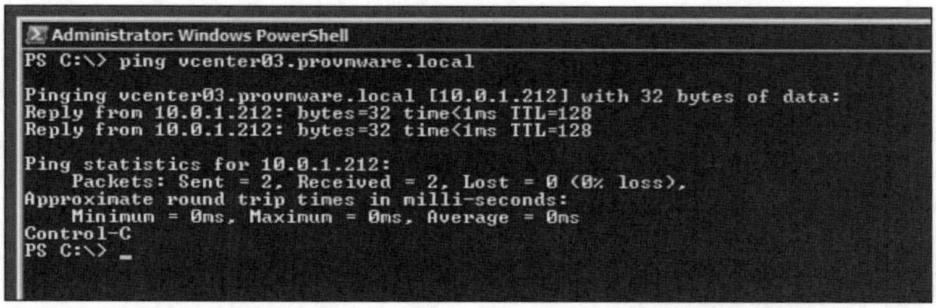
Administrator: Windows PowerShell
PS C:\> ping vcenter03.provmware.local
Pinging vcenter03.provmware.local [10.0.1.212] with 32 bytes of data:
Reply from 10.0.1.212: bytes=32 time<1ms TTL=128
Reply from 10.0.1.212: bytes=32 time<1ms TTL=128
Ping statistics for 10.0.1.212:
Packets: Sent = 2, Received = 2, Lost = 0 (0% loss),
Approximate round trip times in milli-seconds:
Minimum = 0ms, Maximum = 0ms, Average = 0ms
Control-C
PS C:\>

Figure B.15 Name resolution working

Implement Fix

Now that we know DNS is the culprit and have tested the fix using the local hosts file on the vCO server, it is time to reach out to the person responsible for DNS in your organization and ask for the name to be updated.

Scheduled Workflow Failed to Run

In this example, you have scheduled a workflow to run weekly; however, as you can guess from the title, that is not occurring.

Problem Statement

You have a workflow scheduled to run once a week on Sunday. This workflow's job is to clean up the old snapshots in your lab environment. However, you've discovered that it is no longer running. Figure B.16 shows the history of the workflow.

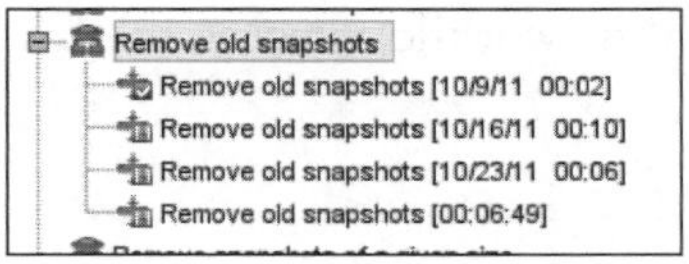

Figure B.16 History of the "Remove Old Snapshots" workflow

What Changed

Well, that is a good question. This being the lab, any number of things could have changed. However, selecting one of the jobs marked in yellow will bring you to the schema screen where the workflow is paused, shown in Figure B.17.

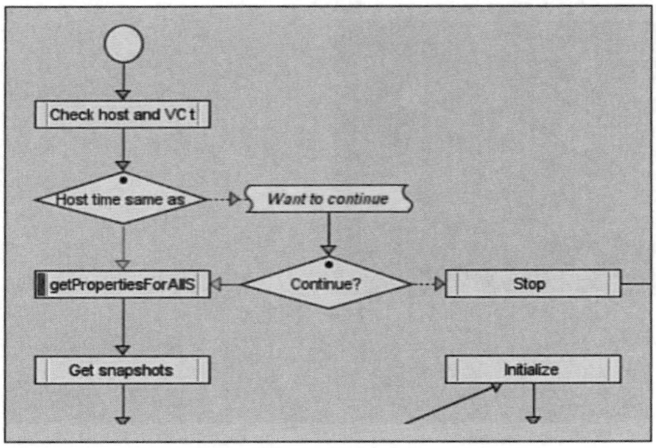

Figure B.17 Schema for the paused workflow

Looking at the surrounding parts of the workflow, you see that the time on the ESXi hosts is different from the time on the vCenter Server. So now that you've found the change, what do you do to fix it?

Identify and Test Fixes

In this case, checking that the time on the vCenter Server and the time on ESXi hosts is the same is key. Further, you want to ensure that both are syncing to the same Network Time Protocol (NTP) server. In our case, they were not.

Implement Fix

For the issue highlighted in this section, we first canceled all the pending instances of this workflow. Next, we set both the vCenter Server and the hosts to sync time from the publicly available NTP server, pool.ntp.org. Finally, we reran the workflow successfully.

Summary

Troubleshooting is quite a broad topic to write a guide on, let alone one that is comprehensive. However, the methodology discussed in this appendix, the ability to find where vCO stores its information around what is broken, and an understanding of the various interdependencies vCO has with your systems should give you the tools you need to effectively troubleshoot any situation that comes your way.

Appendix C

The vCenter Orchestrator vApp

With the 5.0 release of VMware vSphere, the Orchestrator team decided to do something a bit different. They stepped out of lockstep with the official release of vSphere and, in addition to launching the vCO 4.2 standalone install, they launched a vApp, or virtual appliance, to lower the barrier to entry when deploying vCO.

NOTE

If they broke with the vSphere release schedule and launched the vApp, why are we just now touching on it in an appendix? Well, the vApp may have indeed been part of the grand plan when I started writing, but it was not readily available until after I had finished most of this book.

The vCO vApp is a SUSE Linux–based appliance built with VMware Studio and comes complete and ready to run out of the box with Lightweight Directory Access Protocol (LDAP) and its own database back end. In addition, you can configure it exactly the same as the Windows installation to talk to a separate back-end database or external LDAP source.

Downloading

To download the vCO vApp, you need a license for vSphere or must sign up for a 90-day trial. Once you are ready, head over to the download page on vmware.com. You will find the vCO vApp as a separate item, alongside the rest of the vSphere bundle, as shown in Figure C.1.

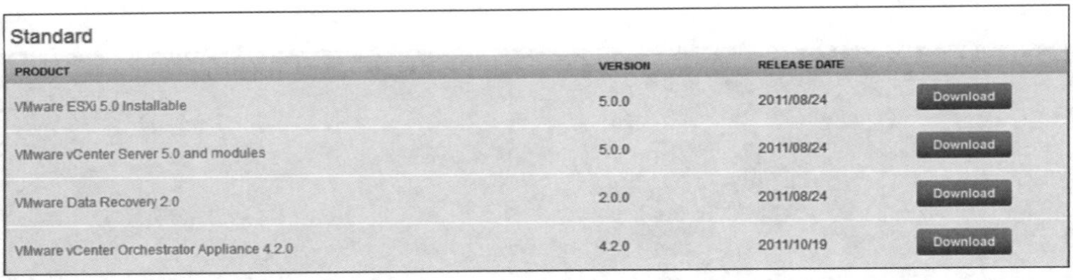

Standard

PRODUCT	VERSION	RELEASE DATE	
VMware ESXi 5.0 Installable	5.0.0	2011/08/24	Download
VMware vCenter Server 5.0 and modules	5.0.0	2011/08/24	Download
VMware Data Recovery 2.0	2.0.0	2011/08/24	Download
VMware vCenter Orchestrator Appliance 4.2.0	4.2.0	2011/10/19	Download

Figure C.1 vCO vApp download

Two files comprise the download: an Open Virtualization Format (OVF) and a Virtual Machine Disk (VMDK). You must place both of them in a location that is accessible to the workstation running the vSphere Client. You also want to note this location for the deployment step.

Deploying

To deploy the vApp, you need to know the location of the OVF and VMDK files you downloaded. After you have that information, complete the following steps in the vSphere Client to deploy this vApp:

1. Open the vSphere Client.
2. Log in as a user with permissions to deploy vApps.
3. Click File, Deploy OVF Template.
4. Browse to the location where you stored the OVF file (see Figure C.2).
5. Click Next.
6. Click Next again.
7. *Read* and accept the EULA, and click Next.
8. Name the vApp and click Next.
9. Choose a resource pool (if you have them), and then click Next.
10. Choose the storage location, and then click Next.
11. Choose a disk format, and then click Next.

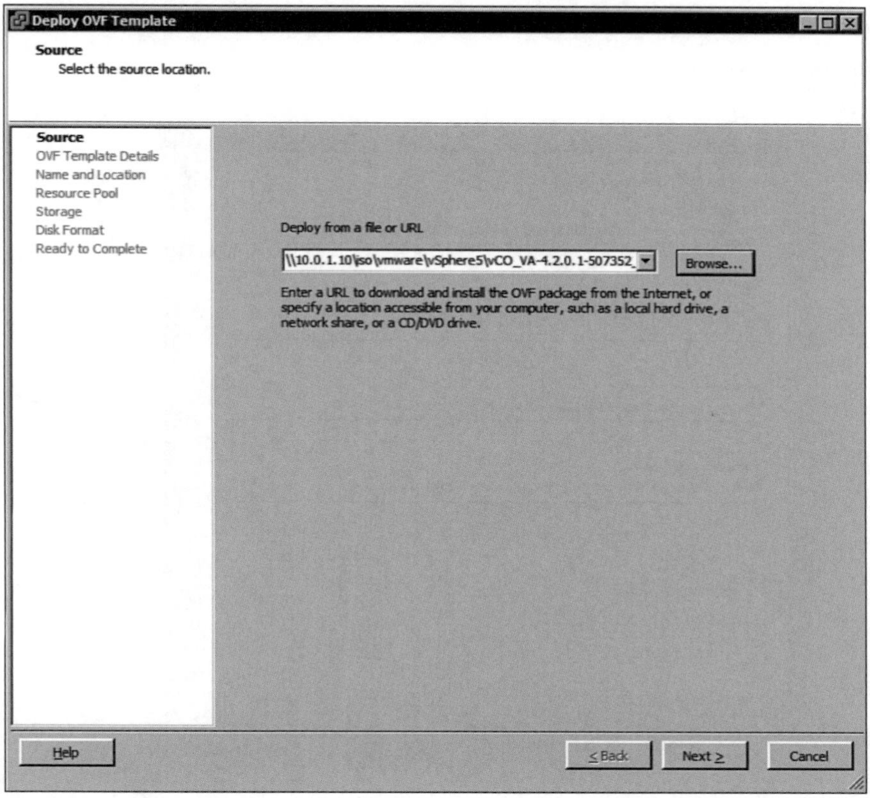

Figure C.2 Location of the vCO vApp OVF

12. On the Properties screen (see Figure C.3), fill in the values for your environment. In my lab, we use DHCP. Click Next.
13. Click Finish.

Get a cup of your favorite caffeinated beverage; this will take awhile.

When the vApp completes its deploy, review its settings and power it on for the next step.

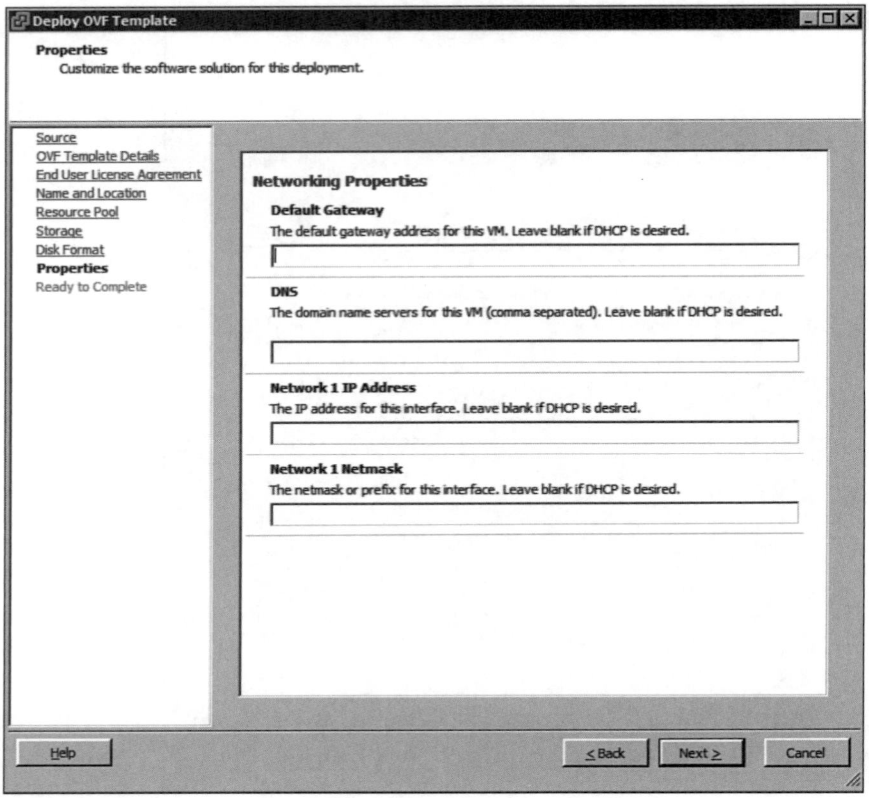

Figure C.3 Configure networking properties for the vCO vApp

Configuring the vApp

The vCO vApp comes mostly ready to go out of the box, but you do need to do a couple more things before you can use the vApp:

- Change the default passwords
- Install the vCenter Server 5 plug-in

Change the Default Passwords

Change the default what? Because the vCO vApp is a generic install and designed to be easy to use, it ships with a set of default passwords that you need to change.

vApp Administration Password

To change the default vApp administration password, follow these steps:

1. In the vSphere Client, select the vCO vApp and view the Summary tab (see Figure C.4).
2. Open a web browser and browse to the IP address listed on the Summary page (see Figure C.5).

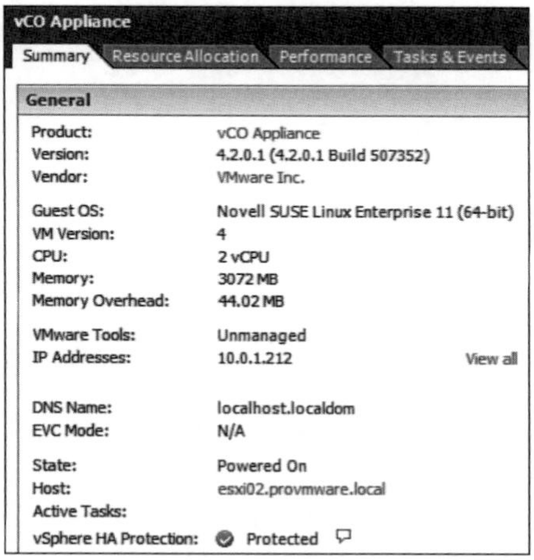

Figure C.4 Summary tab for the vCO vApp

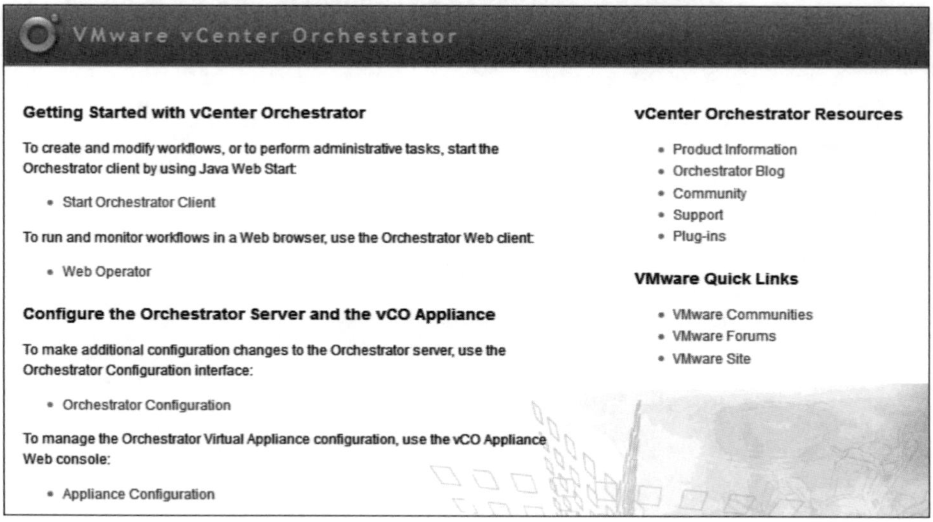

Figure C.5 vCO vApp landing page

3. Click Appliance Configuration.
4. In the resulting page, type and confirm a new password to manage the vApp (see Figure C.6).
5. Accept the SSL certificate.
6. Log in as root (see Figure C.7).

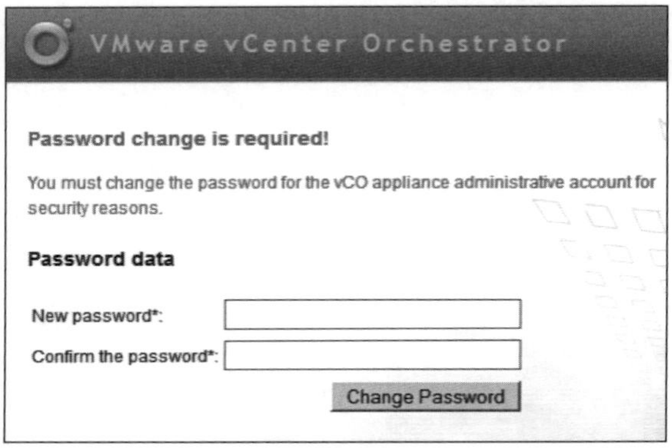

Figure C.6 Changing the password for the vCO vApp

Figure C.7 Logging in to the vCO vApp administration area

vCO Configuration Password

To change the default vCO configuration password, follow these steps:

1. Browse to the vCO vApp landing page (refer to Figure C.5).
2. Select Orchestrator Configuration.
3. Log in with a username and a password of **vmware**.
4. When prompted, change the password (see Figure C.8).

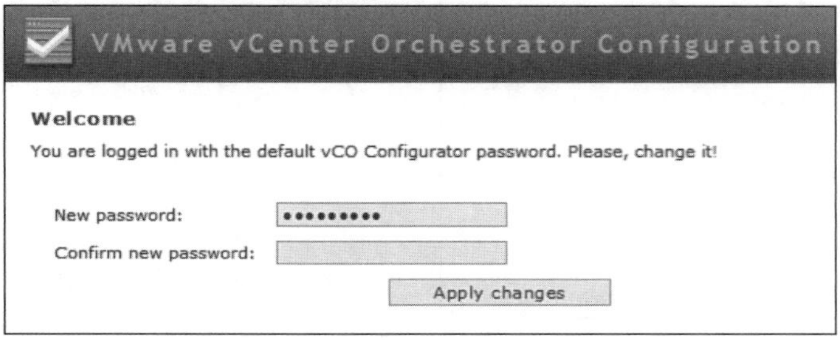

Figure C.8 Password-change prompt for vCO configuration

Now that you have changed the password to access the admin area of the vCO vApp and for the vCO configuration service, the next step is to enable the vSphere vCenter Server 5 plug-in.

Enabling the vCenter Server 5 Plug-In

Unlike the version of vCO that ships with vCenter Server, the vCO vApp ships with only some very basic plug-ins. One of the plug-ins that is included but not enabled by default is the vCenter Server 5.x plug-in. To enable it, follow these steps:

1. Browse to the vCO vApp landing page.
2. Select Orchestrator Configuration and log in.
3. After you have logged in, select Plug-Ins and review the list (see Figure C.9).
4. Select vCenter Server.
5. Click the Apply Changes button.
6. Select Startup Options from the menu on the left.
7. Then Restart service from the resulting page.

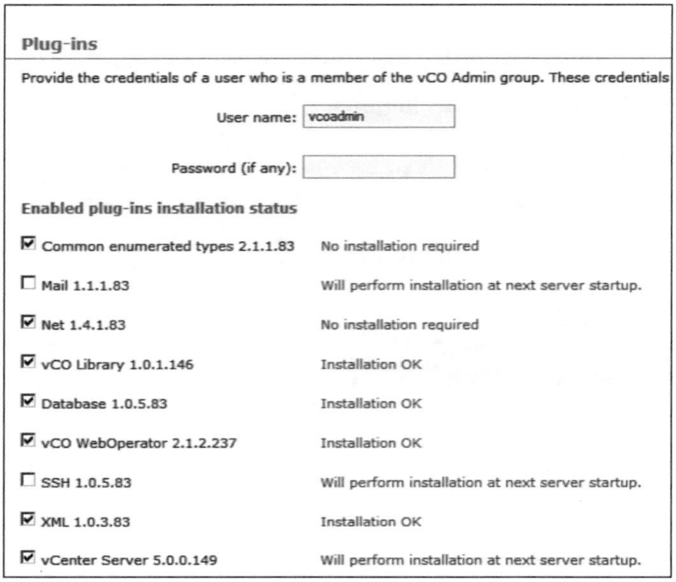

Figure C.9 Plug-ins listing of vCO vApp

At this point, the plug-in is now installed, and you can use the vCO vApp just as you do any of the other deployment methodologies from Chapter 2, "Installing vCenter Orchestrator."

NOTE

Not all plug-ins presently work with the vCO vApp. Therefore, before you install a plug-in, or move wholesale to the vApp, consult the VMware documentation.

Summary

The vCO vApp provides a quick, easy-to-deploy, and easy-to-use way to get vCO up and running in your environment. It also allows for an additional deployment option for those designing an infrastructure where vCO will come into play. This appendix covered the steps you must complete to both obtain and configure the vCenter Orchestrator vApp. You also learned how to enable the vCenter Server plug-in.

Appendix D

VMware VIX Plug-In

Chapter 9, “Amazing Smoothies Day 3: VM Provisioning,” touched on using the VMware VIX plug-in to perform post-installation steps. However, that chapter did not provide much guidance about installing the plug-in. The reasoning there was twofold: 1) The VIX plug-in is not provided by or tested by the VMware vCO team; and 2) the installation process for the VIX plug-in requires a few additional steps to make it work. These two points bring us to this appendix.

This appendix covers the following:

- What VMware VIX is and what you can use it for
- Preparing the VIX installation
- Installing the VIX plug-in

NOTE

The VMware VIX plug-in currently requires a Microsoft Windows–based vCenter Orchestrator install for the plug-in to work.

What Is VMware VIX?

Well, what is VMware's VIX application programming interface (API)? Like VMware Orchestrator, it is one of a few products in the VMware portfolio that is not as high flash or in the limelight as much as its vSphere counterparts. However, because of what it provides, it is no less important.

VMware VIX consists of a number of APIs that provide guest operating system automation and other automation platforms (and all without the user having to log in to the guest OS). The example used in Chapter 9 involved setting IP addresses on newly configured virtual machines. This can be expanded into any provisioning, maintenance, or basic troubleshooting use case. You can find more information about VMware VIX at vmware.com/go/vix.

Preparing the VIX Installation

With all the wonder and promise of being able to automate actions inside of your virtual machine guest operating systems, you still need to complete some work to get the VIX plug-in ready. For this example, we use the VIX 1.10.1 build 266898. As always, this is likely to change over time; see the VMware website for additional information. First you need to prepare the Windows server that hosts your vCO installation. To do this, complete the following steps:

1. Download the VIX plug-in zip file from http://labs.vmware.com/flings/vix-vco.
2. Extract the ZIP file to a temporary folder (see Figure D.1).
3. From the ZIP file, extract VMware-vix-x64-<*version number*>.zip to C:\Program Files\VMware\VMware-vix-x64-<*version number*> (see Figure D.2).

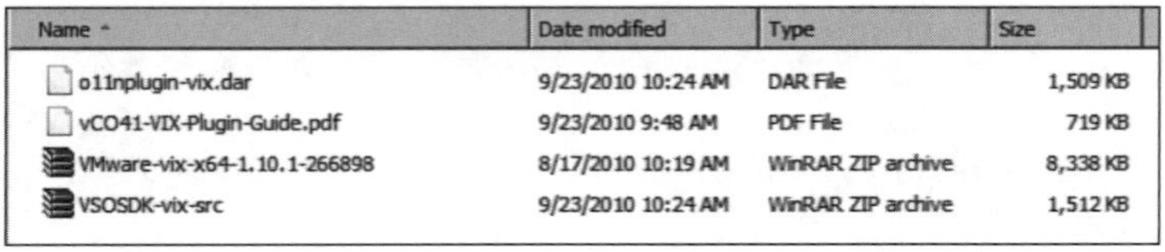

Name	Date modified	Type	Size
o11nplugin-vix.dar	9/23/2010 10:24 AM	DAR File	1,509 KB
vCO41-VIX-Plugin-Guide.pdf	9/23/2010 9:48 AM	PDF File	719 KB
VMware-vix-x64-1.10.1-266898	8/17/2010 10:19 AM	WinRAR ZIP archive	8,338 KB
VSOSDK-vix-src	9/23/2010 10:24 AM	WinRAR ZIP archive	1,512 KB

Figure D.1 VIX download extracted to a temporary folder

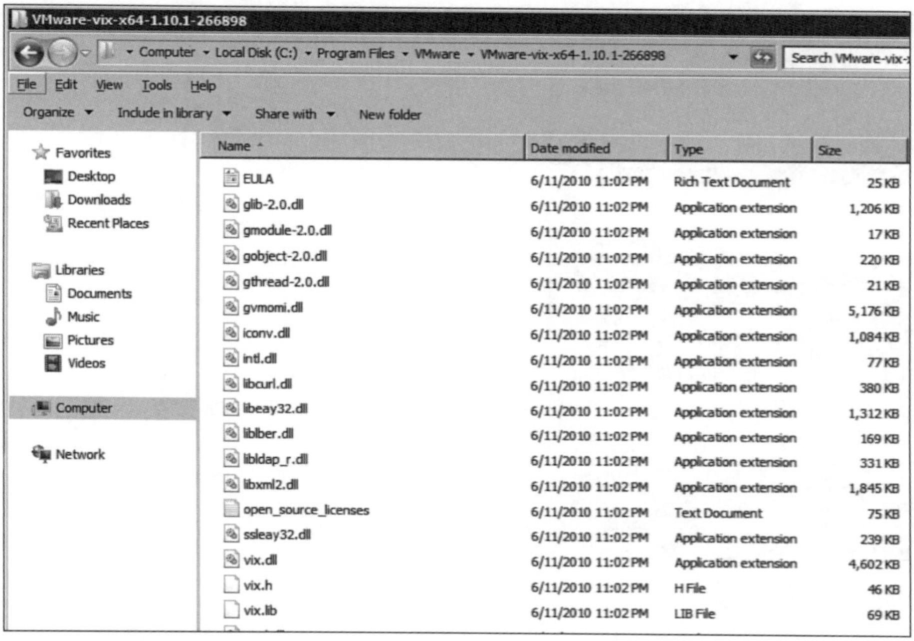

Figure D.2 Files extracted to final location

4. Add the path from step 3 as a Windows system PATH variable:
   a. On Windows 2008, open Server Manager.
   b. Click Change System Properties.
   c. Select the Advanced tab.
   d. Click Environment Variables to open the Environment Variables window (see Figure D.3).
   e. Locate and select the entry for Path in the System Variables list and click the Edit button (see Figure D.4).
   f. Add the appropriate path we composed in step 3 (see Figure D.4).
   g. Click OK and close the remaining windows.

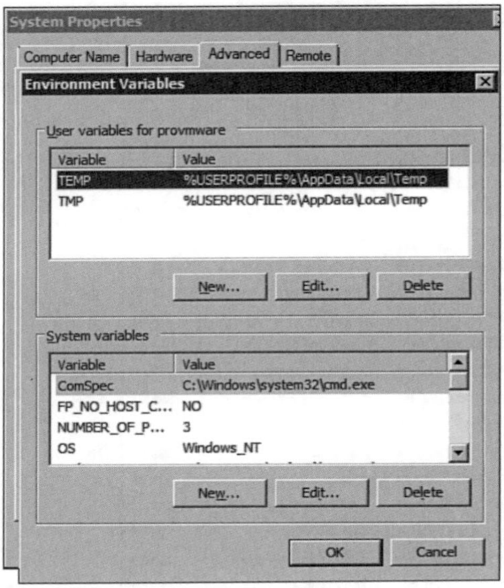

Figure D.3 Environment variables

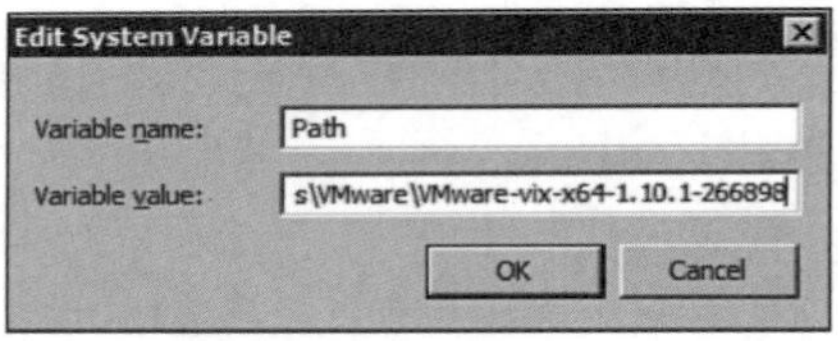

Figure D.4 Modified PATH variable

> **CAUTION**
>
> In step 4.f., when adding to the path, make sure you are appending to the end of the existing path variable and not replacing it. Replacing it might inadvertently cause your system to become unstable or otherwise behave oddly.

After you have the PATH variable updated, you are ready to install the VIX plug-in.

Installing the VIX Plug-In

To install the VIX plug-in, follow these steps:

1. Log in to the vCO configuration portal as an administrator.
2. Select Plug-Ins from the left.
3. Select the text box next to Upload and Install (see Figure D.5).
4. Browse to the temporary folder you extracted to earlier.
5. Select the DAR file and click Open.
6. Select Upload and Install.
7. When the page reloads, select Startup options from the left.
8. Select Restart Service.

When the service restarts, the VIX plug-in will be installed and ready for you to use within vCO workflows.

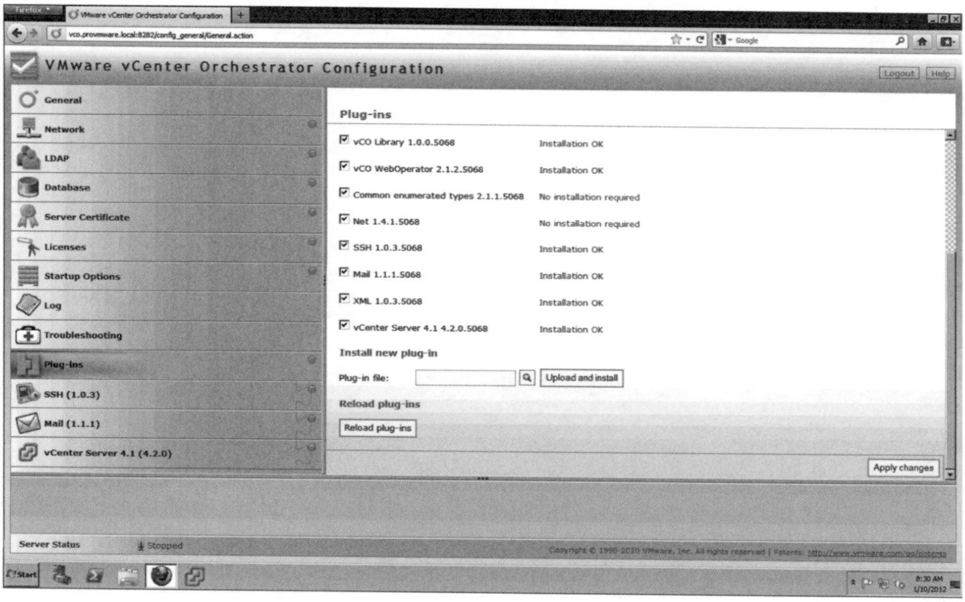

Figure D.5 Upload and install

Summary

This appendix covered what VMware VIX is and what functionality it can bring to your orchestrator workflows. In addition, we prepared and installed the VMware VIX plug-in for use within vCO.

Index

A

B

C

D

E

F

G

H

I

L

M

N

O

P

R

S

T

U

V

W

X-Y-Z

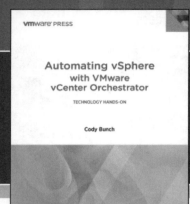